Cecil Rhodes

RHODES' DEATH MASK

CECIL RHODES

BY

Sarah Gertrude Millin

ILLUSTRATED

Harper & Brothers Publishers

NEW YORK AND LONDON

1933

CECIL RHODES

Copyright, 1933, by Sarah Gertrude Millin

Printed in the United States of America

Second Printing

I-H

CONTENTS

vii

Cecil Rhodes

CHAPTER · I

THE MATOPPOS AND BISHOP STORTFORD

I

"YOU worship Rhodes?" George Meredith wrote to a lady. "I would crown him, and then scourge him with his crown still on him."

He wrote on April 22, 1902. The Boer War had a month to go. Rhodes was dead a month. He died at the age of forty-eight, less pleasantly than he had supposed people did die of heart disease. "At any rate, Jameson, death from the heart is clean and quick. There's nothing repulsive about it. It's a clean death, isn't it?"

But they say the heat at Cape Town that summer was a plague. Such summers come to Cape Town. Then the blue hydrangeas climbing up the mountain at Rhodes' command lie pallid in their tracks, the whiteness of his house is a pain to the eyes, the Indian and Atlantic Oceans meet and the wan air is not stirred by the gigantic embrace.

And in such a heat Rhodes, his clothes unbuttoned, his face swollen and purple, his brow wet beneath his grey, tousled hair, wandered from room to room of Groote Schuur, his house, trying to breathe. He lay on a couch in the darkened drawing-room and could not breathe. He crouched on a chair at his desk and could not breathe. He laboured up to his bedroom and about it. He stood at the window that faced his mountain. Below him a regiment of flowers, in big, hard, brilliant, scentless masses, climbed the mountain slope by regular steps, and the trees he had lopped of their branches that screened the mountain, striped with black its purple and blue. But what would a man see of such things who could not breathe?

He was carried to his cottage by the sea, and they made a hole in the wall to let in the air, and laid ice between the ceiling and the iron roof to cool it, and waved punkahs to stir it to life.

Every day for two weeks his coloured man got ready a cart and horses to take him to his farm in the Drakenstein Mountains. But he was not called upon to inspan. Rhodes decided, instead, to go to England. It was cold now in England. Life seemed to be in that coldness.

It was arranged that he should sail on March 26th; a cabin was fitted with electric fans and oxygen tubes and refrigerating pipes. He died on the day he should have left.

A man might think the worshippings, crownings, and scourgings of his world an equal futility who had given his name to a country and could not get a little air.

II

Rhodes was born in an English vicarage on July 5, 1853. He began in the little greenness of a place called Bishop Stortford, and he ended in the granite desolation of a land called after himself.

Rhodes rests in a grave of rock. Here he came to brood on mortality, and here he chose to be laid. Forests, grotesquely piled boulders, hurrying, agitated monkeys lead to it. The ap-

2

proach is alive. But on the other side of this hill of granite, this glacier of black stone so smooth it is hard to climb—on the other side of this smooth, shining, black hill on which there lie carelessly, as if in an abandoned game of Brobdingnags, stones round as sea pebbles and large as houses, a world spreads itself of rough grey rocks spattered out on a desert landscape like the final vomit of planets long since dead.

In a cave near Rhodes sits the skeleton of the Matabele who taught him how a monarch who was also a poet should be buried. As the Matoppos to Bishop Stortford, so Moselikatze to the Williams, Thomases, and Samuels of Rhodes' ancestry who farmed or made bricks or bought land in London and the country; so Cecil Rhodes to the vicar, his father, whose sermons lasted exactly ten minutes.

The meaning of Rhodes' ancestry lies in its very lack of meaning. It proves merely that men like Rhodes come independent of their begetting and also of their land. And Rhodes himself recognized this when he set no name beside his own on his tombstone—not of ancestor or of birthplace. He was that being, Cecil John Rhodes, belonging to nobody, belonging to everybody—self-contained. He exemplified this largeness of spirit, this desire, for good or evil, to go big, which is called greatness and which is the attribute of no nation.

For greatness is a sort of genius—a quality, not an accident or an achievement, a gift and not an inheritance. It inhabits a man like poetry or courage. The great man may not be better than the next man, he has his viscera like anybody else, and as there are minor poets there may even be lesser great men—village, if not world, great men. The point is that greatness is a kind of spiritual growth gland that makes for enlargement. The great man enlarges himself as the poet writes.

3

He is equally conscious of his gift. He knows the mould he has to fill. He is dedicated to the work of filling it. It is the first sign of greatness in a man that he is aware of his greatness. "Be not afraid of greatness!" He is not afraid of greatness! From the beginning he has asked Life, not, like a beggar, for a penny, but, like a creditor, for a pound. When Rhodes is here called great, the quality of bigness is meant.

Rhodes used to say he left England not so much from love of adventure or on account of his health, but because he could no longer stand the eternal cold mutton. What did he mean but that he wanted a larger life? He came to South Africa when he was sixteen.

III

His brother Herbert, the eldest son, was there before him. Cecil Rhodes was one of a family of twelve. He had a half-sister, two sisters, and nine brothers, two of whom died young. Of all this family of big-boned, questing, men and women only two married—the half-sister and Ernest, the brother following Cecil. Does it mean anything in particular for so many people in a family not to marry, anything that would concern scientists? Or is it that things are sometimes just simply what they are, and the Rhodeses were captured by adventure and it would not release them to the prosaic business of settling down? The Rhodes men, descendants, since the beginning of the eighteenth century, of cowkeepers, brickmakers, landowners—not to mention their parson father—were soldiers or emigrants. Their father had wanted them all to become parsons. But they were not of those who remain quietly at home. To this extent Cecil was like his brothers. But his brothers had

4

not his ruthlessness, his imagination, his brains, that capacity for utter absorption in an idea which was his genius and made him Rhodes.

If Rhodes' mind found something to engage it, that was all he could think of, that was all he could talk about, that was the crux (one of his favourite words)—the crux of everything. An idea would appear to him in a certain form, in a certain combination of words, and he could not bring himself to express it in any other but that form or combination. Over and over again the same thought, the same phrase, would come out, not to be abandoned until every possible relation to it had been explored. Rhodes is supposed never to have made a note for his speeches. But, actually, he rehearsed them, sometimes to the point of boredom, in his conversations, for he talked of nothing but what concerned him at the moment. And it merely depended on the kind of thought it was—a minor one or a major one, a thought of few facts or many facts—it depended on how long it took him to explore this thought, whether he held it an hour, a year, or a lifetime. Some thoughts he did not give up in his lifetime. He spoke of them as thoughts. "I am giving you these thoughts." "If I may put to you my thoughts." "I will give you the history of a thought." "Work with these thoughts." "The north is my thought." "Coöperation is my thought." . . .

This force of concentration was the difference between Rhodes and his brothers, between Rhodes and people who are not like Rhodes.

His sister Edith is said to have resembled him. His sister Edith, however, became no Hester Stanhope or Gertrude Bell or Florence Nightingale. To match Cecil Rhodes, that is what she should have become. Unproved potentialities are the spirits

5

of the dead whose limits may be the universe, but they merely tap a table. There are no mute, inglorious Miltons. The point about a Milton is precisely that he is neither mute nor inglorious.

Although Cecil adventured to South Africa to join Herbert, in the end, of course, most of the brothers buzzed about Cecil. One, Arthur Montagu, found himself a farmer near Bulawayo, and after the Matabele rising he put in a claim for mealies destroyed. When it was discovered that the mealies had never existed, he explained that he had an arrangement for supplying the natives with seed-grain and sharing the resulting crops with them. The seed had not been planted, on account of the rising. Therefore he wanted reparation. Cecil wrote across his brother's claim: "This is the most impudent claim that has yet been submitted."

Of his brother Bernard he said: "Ah yes, Bernard is a charming fellow. He rides, shoots, and fishes. In fact, he is a loafer."

He said to one of his secretaries: "I have four brothers, each in a different branch of the British army, and not one of them could take a company through Hyde Park Gate."

Herbert, the chief Rhodes wanderer, camping solitarily in Africa, opened a cask of gin. It caught fire and he was burnt to death.

Frank was a man of charm, popular with men and still more with women. People speak much of his delightfulness. Two months before the Jameson Raid he took the place of his brother Ernest as Cecil's representative in Johannesburg on his gold companies. He found himself caught up in intrigues foreign to his easy nature, and ended as one of the leaders in the movement that led to the Raid. With three others he was sentenced to death, but all four were released on payment of a fine.

Kruger said of Frank Rhodes that he was the only man among the rebels who knew his business. His fellows thought otherwise. They merely said, "Dear old Frankie." Men who knew him in those days still speak of him as Frankie.

The name of Cecil does not yield itself to diminutives. But no one ever called the big Rhodes even Cecil. He was called Rhodes as a boy at school. He was called The Old Man when he was thirty—and by men twice his age.

Frankie was not only popular, but honest. He clearly told the truth at the Enquiry that followed the Raid.

The inheritors of Rhodes' estate in England were the descendants of Ernest, and it was they who were compelled by Rhodes' will to work before entering into their possession.

IV

Unlike his elder brothers, Rhodes had not been sent to Winchester or Eton. There must have come a limit, even for a man wealthy enough to build a church, to sending sons to Winchester or Eton. Cecil went to the Bishop Stortford Grammar School, and his career there may be judged from the blighting fact that he won a medal for elocution.

He left this school when he was sixteen, and read under his father. He had an idea he might like to become a clergyman or a barrister. But then he was found to be tubercular and sent out to Herbert in Natal. He arrived on September 1, 1870, after a seventy days' voyage, and joined Herbert as a cotton-planter. He was entitled, as an immigrant, to fifty acres of land to be paid for in five years.

7

In Natal, for a year, he struggled against caterpillar, bore-worm, and his own inexperience; made friends with a youth related to the Provost of Oriel, and invested his earliest savings in a new local railway. Then he followed Herbert, always the impatient pioneer, to the newly discovered Diamond Fields in Griqualand West. He was now eighteen. At this age Clive was shipped to India. At this age, too, Warren Hastings went to India. And at this age Alexander Hamilton, the Federalist, born an Englishman in the West Indies, wrote a series of papers in defence of the rights of the American Colonies as against England.

Rhodes is not known to have remarked on the man who, a century earlier, helped to federate America as he wished to federate Africa, but he did once speak to W. T. Stead of those Englishmen ("so low have we fallen!") who considered it a good thing that England had lost the United States. "There are some subjects on which there can be no argument, and to an Englishman this is one of them. But even from an American point of view just picture what they have lost. . . ." "Fancy," he writes later in his open letter to Stead, "the charm to young America to share in a scheme to take the government of the world."

The government of the world was Rhodes' simple desire.

CHAPTER ' 2

THE SOUTH AFRICA TO WHICH
RHODES CAME

I

SOUTH AFRICA is no less sentimental than other lands. It likes to refer to itself, first, as a young country; second, as a country made safe and sweet for a white civilization by its ancestry of pioneers. It forgets that, like America, it was settled by people who came from the great civilizations of Europe, and grew uncivilized in the process of pioneering. It ignores the contradiction of the two boasts, their mutual cancellation.

There are no young countries today—no countries rightfully immature. To which country is the past now not an equal inheritance and the present an open declaration? We are alike as old as history, the press that prints, the steam and gas that draw, the wires and the waves that speak. If in this twentieth century a country remains young, it is suffering from arrested development.

And then the pioneers, the early settlers. In South Africa, as in America, there is talk of these pioneers and those settlers. In the United States they say the real America is the Middle West because the descendants of pioneers live there and work the land. These are held to be purer Americans than the inhabitants of New York because the British, Dutch, Swedish, French, German, Scottish, and Irish blood in them is an older mixture. Yet no one has demonstrated why the meaning of a country should lie in its earliest comers unless they have done something besides come first; why, except in a race, there is any merit in doing a thing first apart from that which attaches to the demonstration of its possibility. Nor is the meritorious necessarily the significant.

Pioneering is still going on in various parts of South Africa, and one can see with one's own eyes that pioneers are not always better than other people. The very foreignness of New York may be the essential America. If no white man had come to South Africa before 1870 the South Africa of today would have been, materially, little different, and, spiritually, not, in every sense, worse. Old roots, old bonds, dear traditions, might not have been there, and the dignity of long possession; and among tangible things, some noble houses and furniture. But also a few old hatreds might not have existed; and, courageous and touching as was the advance of the pioneers through the unknown—a thing admirable in itself of which the memory may well be treasured, the actual effect of that advance—the clearing of the land of savages, its tentative cultivation—could now be achieved in two or three years with the aid of a certain number of machine-guns and motor tractors. Nor are generations needed to create a feeling for Africa. It is a land that does not softly melt the heart, but that seizes (as it seized Rhodes) with a swift and passionate grip.

Pioneers—pioneers anywhere—struggling along, living hard and painfully, leave a sentiment, but little else; for they have small help for their minds, and their energy goes out in sweat. Art, thought, and invention come with ease, and are nourished,

as the history of nations through the centuries shows, by prosperity. When the times are stirring and triumphant, desires
arise—body, sense, and spirit alike demand gratification; and
the creator is stimulated to provide that gratification.

South Africa did not exist for the world, and hardly for itself, until its gold and diamonds were discovered.

II

The story of gold in South Africa is an older story than the
story of diamonds. They say the Phœnicians once landed on
the coast of Mozambique and came to dig for gold in the
country destined to bear Rhodes' name, that they worshipped
Baal and Astarte there and sacrificed black bulls as some
African tribes do to this day. Even the gold of Solomon's
Temple, they say, came from Africa, and Southern Rhodesia
they call the very land of Ophir, and from the River Sabi
(they declare) rose Sheba's name.

The stories are pretty, and Rhodes liked to think of them,
but scientists are no longer sure that the ruins in Rhodesia
from which such dreams arise are anything but the work of
Africans, and so perhaps Milton was better informed when he
spoke of Sofala as Ophir:

> Mombaza, and Quiloa and Melind,
> And Sofala, called Ophir, to the
> Realm of Congo and Angola farthest South.

Who knows but that Milton once studied the map of Africa
"done into English by I. S. (John Speed) and published at the
charges of G. Humble Ano 1626," which, among such in-

11

formation as "Here the Amazons are said to inhabit," "The King of Guinea is adored by the common people," "The sons of the Emperor of Œthiopia are held inward in a hill," points out—in the wrong place—"Here is gold digged up in great quantities"?

Diamonds, although Anthony Trollope once heard an American lecturer speak of a mission map, printed in 1750, on which was written "Here be diamonds" ("I have not," comments Trollope, "seen such a map. . . . Such a map would be most interesting if it could be produced")—diamonds were not found in South Africa until 1867.

In this year a Dutch farmer saw a neighbour's children playing at marbles, and one of the stones was white and bright. The farmer admired the stone, and it was given him. He showed it to some diamond merchants, who considered it worthless. He had it sent to a mineralogist, who valued it at £500. At this price it was bought by the governor of the Cape, who allowed it to be displayed. That is the history of the first diamond found in South Africa.

The second was the discovery of the same farmer. It was being used by a native witch-doctor in his wizardry business, and the farmer bought it for 500 sheep, 10 oxen and a horse —all he had. But he knew a diamond now when he saw it. The stone weighed eighty-three carats; he sold it for over eleven thousand pounds to a trader, who resold it for twenty-five thousand. This diamond is called "The Star of South Africa."

There were experts who regarded the two diamonds as freaks. One such expert, whose name was Gregory, reported that there was no diamondiferous ground in South Africa.

Hence a blunder came to be known in South Africa as a Gregory.

And now people began to *look* for diamonds. Two years later they were found in various places over a stretch of eighty miles along the Vaal River. Still another year later they were picked up on the open veld, and the Boers who owned the farms on that veld, which now hold the greatest diamond mines in the world, thankfully sold these farms for two thousand, two thousand six hundred, six thousand pounds, packed their ox-waggons, and again trekked into the emptiness—away from the vultures swooping down on the land and picking bare its bones. And so Kimberley began.

It is reported that, in later years, old man de Beer protested to his wife that he should have asked, not six thousand, but six million pounds for his land:

"But what would we have done with all that money? There are only the two of us, and this house is big enough. We have our front room, and our bedroom, and our kitchen. What more do we want?"

"We could have had a new waggon."

"We have enough to buy twenty new waggons."

"And a new Cape cart to go to service—to Nachtmaal."

"That, too, we can afford. . . . Ach, my little heart, be easy. What have we to trouble about? We have enough."

But the people who followed old de Beer and his wife could never have enough. All over South Africa there are those who made fortunes in Kimberley and could not have enough; who, like the fisherman of the fairy-tale, began in a hovel and wished for more and more until the world itself was too little for them, and the charm broke and they were back in their little old hovel again.

It is appropriate that Rhodes should have come to Kimberley in the very month of England's proclamation to her rivals and the world that Griqualand West—Kimberley—the Diamond Fields—was British territory.

What right had England to the Diamond Fields? What right had anybody? There are a people in South Africa who complacently call themselves the Bastaards (officially the Griquas) because the blood in them is a mixture of white, Hottentot, and Bantu. Early in the century missionaries had helped them to settle in the land that is now Griqualand West, and there they had killed off the Bushmen and established a government. They had then wandered this way and that along the Orange River; claimed rights in what is now the Orange Free State; sold them to the Boers for four thousand pounds; and finally crossed the dangerous Drakensberg to found the new dominion of Griqualand East.

When diamonds were discovered in Griqualand West England said Griqualand West was the possession of one Nicholaas Waterboer, of the royal line of Bastaard Waterboers, and that Waterboer wanted England to take over his country. Against this the Orange Free State, existing at the moment on paper money, protested that, since she had taxpayers there, Griqualand West was hers; and the Transvaal, recently unable to float a loan of three hundred pounds, said no, there were certain concessions, it was hers.

At a village on the Vaal River the diggers hoisted a republican flag and elected as president Stafford Parker, at one time an able seaman in the British navy.

From this distance of time it all seems merely comic: hereditary ruler Nicholaas Waterboer, the Bastaard; President Parker, A.B.; the failure of the three-hundred-pound Transvaal loan flotation; the cessions of kingdoms by this vagrant half-Hottentot or that. But behind the comedy was the first wealth that had ever come to South Africa, hitherto a poor and humble country, whose golden air was no use for barter. Much bitterness flowed from the rivalry for the Diamond Fields. And although the Transvaal withdrew her claim without much further talk, and President Parker hauled down his flag to make way for England, the Free State has not yet overcome the feelings with which she accepted from England, in full settlement of her rights, the sum of ninety thousand pounds.

Into this atmosphere of treasure and intrigue, of concession, claim, and Imperial passion, walked the tall, thinking youth, Cecil John Rhodes.

IV

To this Imperial passion, despite the fact that he himself never matched his ideal of an Englishman, to such a passion Rhodes could not have been a stranger when he arrived in Kimberley.

He may have had—he did have—the kind of genius that entranced the legal world when Rufus Isaacs, without reference to his documents, cross-examined Whittaker Wright for hours on questions of finance. Rhodes, too, learnt to do that sort of thing. His speech concerning the amalgamation of all the diamond mines and the buying out of his rivals is nine thousand words long, it is as detailed as it seems clear and simple, and he made it, so they say, without looking at a note.

Nor was this the sort of speech to be rehearsed, as others, in conversation. . . .

Again, if photographs and anecdotes are any guide, Rhodes may have developed the face, not so definitely as he imagined, of a Roman emperor as of a rather impressive Hebrew financier (a secretary of his tells how he was once mistaken for a Jewish trader by his own Rhodesians).

Still, Jewish genius or Jewish face, a Jew he was not. He was, on the contrary, the son of a Church of England clergyman. He belonged to a family that, in the English manner, sent its sons from parsonages to playing-fields and battlegrounds. The family even moved in those circles that are called "county." As it happens, he himself was of those natural merchants at sight of whom, according to Emerson, Nature herself seems to authorize trade; whom, indeed, as he says, she elevates from the ranks of private agents to be her very factors and Ministers of Commerce. Rhodes could not, therefore, be so limited as to express in his person merely a national ideal. Nevertheless, he had always in his mind the sense of his English background. It directed his aims and strengthened his dealings.

When, for instance, there was the question as to who should control the diamond mines, he or the East End Jew, Barney Barnato, Rhodes played as one of his trump cards membership of the Kimberley Club. For Barnato might be a millionaire; he might buy a house in Park Lane; he might, in the year whose end was to see also the end of Rhodes' triumphant ascent, avert, through his dealings, a panic on the London Stock Exchange—he could not, until Rhodes worked it, achieve what a man who had an old England behind him found waiting in

16

his path: he could not get into the little iron-roofed Kimberley Club.

Membership, then, of the Kimberley Club was one of the things Rhodes offered Barnato when they were playing for the diamond mines. It went into the scale. "This is no mere money transaction," he said to Barnato. "I propose to make a gentleman of you."

It seems incredible that a gentleman should have said it, or a man accepted it. One has to allow much for the mitigating smile or gesture. The fact remains that Barnato agreed to let Rhodes make a gentleman of him by getting him into the Kimberley Club.

Barnato had as good a business head as Rhodes. But Rhodes, and not Barnato, came to control de Beers, because Rhodes had this advantage over Barnato: he could play with other things than money. Barnato had only money, and in the end he found it not enough.

If Rhodes did not realize the advantage of being English in blood and bone before he arrived in Kimberley, he learnt to appreciate it there. In this cosmopolitan hotbed being English seemed more than an advantage, it seemed a rare and lovely virtue.

The time came when Rhodes could say of a man (it was his friend, Earl Grey): "Take heed of him, all of you, for in him you see one of the finest products of England . . . an English gentleman."

It was in Kimberley that Rhodes learnt many things about England, and first of all, by immediate example, how England went about annexing countries, and, second, how she justified such annexation.

Kimberley is an ugly town. It is an ugly town today. But when Anthony Trollope saw it six years after Rhodes sorted his first wash he said that an uglier place he did not know how to imagine. There had been no rain, Trollope reports, for months. The temperature was a hundred and sixty degrees in the sun and ninety-seven degrees in the shade. There was not a tree within five miles, nor a blade of grass within twenty, nor a house of anything but corrugated iron, nor food fit to eat. There were no pavements. The roadways were of dust and holes. The atmosphere was of dust and flies. "I seemed to breathe dust rather than air. . . . I was soon sick of looking at diamonds."

Yet it was not this barrenness of Kimberley that struck Rhodes' imagination, making him think of softer, greener lands. Rhodes loved Kimberley. When life failed him—perhaps, more significantly, when he failed life—when, in his later years, he needed assuagement, he came for it to Kimberley. He had a house opposite the Kimberley Club in the main street of Kimberley, where today there are only shops. The house was small, ugly, hot, and uncomfortable—a working-man, at thirty pounds a month, would demand a better. Sir James Rose Innes, later in Rhodes' Cabinet, and still later Chief Justice of the Union, describes how, in the year Rhodes entered Parliament, this house looked. A corrugated-iron shanty. Soiled and tumbled bedclothes on an iron bed. A Gladstone bag for a bolster. . . . It was one of the Kimberley spectacles—how a man lived who was in Parliament and had just floated a company for two hundred thousand pounds.

But Rhodes was happy in it. All over South Africa one may

still meet men who loved Kimberley in its first days and love it now. It is perhaps their youth in Kimberley they really love, the eagerness that will not come again, the thought of those days when wealth dropped on men as in dreams, and they could be young and rich who are now merely old and rich. But, whether it is this or that, still their hearts draw them to Kimberley.

So it was not the ugliness of Kimberley that set Rhodes dreaming of English things. It was not the town itself, but it was, very likely, almost certainly, the people in it.

VI

What sort of people—the natives apart—came to dig in Kimberley? They are described by old-timers, by one or two scurrilous writers of those days, by several not so scurrilous, also by Froude and Trollope.

Froude compares them to a squalid Wimbledon camp. "Bohemians of all nations," he says—American and Australian diggers, German speculators, traders, saloon-keepers, professional gamblers. . . . "They may be the germ of a great future colony, or the diamonds may give out and they may disappear like a locust swarm. It is impossible to say. The diggers were in a state of incipient insurrection when I arrived."

Trollope comments on the vacuousness of their existence. "I am often struck by the amount of idleness," he says, "which people can allow themselves whose occupations have diverged from the common work of the world. . . . I can conceive no occupation on earth more dreary—hardly any more demoralizing—than this of perpetually turning over dirt in quest of a peculiar little stone which may turn up once a week or may

19

not. I could not but think . . . of the comparative nobility of the work of a shoemaker who by every pull of his thread is helping to keep some person's foot dry."

One may judge by these descriptions, particularly by Trollope's comment on the idleness of the digger, that the early Kimberley must have been much like the diggings of today. Indeed, even worse. For today there is the cinema, the train, and the motor-car. The digger is not cut off from the world. In Rhodes' time in Kimberley the diversions were drinking, gambling, coloured prostitutes, an occasional boxing-match, dance, or amateur entertainment. And the diggers (except for the occasional decent youngsters, gaily adventurous, and the anxious strivers that go everywhere) the diggers were the derelicts of other worlds and other occupations; men reckless, feckless, unable to work for themselves, unable to work for a master, with nothing to lose and only luck to hope for. As soon as this luck gave out they would expect to hurry away, and their conduct would not be regulated by the fears and responsibilities of the citizen who remains where he must answer tomorrow for his actions of yesterday.

When one reads in the shabby chronicles of those days of the practical jokes, the adorable bar-ladies, the houses of ill-fame, the girls, "slightly off-colour," put up to auction, the drinking, prize-fighting, concerts, racing, gambling, rushing around—it seems that the old Kimberley life may have been a vicious life, but it was also a bright life, full of movement. So, probably, those who think wistfully of the old days remember it. The facts are otherwise. People naturally select or invent the interesting things to write about. They do not, they cannot, record the procession of those days on which nothing happened. Men drink and gamble and go with native women in such places as the early Kimberley because life there is as boring as existence on an airplane. To wait for luck is the most tedious, heart-lowering of experiences. To wait for luck is the lot of the diamond-digger in these days, and it was the lot of the diamond-digger in Rhodes' days. Nor did this luck come to all. Nor, before it was found that the real hoard of diamonds was in the blue ground below the yellow ground, were great fortunes made. "A man with a thousand pounds was considered well off." Rhodes' own brother Herbert, the first Rhodes in Africa and on the Fields, the one who was later burnt to death, gave up diamond-digging and went to look for his fortune in the newly-discovered goldfields at Pilgrim's Rest—in that large, rich district of Lydenburg which the Boers bought from the Swazi natives for a hundred head of breeding-cattle. His brother Frank, who had come out on his advice, returned to England to take up his commission in the cavalry.

Certainly men made fortunes in Kimberley. A score of men —more than half of them Jews—made extremely large fortunes. But not at once, not in the early 'seventies, not in the days when Rhodes pumped water and sold ice-cream and bought the claims of those prepared to abandon them.

CHAPTER ، 3

FROM KIMBERLEY TO OXFORD

I

THERE is a photograph of Rhodes which shows him at the age of about twenty. In this photograph the face is thin and delicate, it is a face very different from the big, ruthless, powerful face of the later Rhodes. They say (it sounds well) that Rhodes brought to the Diamond Fields from his farm in Natal his digger's tools, some volumes of the classics, and a Greek lexicon.

And this, they say, is how he looked: a tall, fair boy, blue-eyed, aquiline-featured, in ill-washed, shrunken white flannels; a sullen, silent boy scraping at his pebbles, débris around him, windlasses turning, buckets crashing, natives picking, heaving, chanting as they worked in the quarry (diggers would call it the paddock) below him. From the mound on which he sat Kimberley displayed itself to him: the white tents of the diggers, the bars, the shops, the sheds of the diamond dealers— all of corrugated iron and shocking to the eyes in the glare of that bitter sun. . . .

"The silent, self-contained Cecil John Rhodes," writes a contemporary. . . . "I have many times seen him in the main street, dressed in white flannels, leaning moodily, with his hands in his pockets, against a street wall. He hardly ever had a companion, seemingly took no interest in anything but his thoughts, and I do not believe if a flock of the most adorable women passed through the street he would go across the road to see them."

It is probably true that Rhodes did not freely yield his interest to women. When he arrived in Kimberley there were indeed no women there—that is, no white women. They came later. In those old Kimberley days he danced, he said, for exercise. If he danced as he walked, heavy, rolling, pigeon-toed, it was as well he was also little concerned about his partners. It did not matter to him who they were or how they looked.

"I don't want them always fussing about," he said of women, little knowing that his words were being noted in Olympus and that a most preposterous woman was to be the last chagrin of a life heroically designed.

But it is strange that Rhodes should be so constantly reported as a solitary. He seems always to have had friends and to have loved and trusted them. There was the youth in Natal, the relation of the Provost of Oriel, with whom he read classics and with whom he arranged to go to Oxford, though, in the end, he alone did so.

There were Rudd, Beit, Maguire, Jameson—the men who were by him in his beginnings, his schemings, his fortunes, his failure, and his end. Jameson ruined him and was forgiven. Beit served him in life and after death, and once, during the great diamond amalgamation, when Beit faced trouble through helping him, Rhodes gave him half a dozen promissory notes signed in blank, saying: "Whatever I have got is yours, to back you if you need it."

There were the four he used to meet that they might debate

Imperial problems and teach Disraeli his business—they wrote to do so.

There was Sidney Shippard, the Attorney-General of Griqualand West, destined to have power in a place and at a time when Rhodes needed some one to do a bit of queer work for him. To this Sidney Shippard, in conjunction with the British Colonial Secretary, Rhodes' first will assigns all his possessions that they may use it to spread Britain over the world.

And there was the young Neville Pickering, secretary of de Beers, to whom, in his second will, he leaves everything for the same purpose.

Pickering died young, and, to ease his dying, Rhodes abandoned his larger prospects on the goldfields and left Johannesburg for Kimberley. But it was a sacrifice, so he said, that he never regretted.

Though he never cared for another human being—not even Jameson—so much as for Pickering, he continued to the end of his life making vehement friendships, always with men. He had something more than a political alliance with the Dutch leader, Jan Hendrik Hofmeyr, which the Raid broke. The confidant of his maturity was W. T. Stead. There was Grey, whom he spoke of as that finest of English products—an English gentleman.

Friends naturally came to him as his career blossomed out; he was surrounded, of course, by seekers and toadies. And sometimes he treated them with impatience and contempt, but yet they were his intimates.

The loneliness of Rhodes, his spiritual solitude, is mere romanticism. Isolation seems to fit the character of a great man, that is all. With Rhodes the contrary was the truth. Apart from those phases of brooding and introspection natural to a man of temperament, he was dependent on company. He hated even a meal by himself. He loved to speak. So far was he from being the reserved Englishman of tradition and W. T. Stead, who said of him, among other absurdities, that he dwelt apart in the sanctuary of his mind into which the profane were not admitted—so far was he from this cloudlike loneliness that he was always explaining his feelings to people.

Rhodes had a passion for self-revelation. He talked (they sometimes say "shyly"—it is the conventional thing to say about a big man) of what most human beings keep secret. He was as eager to confess—not as a child, for children do not tell, but as an adolescent, a traveller on a long voyage, sometimes a genius. If it was not to Jameson, Beit, Hofmeyr, Grey, Stead, his intimates, it was to General Gordon, it was to General Booth, it was to any little group of people, it was to any large group of people, it was to his settlers, his shareholders, his constituents, his fellow-undergraduates, his parliamentary followers, his hosts, his guests; to Britons, to South Africans, to whites, to blacks, to those for him, to those against him— to anyone, in short, who would listen to what he had to say— which, when a man is Rhodes, means everyone. There his sayings are, treasured by his contemporaries. There his speeches are, reverently collected. There his Open Letter stands, which he asked Stead to publish. There his letter is that he wrote to Sir William Harcourt after the Raid—the letter of some one forever nineteen. If posterity chooses to misunderstand Rhodes, it is not because Rhodes lost an opportunity of explaining himself.

25

Not that he was, generally speaking, a great letter-writer. He wrote documents of letters to Alfred Beit, but, on the whole, he belonged to the category of those who send telegrams. His letters that remain are not many, and they have a business-like air—they are hardly what one would call heart-spillings. Secretaries, in the days of his fame, answered the politicians, soldiers, sailors, missionaries, explorers, needy men and questing ladies who wrote to him. His early letters to his mother—the letters, after all, of a son sent out sick and very young to a barbarous country, are more connected with the activities around him than with family intimacies or the state of his own being. Rhodes' confessionals are not paper.

He describes Kimberley to his mother much as Trollope describes it. "Fancy," he writes, "an immense plain with right in the centre a great mass of white tents and iron stores, and, on one side of it, all mixed up with the camp, mounds of lime like anthills; the country round all flat with just thorn-trees here and there: and you have some idea of Du Toits Pan, the first spot where dry digging for diamonds was begun. . . ."

It was, however, at another camp Herbert Rhodes was digging—at Colesberg Kopje on the farm appropriately named Vooruitzicht—Foresight—by the Boer who sold it with all its diamonds for six thousand pounds. Now the camp was known as de Beers New Rush to distinguish it from the earlier camp of Old de Beers. This became soon merely New Rush. And, in the end, since Lord Kimberley, the Colonial Secretary of the day, deprecated the name Vooruitzicht because that was unpronounceable, and New Rush because that suggested wildness

—in the end, and finally, it received the name of Kimberley. The camp grew to the town. Along the Vaal River, and in Griqualand West generally, one may still meet old natives and Boers who, when they use the Dutch equivalent of the term New Rush, mean the town of Kimberley.

III

When Cecil Rhodes joined Herbert the camp was still called New Rush. And there, on a kopje, thirty feet above level country, one hundred and eighty yards broad, two hundred and twenty yards long—on this kopje, divided into six hundred claims, Herbert had his three claims. A claim was, by regulation, thirty-one feet square. It was divided into four sections. On each section several blacks and whites were working. In this small space, therefore, on the kopje, ten thousand people were assembled.

And they had to dispose of the débris, they had to sort and sieve. Rhodes writes how mules and carts, going along the narrow and unrailed roads, were always tumbling into the chasms below. At the same time he views with complacency his life at New Rush. "I average about £100 a week," he tells his mother, and he signs his letter, without any affectional to-do, "Yrs. C. Rhodes."

He is eighteen, but he is not like his elder brothers, at Winchester or Eton. On the contrary, he averages a hundred a week. He is tubercular—a few years later a doctor gives him not six months to live, yet in a strange world, among strangers from all over the larger strange world, he is able to maintain himself. When his brother Frank joins Herbert at Durban, and together they arrive at Kimberley, it is to find Cecil with

27

a lawyer measuring his ground to prove that a digger next door is encroaching on his claim.

Rhodes had thus his reasons for saying later in life that children should be given a sound education "and then kick all the props away. If they are worth anything the struggle will make them better men; if they are not, the sooner they go under the better for the world."

IV

What did Rhodes consider a sound education? Not, ap-(parently, the sort of education that would please a Wells or a Bertrand Russell. Not a scientific training, not a commercial training, not the sort of training that may be acquired in what is called the school of life where the same lessons produce such incalculably varied results. Rhodes considered that education a sound education which his father, the Vicar of Bishop Stortford, would have considered a sound education. His genius was a thing apart from his roots, but his tradition was not.

Right from the beginning of Rhodes' life in Africa his dream was Oxford. In his first year in Natal he was speaking about Oxford to his friend, the relation of the Provost of Oriel. He must have come to South Africa with that dream, or what was he doing here with his classics and his Greek lexicon? Why had he brought them across the seas and carried them by Scotch cart and oxen all the slow, lumbering way from Natal to Griqualand West—just (let us believe the story) these books and his digger's tools? It seems clear that, in the days when Rhodes' brothers thought of Sandhurst, he thought of Oxford. It was his first love, and remained his last.

V

The dream began to shape itself a year or two after his arrival at Kimberley.

He was now nineteen and financially at ease; he had had the first of those heart-attacks that were to be his undoing; his brother Herbert, a restless man who could never stay long in any place or any activity, wanted to give up diamond-digging and try the new business of gold-digging. The two brothers bought an ox-waggon and started out for the Transvaal.

It takes a long time to travel by ox-waggon from Kimberley to Pilgrim's Rest, where Herbert was going to dig for gold. Time faints in the sun and forgets to rise again while one travels across Africa by ox-waggon. The oxen walk as if in sleep, chewing, with sideways-moving, rhythmic jaws, and a Kaffir goes in front with a long whip which he lashes at them, crying their names—Blackboy or Whiteface or Scotchman or something like that—and they wake up for a moment and then fall again into their ruminative sleep-walking.

To journey by ox-waggon across the veld is a manner of existence incredibly monotonous, but in the end it lifts one into a sphere which is a thing in itself, a life somewhere between hell and heaven, yet hardly of earth.

And so, by the end of a day, fifteen miles are done, and the oxen are released to wander over the veld, and sticks are gathered to make a fire within a circle of stones, and wild flesh is roasted, and a burning stick is plunged into the coffee that sends into the soft air its friendly, innocent-seeming invitation.

And when the dark comes, the farthest nothingness is punctured only by stars, like light shining through little holes in the worn material of a blue-black tent, and there is no sound but that of a cricket or a frog or a distant hyena, and thin, faintly-bitter scents rise from the earth like threads of memory or of longing.

In such nights, forgiving the hot, dull days, one dreams. In such nights, repeated over eight months, Rhodes dreamt. He thought, as he came to say, of the gold and diamonds and other precious stuff under the earth, of fertility and browsing cattle above it. How long had this bigness remained inviolate? How much longer would it remain so? Who, finally, would master it? And why, he thought, not he, Cecil John Rhodes, in the name of England? Why not, in the end, through this conception, all the world for England?

When Rhodes returned to Kimberley from his long trek he knew what he wanted of life, he had his grail.

In Kimberley he replaced his brother Herbert with one C. D. Rudd, destined to be his partner in the largest of his enterprises, and, having thus arranged for his affairs to be watched on the Diamond Fields, he sailed with Frank for England.

Frank was going to take up his commission in the cavalry, and Cecil was going to Oxford.

VI

Rhodes used, in after-life, to tell how he came to Oriel. One might have imagined his talks with his Natal friend who was related to the Provost of Oriel would have had something to do with it. But it appears not. The story is this: The college Rhodes wanted to enter was University. But the master would not take him when he heard he meant to read only for a pass degree. He had failed, too, his matriculation.

He protested to the master that he ought to be exempted

30

from ordinary rules. He explained his life in Kimberley—how hard it was for him to achieve what boys in England could carry on their way. "I am not what they are. I am a man."

He was twenty.

But the best the master could do for him was to write to the Provost of Oriel. "They are less particular there," he said.

The Provost, says Rhodes, read the letter while he waited. He stared down at his table in hostile silence, and, afraid for his dream, Rhodes waited. "All the colleges send me their failures," said the Provost at last.

In this way Rhodes was admitted to the college of Raleigh, the first Chartered Empire-Builder, and to Oxford. He did eventually matriculate.

CHAPTER ꞌ 4

THE DISCIPLE OF RUSKIN

I

GREAT men begin early and are long young. At the age of eleven Alexander Hamilton, a man in youth but forever a boy, became a warehouseman's assistant. At thirteen he was managing the business—correspondence, staff, and cargo dealings. At fifteen he sent himself to school.

Rhodes was not quite so precocious. He was a farmer at seventeen, a diamond-digger at eighteen, a man of means at nineteen, and an undergraduate at twenty.

That in itself is not so remarkable. Many men have worked before going to college, and in order to go to college, and to keep themselves there. What is remarkable is the way Rhodes now arranged his life. He conducted it simultaneously in two continents. In one he knew the out-flung, bobbing, careering, far-swept flotsam of thirty nations, and in the other the fruit of generations of care and particular tradition. He experienced side by side a youth and a manhood. He was together earthy and airy. At Oxford he was concerned with the fortune-snatching of Kimberley, and at Kimberley with the philosophizing of Oxford. In the dust of Kimberley he read his classics, and beneath the poetized spires of Oxford he negotiated for his pumping-plants.

The return journey from Kimberley to Oxford was, in those days, a matter of three or four months' travelling.

One might imagine that such a course of life would provoke attention. Yet neither the college that rejected him nor the college that accepted him seems to have thought that here was something notable. The memories concerning Rhodes at Oxford are meagre and dull. The most interesting, because the most candid, recollection of Rhodes by a contemporary has it that, although there were among Rhodes' fellows some of whom one might have expected to hear again in a world "some degrees larger than Oxford," even Rhodes himself would admit "that if he personally felt as young men are apt to feel, that he had it in him to be, or to do, something great, he did not betray his secret."

Twenty-five years later, says this writer, Rhodes told him that he was wrong. Already at Oxford he had been filled with the ideas which came to inspire his effort and life.

That Rhodes was not lying may be judged from words he wrote at Oxford, his mind buzzing with the exhortations of Ruskin and the ethics of Aristotle.

"You have instincts, religion, love, money-making, ambition, art, and creation, which, from a human point of view, I think the best, but if you differ from me, think it over and work with all your soul for that instinct you think the best."

There was a lecture Ruskin gave at Oxford in which he spoke of "a destiny now possible to us, the highest ever set before a nation to be accepted or refused. Will you youths of England make your country again a royal throne of kings, a sceptred isle, for all the world a source of light, a centre of peace . . . ? This is what England must do, or perish. She must found colonies as fast and as far as she is able, formed

33

of the most energetic and worthiest of men; seizing any piece of fruitful waste ground she can set her foot on, and there teaching her colonists that their chief virtue is to be fidelity to their country, and that their first aim is to be to advance the power of England by land and sea."

Here, it seems, were the words that gave form to Rhodes' desert dream.

Strange to think of this geyser spouting up just fifty years ago. The Ruskins of our day toll a knell with Isaiah, "Thou has multiplied the nation, and not increased the joy."

But so it had to happen. A man born most English had to be driven by illness to a far continent. And in the very year of his coming precious stones had to appear that he might be enriched for what was to follow. And illness again had to send him on a long journey through brooding wastes, and in the hot, bright silence the desire for these wastes had to fever his blood.

Then he had to voyage back to merge himself once more in the traditions of his kind. And here he had to be in a place where, at just this time, an apostle of beauty must choose to speak not only, as by right, of pictures and stones and workmen, but also of such dreams as had once been Raleigh's.

Who dare now chant with Shakespeare of royal thrones of kings and sceptred isles, and with Ruskin of fruitful wastes to be seized for the advancing of a nation's power? It was easy to shout glory in Ruskin's time when life was at its swell, and the vanity of nations brought sorrow only to the weak. Not every nation had yet experienced the older prophecy: "Woe to the multitude of many people, which make a noise like the noise of the seas; and to the rushing of nations, that make a rushing like the rushing of mighty waters. . . . They . . .

shall be chased as the chaff of the mountains before the wind, and like a rolling thing before the whirlwind." The boy Rhodes was ripe for Ruskin's heroic message; it was the time also of Disraeli.

To the words of Ruskin he linked the thoughts of Winwood Reade and the discoveries of Darwin, and out of this curious compound evolved his creed.

II

This was his reasoning:

He began by assuming, says W. T. Stead, that there was a fifty-per-cent chance a God existed.

Take it a God did exist.

What would this God want of man?

It was a question Rhodes was prepared to answer. God would want man not only to look like him, but to act like him. Man, therefore, had to find out what God was doing, and do the same.

What was God doing? Darwin had said it. God was perfecting the race through natural selection and the weeding out of the unfit. It remained merely for man to follow this lead and God's will was done.

The eyes of Rhodes were after God. He looked to see what, in this process of selection and elimination, God had achieved. Which, among all the peoples, had he brought to flower?

With all modesty, Rhodes could not help admitting that it was the English-speaking peoples that followed the highest ideal of Justice, Liberty, and Peace: the people of Great Britain, her dominions and America.

The conclusion was clear. If Rhodes wished to please and

follow God, he had, in whatever way he could, to promote the unity and extend the influence of the English-speaking race.

To himself, personally, he allotted the task of Africa.

III

In Rhodes' second term at Oxford his lungs, not yet strong enough to withstand the damp of England, were injured afresh by a chill caught while rowing. It was now a doctor wrote down in his case-book (Rhodes himself later saw it) that he had not six months to live.

Rhodes gave up Oxford for two years, returned to Kimberley, and there began to work out a plan of life.

In 1876 he returned to Oxford. In 1877, spending the long vacation in Kimberley, he composed a document which, many years later, he sent to W. T. Stead.

"It often strikes a man," says the document, grappling still, in the worrying Rhodes way, with his Ruskin-Darwin-Aristotle theme, "to inquire what is the chief good in life. To one the thought comes that it is a happy marriage, to another great wealth, to a third travel, and so on, and as each seizes the idea, he more or less works for its attainment for the rest of his existence. To myself, thinking over the same question, the wish came to make myself useful to my country. . . . I contend that we are the first race in the world, and that the more of the world we inhabit, the better it is for the human race. I contend that every acre added to out territory provides for the birth of more of the English race, who otherwise would not be brought into existence. Added to which the absorption of the greater portion of the world under our rule simply means the end of all wars."

36

And here and now he decides that he will work "for the furtherance of the British Empire, for the bringing of the whole civilized world under British rule, for the recovery of the United States, for the making of the Anglo-Saxon race into one Empire. What a dream! But yet it is probable! It is possible!"

In the same year, accordingly, he draws up the first of those six wills in which, in one form or another, he bequeathes his fortune to the purpose of extending British rule throughout the world.

In this particular will a secret society is to carry out his scheme, and a system of emigration is to be perfected for colonizing "all lands where the means of livelihood are attainable by energy, labour, and enterprise." The whole continent of Africa is to be settled by Britons, and also the whole continent of South America, the Holy Land, the Valley of the Euphrates, the islands of Cyprus and Candia, the islands of the Pacific not heretofore possessed by Great Britain, the Malay Archipelago, the seaboard of China and Japan, and, finally, the United States. In the end Great Britain is to establish a power so overwhelming that wars must cease and the millennium be realized.

This will, like its explanatory credo, he gave to W. T. Stead, with instructions that it was not to be opened until after his death.

Remembering that at the time Rhodes made the will he was twenty-four, an undergraduate at Oxford, and not unique among the young moneymakers of Kimberley, one may forgive oneself for finding this provision—the provision that the will is not to be opened until after Rhodes' death—the only sane one in the whole scheme. Children of eight or ten are given to speculating on what they would do if they had twenty million pounds. It is perhaps well that, as Stevenson says, "most men are so wise (or the poet in them so dead) that they keep their follies to themselves." An inhibition or two is cheap at the price. Imagine a man of twenty-four solemnly donating a fortune not yet made to the end of Britain's absorption of the globe!

The will itself is not more astounding than the fact that Rhodes leaves the money which is to alter the fate of all the world to two men—the Secretary of State for the Colonies at the time of his death, and Sidney Godolphin Alexander Shippard, an Oriel man, until 1877 Attorney-General of Griqualand West, later a judge, then an administrator in a place and at a time very important to Rhodes, and, finally, a director of the Chartered Company. These are the actual legatees.

It was what Rhodes was always doing in his wills—he bequeathed his money to one or two or more individuals and left it to them to carry out his plans.

It is generally said that Rhodes was a cynic. He did become a cynic; his life made him one. And yet he never lost his natural romantic trustfulness. He was prepared to leave the day's output of diamonds at de Beers in the unchecked charge of one man merely because he was an Oxford man. His second will reads, simply, "I, C. J. Rhodes, being of sound mind, leave my worldly wealth to N. E. Pickering." A covering letter adds that the conditions of the will can only be carried out by a trustworthy person, and "I consider you that one." "You fully understand," he adds in a postscript, "you are to use the interest of the money as you like during your life."

In other words, this young Pickering, one of Rhodes' clerks, no sort of genius, merely some one Rhodes loved, is to arrange

38

that, by means of Rhodes' money, the world shall become British. Nothing more!

The human brain is an awesome bit of flesh. Where would one expect the author of such a conception to be working out his destiny? . . .

But not so fast. By the time Rhodes signed this will in 1882 he had formed his de Beers Company, entered Parliament, and taken his degree at Oxford.

In 1888, the very year he amalgamated all the diamond mines of Kimberley and achieved the Rudd-Rhodes concession over the territories of Lobengula, he made his third will (young Pickering having died), leaving his estate once more to a friend—again to the same purposes.

In 1891, chairman now of de Beers and the Consolidated Goldfields, managing director of the Chartered Company, Prime Minister of the Cape, he added, in his fourth will, the name of W. T. Stead to that of the previous sole legatee.

In 1893, the year in which he took Matabeleland from the Matabele and so consolidated the whole of the territory that was to be named after him, he made his fifth will.

And in 1899, three years after the Jameson Raid and his downfall, in the year that was to mark the beginning not only of the Boer War, but also of England's troubles, he made his sixth and last will. And the old dream is still alive. But its expression is at last that of a man who has discovered, as he said, that Napoleon "remade boundaries and tried to recast the fate of empires, yet left France no larger than he found it," who knows now the limitation of the human instrument, and realizes that even he is such an instrument. It needed the actual evidence that he was not a god to make Rhodes feel this globe called the earth was more than his toy.

39

It will be seen, then, how, by the side of Rhodes' fantastic broodings ran his concrete performances, how, indeed, they were dependent on one another. Even through the hazes of his first exaltation at Oxford he saw clearly the material fact of money. He not only, after his lungs became strong enough, kept his terms at Oxford, he also ate his dinners at the Temple (though he was never called), since "on a calm review of the preceding year I find that £3,000 has been lost because, owing to my having no profession, I lacked pluck on three occasions, through fearing that one might lose and I had nothing to fall back on in the shape of a profession. . . . I am slightly too cautious now." And even while at Oxford he was inviting undergraduates to dinner, and, as one of them reports, making speeches to say that every man ought to have an aim in life, and his own was to work for the British Empire, he was also buying shares in a new railway in Natal, picking up an investment in Hampstead on which he made eight hundred pounds, and calling on secretaries of rival diamond companies and on diamond merchants in Hatton Garden.

Did he, already at that time, want money for nothing but his Imperial schemes? Or—"Philanthropy plus five per cent," as, in a moment of frustration, he came to say sneeringly of British policy—did he want a royalty on his imaginings? It may be taken that he was human and he did: for many years, and despite all rosy talk, his five per cent and more.

And still, not towards the end. When Rhodes gave his name to a country, and England worshipped him, and the natives he had betrayed called him father, and the young men he had led called him The Old Man—in those days when the bliss of triumph swelled his being until he felt himself, as was after-wards said, the equal of the Almighty, then, despite the Matabele War, his political corruption, his ruthless dealings with money and men, the Jameson Raid and all that followed, Rhodes saw his destiny as something above the gathering of possessions. . . .

Enthusiasm is inspiring even when it is selfish. It dazzles the mind and deflects the eye of experience. Let Henry Ford and Northcliffe present their creations, and who can clearly discern the Ford car and the *Daily Mail* of fact? They are Heaven's Golden Chariot and the Tables of the Law. One is enslaved by the men's own conception of their achievements.

In Rhodes Spengler sees the captain of industry become statesman, a man who "has really ceased to feel his enterprise as his own business, and its aim as the simple amassing of property." Rhodes is actually the example Spengler gives of this enlarged being.

The world worshipped Rhodes and his Idea, and he saw himself a man heroically dedicated. It came to this, that his Idea transcended not only conventional desires, it rose also beyond the common acceptations of goodness and honour. Everything had to yield before it.

In a way, Rhodes was a greater man in the days when, seeing the shortness of his time, he cut through caution and right and human feeling to reach his goal. But it was in the Nietzsche-Dostoevsky way. He undid himself—if not in the manner, then in the spirit—of Dostoevsky's Stavrogin, that he might rise above himself.

CHAPTER · 5

THE TREKKING BOERS

I

WHAT was this South Africa of Rhodes' destiny? What those people flying before him, dark against a burning sky, and crawling back to kneel to him? Who these men, called Boers, bearded, sable-clothed in Parliament, loose-seated, straight-legged, in their saddles on the veld? Who the Englishmen that opposed them?

It was more than four hundred years since the Portuguese, the adventurers of those times, had found South Africa; more than two hundred and fifty years since the English had planted in it King James' flag; more than two hundred years since the Dutch, absorbing other emigrants from Europe, had settled it and beaten off and out the little yellow Bushmen and Hottentots; not so long since those Dutch had come to grips with black men, flowing down the continent, who had in them much Negro, a bit of Hottentot, and something of such people as the Arab, whose name for them was Kaffir—Unbeliever.

Towards the end of the eighteenth century the Prince of Orange, a fugitive in London, had asked England to guard this African outpost of his—the Cape—from the French invader. Eight years later, following the Peace of Amiens, England handed it back. In 1806 she took it again. In 1814, after the Congress of Vienna, she bought it, with some other Dutch settlements, for six million pounds.

There were Dutch settlers who disliked this constant unsettling, and they moved away; they did as they had been doing for the last hundred years when they were dissatisfied; there was room enough in Africa: they trekked.

Those more deeply rooted farmed with their slaves until England, as a final hurt, abolished slavery and, most well-meaningly, ruined them. Now many of these, too, trekked. They complained officially of their losses through the emancipation of slaves, of their fear and hatred of Kaffir marauders, of the persons who, "under the cloak of religion," cast odium on them. . . . To this day the missionary is to the Boer the fundamental traitor, the white man who stands for black against white. . . . "We despair," said the manifesto, "of saving the colony from those evils that threaten it."

And so they trekked. They called themselves the Voortrekkers—those who go before. This was, indeed, the trek of treks, the Great Trek. Some trekked north-east across mountains they named the Mountains of the Dragon; fought bloody battles with the Zulus (there exist still the town of Weenen—Weeping, and a Blood River); and stayed in Natal until England told them they were British subjects there no less than at the Cape, when they trekked again, this time towards the Vaal River.

To the lands through which this same Vaal River flowed the other trekkers had meanwhile journeyed. They had arrived at the source of a river which they took to be the River Nile (five hundred miles across Africa by ox-waggon might well seem five thousand); they had driven farther north still that Moselikatze, who was to teach Rhodes how a conqueror of imagination should rest in death; they had settled themselves on both sides of the Vaal, hoping that at last they were free of England. . . .

But they were not. England knew her children. The Boers had been, they remained, England's children. She claimed her own. The Vaal was crossed and recrossed in motherly pursuit. There was talking, fighting, talking, fighting—possession, release—at last, weariness. England gave up. On one side of the Vaal there came into being the South African Republic (the Transvaal); on the other the Orange Free State. Conventions recognized their independence. Natal, hitherto attached to the Cape, became a separate colony. The Cape received a constitution.

All these things took place in the 'fifties. A few years before the land of the Kaffirs—Kaffirland, or Kaffraria, a region sharing with Cape Colony the foot of South Africa, had become a crown colony. There were now three British colonies and two Boer republics.

Among the Voortrekkers, a boy of ten, journeyed Paul Kruger.

II

So much for the trekkers. There were now the Boers in the South African Republic, the Boers in the Orange Free State, the Boers who had preferred not to trek and were Cape Colonists. The Boers who had trekked north hated with a deep and contemptuous hate the Kaffirs they had fought against on their terrible journeyings; they hated—respectfully, and not unanimously—the English from whose embrace they had wrenched themselves to experience those terrible journeyings.

44

They developed the virtues of pioneers and lost the civilization of cities.

The Boers who had remained—it follows from their remaining—were suave and not rebellious; they regarded themselves, many of them, as the old families, the aristocrats of the Cape.

They were all of them, those who went and those who stayed, equally earnest and political-minded. Beneath everything they felt their common blood.

There were, indeed, some, even in the north, who still wanted to be linked, in their lonely helplessness, with those they had left behind. The Free State had barely achieved its independence when it was craving the intervention of the British against the Basutos, and was passing resolutions in favour of a union or alliance with Cape Colony.

The request came at the very time the Governor of the Cape, Sir George Grey, was asking England to take measures "which would permit of the various states and legislatures of the country forming among themselves a federal union."

Bulwer Lytton, the novelist, was the Colonial Secretary of the day, and he rejected the proposal. His Government, he said, were not prepared to depart from the settled policy of their predecessors. England, at the moment, did not want to saddle herself with distant, unprofitable lands.

Thirteen years later she found that at least one piece of Africa was profitable, and she annexed Griqualand West with its Diamond Fields. In the same year a young Cape Dutchman, Jan Hendrik Hofmeyr, revived this talk of union. At this time Rhodes had only just arrived at Kimberley, he was eighteen against Hofmeyr's twenty-six, he was not ready, for many years, to fight beside Hofmeyr for the cause which, in Hofmeyr's eyes, he was later to betray.

In the Transvaal Burgers, once a Dutch Reformed minister too advanced for his flock and now the Transvaal's President, came to speak of himself as "an ardent Federalist."

In England the fashion was Disraeli and that Imperialism which had enchanted Rhodes in his Oxford days. There was an example to South Africa in the federation of Canada. As against the conservatism of Bulwer Lytton, another writer, the historian Froude, had been sent out by the Colonial Office and was going about the country passionately advocating its union. And though, by the time Froude had done talking, South Africa was begging to be allowed to mind its own business, everything seemed to be fairly set for a consummation, generally desired and apparently inevitable, when, in 1877, Sir Theophilus Shepstone, the Secretary for Native Affairs in Natal, rode into Pretoria with eight civil servants and twenty-five policemen and annexed the Transvaal.

That, as the saying is today, tore it. That did tear the silver cord. The word blood came to be used as it had not hitherto been used between the Dutch of the colonies and the Dutch of the republics. "Do not," cried Kruger, "wash your hands in the blood of your brothers."

It was a story destined to be repeated twenty years later in the Jameson Raid.

Kruger sailed for England to protest against the annexation, and for the Continent to seek intervention.

III

A third writer makes himself heard. Shepstone's commission had been to annex the Transvaal "if it was desired by the

46

inhabitants and in his opinion necessary." The ubiquitous Trollope was travelling in South Africa. Now, in the Transvaal at exactly the right moment, he comes forward to testify that it *was* desired by the inhabitants, and highly necessary.

He describes the condition of the country, the rebellious natives, the impotent President, his stiff-necked and ignorant Parliament . . . hardly any education, hardly a mail service, property worthless, no revenue, no order, no obedience, no longer even a fighting spirit.

As for the feeling of the Boers, he never, he said, except from Burgers, heard a word of protest, and even Burgers thought that "the wrong done would be of great advantage to everyone concerned." "My conviction is," says Trollope, "that, had not the English interfered, European supremacy throughout a large portion of South Africa would have been endangered. I think annexation was an imperative duty."

He goes farther. The Boers are still, in his view, England's "migrating subjects" who have the right to English government. If England denies this, let her abandon them and be done with it. It cannot be, he says, now "Rule Britannia!" and now "Economy!" Now "Protect the native!" and now "Let the native look after himself!" He points out that there are, at this date, eleven living Colonial Secretaries, all honourable and deserving well of their country, and as many equally admirable "at peace beyond the troubles of the Native Question." If only, actuated as they are "by every virtue which should glow within the capacious bosom of a British statesman," they knew their own policy! . . .

Trollope, then, seems to defend Shepstone's action. It is at least decisive. There is one thing, however, against his reasoned conclusion—his premises are wrong. He does not understand the feeling of the Boer, which he finds so meek and acquiescent.

Nor did Rhodes understand it when he said, many years later, that, for all Shepstone's impetuosity, the Transvaal would have been happy under British rule had not the Imperial Commissioner who now came to take charge of the Transvaal "conducted the business on the lines of a second-rate line regiment." If Rhodes had understood the real feeling of the Boer about the Shepstone annexation, the Jameson Raid might not have happened. . . .

The temper of the Boer is slow. He says nothing. He does nothing. It is all going, one thinks, very smoothly. . . . A shock! His chance comes, and the whole time, one sees now, he has been remembering. . . .

The fighting spirit Trollope thought dead was no more than sleeping. It had been awakened by outrage and strengthened by resentment. It was gathering itself together. It was rising. There needed, at last, little to spur it to urgent activity when that little came to it—from Scotland.

IV

Gladstone's Midlothian campaign is still spoken of in South Africa.

When, thirty years after, Gladstone's son came out to be the first Governor-General of the Union, his name was a hindrance rather than an asset to him.

The Midlothian campaign had one supreme object—to get out Disraeli. To that end Gladstone was prepared to do everything Disraeli was not. If Disraeli wanted to expand the Empire, Gladstone wanted to contract it. If Disraeli was, as Harcourt said, "recklessly pursuing an Asiatic policy," Gladstone's "drenching oratory," as Disraeli called *that*, was out to quench it.

Shepstone's annexation was to hand. Gladstone spoke of "the free subjects of a monarchy going to coerce the free subjects of a republic to compel them to accept a citizenship which they decline and refuse." "If Cyprus and the Transvaal were as valuable as they are valueless," he vowed, with that unknowingness of the immediate future which is so ironically pleasing to later generations—"if they were as valuable as they are valueless I would repudiate them because they are obtained by means dishonourable to the character of the country."

Nothing could so have heartened the arising Boers as this evidence that the Lord, as represented by Mr. Gladstone, was with them. They wrote, hoping he would be victorious in his campaign, and that, "by the mercy of the Lord, the reins of the Imperial Government would be entrusted again to men who look out for the honour and glory of England."

Their hope was fulfilled. The Lord was merciful. The reins of the Imperial Government were duly entrusted once more to Gladstone. They asked him (Kruger, as he reports in his Memoirs, made the appeal) not to compel them to accept a citizenship which, in the words of the campaign, they declined and refused. Seven thousand Boers—practically the whole electorate—supported Kruger. Gladstone regretted his inability to help the Boers. Inspired by Joseph Chamberlain, he could not, he felt, desert the natives. The annexation might not, he said, be annulled.

On December 16, 1880, then, on the anniversary of the day even now held sacred to the memory of the victory of the Voortrekkers over the Zulu Dingaan—on this day the Boers proclaimed again their republic. They took up their arms. In February, 1881, they utterly routed a small English force at Majuba and killed the general in command.

Now, at last, Gladstone returned the Boers their independence. It was a qualified independence, the kind of self-government which, as Kruger expressed it, meant that "first you put your head quietly in the noose so that I can hang you, then you can kick your legs about as much as you please."

The English were no less dissatisfied. The defeat of Majuba stayed unavenged. Shamed, resentful Englishmen, when they heard of the settlement, dragged their flag through the dust of Pretoria.

v

Two months after the battle of Majuba Rhodes took his seat for the first time in the Cape Parliament. In 1880 the district of Griqualand West had been added to the Cape, and at the election that followed, and even before getting his pass degree at Oxford, Rhodes had stood as an independent candidate for the river digging district of Barkly West, and been elected. He represented Barkly West till he died.

He had not cut a great figure at Oxford. He never took rooms at college. He went little into Oriel. He was no sportsman. He belonged to no important group. And as to his work, he seldom attended a lecture, was not known to be anything of a student, and was warned against his idleness. He said then that if he were let alone he would pull through somehow, and somehow he did.

He had at Oxford, as always and everywhere, the habit of discussing exclusively, exhaustively, repetitively, shamelessly, a subject that interested him. He told his friends, a number of whom afterwards became successful men, how things were in

50

Kimberley, what he understood by life, how one might seek it and experience it in a remote continent.

The anecdotes concerning Rhodes' time at Oxford are few. The most interesting is that, at a dinner following his initiation as a freemason, he cheerfully, ignoring anguished protests, made a speech revealing the secrets of his craft.

He was, by turn, romantic and cynical. He was a man who sharply took his tone from his surroundings and his associates, but as, beneath it all, he held to a few inviolable principles, this was not recognized.

He came away from Oxford having learnt (1) that Oxford was great, (2) that England was great.

He was a rich man by the time he had his degree. Already, in 1874, he and Rudd had taken in another partner. In his last year the three partners had become six, and they had floated the de Beers Mining Company with a capital of two hundred thousand pounds.

Rhodes entered Parliament still wearing, as he pointed out, his Oxford tweeds. "I think I can legislate in them as well as in sable clothing," he said.

Sable clothing was the form in the Cape Parliament of those days. It was what the good old-fashioned English members wore, and certainly what the Dutch wore.

Rhodes' Oxford tweeds really meant a new way of life in the governing of South Africa.

South Africa was soon to know it.

C H A P T E R ˏ 6

RHODES IN PARLIAMENT

I

IT MAY be seen that when Rhodes entered the Cape Parliament the air was charged with resentments, suspicions, hostilities. The Dutch of the Free State could not forget the annexation of Griqualand West, their loss of the Diamond Fields. The Dutch of the Transvaal could not forget the Shepstone annexation. The Dutch of the Cape felt for their northern brothers. In the middle of 1880 a new scheme for confederation had been before the Cape Parliament, and to Cape Town had come Paul Kruger, inflamed by the betrayal of the Gladstone Government, to speak against it. The Jan Hendrik Hofmeyr who, for years, had preached South African union, now opposed it until the annexation was annulled.

But then, mollified, he linked his Farmers' Defence Association to a society run by a Dutch Reformed minister called du Toit, whose principles were "A United South Africa under its own Flag"—but not under England—and together the two societies formed a body which called itself the Afrikaner Bond, which felt itself to be, defensively and protectively, Dutch, and which, as Hofmeyr's rancour faded, ceased to be hostile to England and became (exit the Rev. du Toit) Hofmeyr's instrument for his own particular brand of union.

The influence of the Bond spread to the Free State and the Transvaal. Hofmeyr's word became its law. The Bondsmen voted as Hofmeyr instructed them to vote. Ministries were formed subject to Hofmeyr's approval. For thirty years, although he only once, for a short period, took office, he was the autocrat of his party. He was called, for his subterranean methods, the Mole. But he was a sickly man, and, slightly varying the Duke of Plaza Toro's method, he led his regiment from below because he found it less exciting. He was one of the ablest of South African statesmen, and is remembered in South Africa as Onze Jan—Our Jan.

It did not take Rhodes long to decide that Hofmeyr was his man. Hofmeyr, for his part, saw in Rhodes what he could see in no other Englishman. They found, very soon, that they could work together.

II

The English of the Cape, generally speaking, were not so amiably inclined towards the Bond as was Rhodes. For, if the Dutch colonists had feelings about the Transvaal, so had they; if the Dutch could not forget the Shepstone annexation, neither could they forget the humiliation of Majuba.

Then there was a depression in the country such as had not been known since the finding of diamonds, and, naturally, that made people hate and blame one another.

Then there was the perennial Native Question, concerning which there had been enmities between English and Dutch from the beginning of the century. Nobody really knew what to do about the Native Question, and here was a fresh manifestation of it: should, or should not, the Basutoland natives be disarmed?

53

The Basutos themselves did more than talk. They fought. Already this disarmament policy had cost the Cape a war, the lives of men, millions of money, and a certain reputation for fair dealing.

Rhodes had seen in Kimberley what guns meant to the natives. It was the reason they came to Kimberley, walking hundreds of miles on their pale, hard soles, sweating, far from their kraals and women, on the floors of great ditches, that they might earn the money to buy the white man's magic. They would work half a year and more for a gun. The guns were their investment, their claim to modernity, their title to power among those who knew only the old-fashioned assegai. They had found it beyond justice to be asked to give them up, they had fought rather than give them up, they had not given them up.

Rhodes' speech concerning the disarmament of the Basutos was his first in Parliament. He had three reasons, besides the feelings of the Basutos, for speaking against this policy. The first two he mentioned, the third he did not. He said it was no time to throw away millions. He asked who were they, in South Africa, to play about with native policies: "Are we a great and independent South Africa? No, we are only the population of a third-class English city spread over a great country." He did not point out that if the natives were not allowed to carry arms they would lose their chief inducement for coming to work on the Diamond Fields, and that would be a great nuisance for Kimberley.

On the other hand, he did, on behalf of the Diamond Fields, say that if Kimberley were not given a railway he would smash the Ministry. The railway was refused and the Ministry fell.

He then went himself to Basutoland to investigate the claims of loyal Basutos. It was in Basutoland he met General Gordon, who had come out as military adviser, and they became friends. England took over Basutoland, a rocky little country full of natives, for it was land the Cape needed, said Rhodes, and not natives. What with disarmament and railways, it was something like a political triumph for Rhodes. He was, for a few weeks before its end, Treasurer-General in the Ministry that followed.

III

But as if South Africa had not already enough racial troubles—Boer against Briton, black against white—racial troubles must needs now begin to come in from outside. For suddenly the European nations had discovered what Rhodes had discovered at the age of nineteen, on his long trek from Kimberley to Pilgrim's Rest—that the only great untaken lands left in the world were in Africa; and they were all snatching at Africa, rousing agitation and the spirit of rivalry in South African bosoms. The Belgians, led by the explorer Stanley, were in the Congo. The French, led by the explorer de Brazza, were in the Congo. Italy was colonizing. Portugal was colonizing. Germany was colonizing. It was more than Kruger, now President of the South African Republic, could bear. His Republic was young, feeble, poor, harassed by debts and natives; its wealth of gold was barely, as yet, realized; it was already too big for its scattered people. But what country is ever big enough? Kruger's Boers wanted to have so much land that they need do nothing but let the cattle browse on it. It was their dream not to have to see the next man's smoke. Kruger could hardly stand by while everybody else was taking Africa from the natives, and do nothing himself. Kruger was in it, too.

There were, as Kruger tells the story, two native chiefs of Bechuanaland who were at war with one another. Each had an ally. Each sought also white assistance. One offered land to English settlers in return for their help, the other offered land to Boer settlers in return for *their* help. A Royal Commission following Majuba had laid it down that the Boers were not to interfere with the natives. So Kruger, he says virtuously, forbade his Boers to join the natives. The Boers were tempted, however, he says, by the land, renounced their burgher rights under the Republic and, consequently, his authority, and did join.

The chiefs supported by the Boers won. The Boer mercenaries claimed their reward. They got the land. They were joined by other Boers, and founded the Republics of Stellaland and Goshenland, which immediately began to quarrel with one another and their native allies.

That, according to Kruger, is how the Boers happened to be in Bechuanaland.

Others tell a different story. They remember that already in 1870 Kruger had offered to ally himself with the Chief Montsioa, and the chief Montsioa had declined, saying, "No one ever inspanned an ass with an ox in one yoke"; how, four years later, Montsioa begged the British to help him against the marauding Boers; and how, in the end, the Boers had so much power over the natives that England was compelled to warn them off.

Whichever story is right (and, as far as they go, they are both probably right), Rhodes had not been long in Parliament when not only were the nations of Europe, and notably Ger-

56

many, snatching at Africa, the Boers also were entrenching themselves in Bechuanaland.

Rhodes knew something of Bechuanaland. The district of Griqualand West which held his Kimberley was geographically a part of it. Even now there were heartburnings over a piece of the chief Mankoroane's ground that had been wrongly assigned to Griqualand West. Bechuanas came to work in the Kimberley mines. Trade went out from Kimberley into Bechuanaland. Rhodes saw Bechuanaland and its meaning where it lay on the map of Africa. He loved maps. Still, today, there rests on a small massive table in the middle of his bedroom an enormous atlas. His house is full of maps.

He arranged to have himself sent up to Bechuanaland on a commission that was to enquire into Mankoroane's rights.

But he did more than investigate Mankoroane's rights. He investigated the possibilities of annexing the country; the possibilities that Kruger, about to go on a mission to England, might lure, from innocent or indifferent statesmen, the power to annex it himself. "Don't part with an inch of territory to Transvaal," he wired urgently to Cape Town. "They are bouncing. The interior road runs at the present moment on the edge of Transvaal boundary. Part with that and you are driven into the desert." Not an inch, not an inch, iterates the long impassioned message. "You can take the country without costing you a sixpence."

He made touch with van Niekerk, the Boer Administrator of Stellaland, and when he returned to Cape Town it was with a petition from the white inhabitants of Stellaland for the protection of the Cape. He had also spoken smoothly to Mankoroane and asked him to cede to the Cape, for Heaven knows what consideration, his disputed land. Now he demanded the backing of the House. "You are dealing," he urged, "with a question upon the proper treatment of which depends the whole future of the Colony. I look upon this Bechuanaland territory as the Suez Canal of the trade of this country, the key of its road to the interior. . . . Some honourable members may say that this is immorality. . . . 'The lands,' they may say, 'belong to the chief Mankoroane. How improper! How immoral! We must not do it!' Now I have not these scruples. I believe that the natives are bound gradually to come under the control of the Europeans. I feel that it is the duty of this Colony when, as it were, her younger and more fiery sons go out and take land, to follow in their steps with civilized government. Is not this also the principle of the British Government? . . .

"If we do not settle this ourselves we shall see it taken up in the House of Commons, on one side or the other, not from any real interest in the question, but simply because of its consequences to those occupying the Ministerial benches. We want to get rid of the Imperial factor in this question and to deal with it ourselves, jointly with the Transvaal. . . . What did we build railways for? To secure the trade of the interior. . . . I solemnly warn this House that if it departs from the control of the interior we shall fall from the position of the paramount state in South Africa, which is our right in every scheme of federal union in the future, to that of a minor state."

IV

It is said, even by the admirers of Rhodes, that he was not a good speaker. They admit he was effective because his matter was good, and he could now and then flash a phrase. But he

58

began and ended awkwardly. He was rambling and repetitive. He had a voice that broke startlingly into a high falsetto.

We are, on the other hand, assured that his speeches, which are here quoted, were not edited. But, unless his manner was quite inescapably bad, there can be no explanation of why those speeches seemed so indifferent when they were delivered and read so well now, except that fashions in oratory have changed in the last fifty years.

For Rhodes' speeches are not only bold, wise, direct, and epigrammatic in the reading; they give an impression of almost contemptuous sincerity. Here is a man, one feels, who, in his successful twenties, had already discovered what Samuel Butler felt bound to tell himself after a lifetime of the pain that comes from the consciousness of neglected merit: "The world will, in the end, follow only those who have despised as well as served it."

When Rhodes made this, his first speech on northern expansion, he was thirty. But he was already in what Conrad, thinking of a man's forties, used to call "the force of his life." In experience, achievement, habit, thought—and body, too—he was a middle-aged man.

He had always, since his arrival in South Africa, been ahead of his years. At an age when his contemporaries were still schoolboys, he was managing a farm, he was "averaging about a hundred pounds a week" as a digger. When they were undergraduates he was an undergraduate, too, but he was also a many-sided commercial adventurer. He knew his mind and had a plan of life at the age of twenty. When he entered Parliament his income was said to be twenty thousand a year. He had come to Parliament with a definite purpose which was nothing less than to make Africa British. ("I went down to the Cape Parliament thinking in my practical way, 'I will go and take the North.' ") He was then twenty-seven.

And he was something of a cold brute, was he not? in his speeches, a trampling realist: "Are we a great and independent South Africa? No, we are only the population of a third-rate English city spread over a great country" (1881). "Some honourable members may say that this is immorality. . . . Now I have not these scruples" (1883). Yet, in the year between these two offerings to Parliament, he makes a will leaving all he possesses to one inexperienced young friend because his conditions "can only be carried out by a trustworthy person, and I consider you one," and this young friend is to see that the money is used for the "foundation of so great a power as to hereafter render wars impossible and to promote the best interests of humanity." Nothing less.

Can two such conflicting attitudes both be honest? Was Rhodes presenting a false front to humanity or a false inside to himself? Did Rhodes make his wills as children write their secret diaries—for the joy of impressing with his virtues a world to which he now chose to show himself sneeringly indifferent? Was he a realist or an idealist? . . . Was King David a realist or an idealist? Was the Shakespeare of the Sonnets a realist or an idealist? Which human being is wholly the one or wholly the other—a straight flush, all the cards one colour, one kind, one sequence—that is outside a house for the insane? . . .

And he had not only, so soon, lived far into life, he looked a man past youth. At thirty he looked forty; at forty, fifty; at his death, even more than sixty. The portraits of his thirties show him a man, sensual-mouthed, double-chinned, heavy in stance, heavy in seat, big, thick, square, his very hands big and thick and square. But they show him, too, with the head, hair, brow, eyes, mien of a man beyond his fellows. Take up a picture with Rhodes in it—inevitably in the front, in the middle, of a group of men significant in their day—and he demands the eye, something different, something, for both good and evil, unique. "The reason why this or that man is fortunate," says Emerson, "is not to be told. It lies in the man. . . . See him, and you will know as easily why he succeeds, as, if you see Napoleon, you would comprehend his fortune." That is not well written, and it is not inevitably true. But it is true of some, and it is true of Rhodes. The history of Rhodes does overtly lie in his body, and, as it is clear now, it was clear in his own time. He commanded attention, he drew curiosity. "Who is the young man," writes a traveling Baron von Hubner, once Austrian ambassador in Paris—"the young man with an intelligent look, a grave deportment, and a sympathetic air?" . . . The sympathetic air is not generally reflected in Rhodes' portraits, but the Baron answers his own question correctly enough: "The path which he has taken, and means to take, marks him out to me—" and so forth. Even then it is not a totally unknown young man he considers; it is a young man already notable for "the path which he has taken."

And Rhodes was now in good health. He was not destined to be so for long. But just at this time the germs of disease were not eating his flesh, a straining heart was not swelling it out. He was full of vigour. He was full of schemes. He knew what he wanted. He felt he must get it. More. In the way of men who have strong desires, he felt it his duty to the world to get it. In this very speech of his, the first on northern expansion—actually within the few lines here quoted from it—

61

there are ranged all the things that came to make up Rhodes' plan in life.

v

There are, first, those expressions: The Suez Canal to the interior, the Imperial factor. There is the impatience of professional politicians. There is the haughty "I have not those scruples." There is the question of the rights of the natives—the control of them by this or the other power; the conviction that they must give way before the white people. There is the theme of colonization—the going forth of the young and fiery sons. There is the understanding that coöperation with the Dutch is essential. There is the thought of railways and pursuant trade. There is the promise of union—consummation—increase. . . .

It is an overture, a Wagnerian overture. The conductor lifts his baton; we have a prophecy of all the themes in the drama to come.

CHAPTER · 7

WHO SHALL HAVE BECHUANALAND?

I

RHODES used to call this piece of Bechuanaland that contained the Republics of Stellaland and Land of Goshen, sometimes the neck of the bottle, and sometimes the Suez Canal to the interior.

This, roughly, is how the map of South Africa looked when Rhodes began to assail it:

At the foot of it lay the Cape Colony, on the east coast Natal, and higher up Portuguese East Africa. Almost opposite Portuguese East Africa, on the west Coast, lay Portuguese West Africa.

North of the eastern part of the Cape was the Orange Free State and its little mountainous neighbour, Basutoland. North of the Free State was the Transvaal. Rising from the middle of the Cape border, right in the heart of what South Africans call the sub-continent, at no point anywhere near the sea, spread the land of the Bechuanas that led to the lands of the Matabele, the Mashona, the Barotse, and so on—all the lands that were presently to become Rhodesia.

Then came the Congo Basin, then the Great Lakes, and, above these lands again, a great bare continent through which England might break a path, if she chose, that reached to Egypt.

63

Bechuanaland, in short, four thousand feet above sea-level, more than a quarter of a million of square miles large, had as designing neighbours the two Dutch Republics; the colonies of England and Portugal; those marauding offshoots of the great Zulu nation—the Matabele, and their despised vassals, the Mashona. They all saw the oncoming of Bechuanaland. They all wanted it, not for the beauties it did not possess; for the streams that had ceased to flow and the forests that were no more; for its terrible summer heat and its terrible winter cold; for its dwindling rainfall, its sands, its droughts, its deserts; for its little yellow-brown people who were not of the Zulu-Xosa, but of the Basuto, type, and with some Bushman and Hottentot blood in them. . . . The chief town of Bechuanaland is Mafeking, which was besieged in the Boer War and which lies in the midst of that barrenness whose sands rise up to grit the teeth of the traveller to the Victoria Falls.

Rhodes used to say that the country was not of much use to the Bechuana, but white farmers could preserve the water and cultivate the land. Yet it was not, in truth, for its own sake the nations, and most passionately Rhodes, wanted Bechuanaland; it was for what lay beyond it.

II

Beyond it lay this Africa Rhodes called, first, the Hinterland, and then, when the thought of it absorbed him altogether, My North. There is a statue of Rhodes which shows him pointing northwards and saying, "Your Hinterland is there."

But what is this about the Imperial factor? Why did Rhodes, the excessive Englishman, now not want British interference?

The trouble was, very largely, missionaries.

It has been remarked already that the missionaries and the Dutch hated one another.

Now what the Dutch of those days could not understand was, as Trollope suggests, the hypocrisy of the English. They did not apprehend that hypocrisy might be, not the deliberate desire to deceive, but merely a failure to live up to an ideal. They saw only the double-faced result. The Kaffir must not be a slave! No, but you could take away his land and so compel him to work for you as if he were a slave! Was ever anything more illogical, more essentially false?

And yet even such an attitude (thought the Dutch) had some merit. It did at least recognize the fact that the black man had been put on earth by the Lord to toil for the white man. What did the Bible say? Did it not say: "Cursed be Canaan. A servant of servants shall he be to his brethren. . . . God shall enlarge Japheth, and he shall dwell in the tents of Shem, and Canaan shall be his servant"?

Was that clear, or was it not? Yet now came the missionaries and insisted that the black people and the white people were brothers. Were they brothers? Did they look like brothers?

There was a missionary going about Bechuanaland whose name was John Mackenzie. He was the successor of Livingstone. He found the Bechuana amiably inclined towards his religion, and he instituted himself not merely their spiritual, but their political, guide.

And he hated the Dutch. He said the Dutch ill-treated the natives. He said they had a plot to make the whole of South Africa into one great Boer republic. He begged England to take the Bechuana under her own protection.

He was a virtuous, vehement, courageous, and determined man. By the time he had finished doing his duty to the Bechuana a number of people in South Africa were thoroughly hating and distrusting one another, and, still more, the professed servants of God.

These are the things that happened while the Rev. John Mackenzie was doing his duty to the Bechuana:

The Bechuana went marauding and then overcame a punitive expedition led against them by that same officer (Lanyon, the Administrator of Griqualand West) who later, as Rhodes put it, caused all the trouble in the Transvaal by running it on the lines of a second-rate line regiment. Rhodes himself was in that punitive expedition, hence his bitterness.

Afterwards a Colonel Warren was sent out to restore order, but did nothing much more than receive petitions for the protection of one tribe from another.

Those happened to be the days of Imperial contraction; therefore, instead of the British coming in, the Boers came in and established the Republics of Stellaland and Goshenland.

The Rev. Mackenzie saw in this a Dutch plot to take the whole of South Africa, with results terrible to the natives and the cause of civilization, and went to England to protest. He engaged the sympathy of the Aborigines Protection Society, so that Rhodes, for the rest of his life, lost no opportunity of jeering at them; opposed the granting of certain concessions Kruger was now seeking in London; and, to the chagrin of all those he had calumniated, was duly sent back to Bechuanaland as Deputy Commissioner.

He answered the call with energy. He raised the Union Jack in Stellaland in the faces of the furious Dutch. He carried his flag to Goshenland, and while he was reading his proclamation the Boers rode away and looted, so it is said, the cattle of the natives who were respectfully listening to the proclamation. But it is also said the Boers went out to repel a native raid on their capital.

Whichever way it happened, it is clear that Mackenzie found himself in a ridiculous and intolerable situation, and returned, with a force of police, to Stellaland, to find the flag he had set up there pulled down, and the republicans applying to be taken over by the Cape that they might be saved from him. He sent a bitterly complaining telegram to the High Commissioner, Sir Hercules Robinson, and received in answer the news of his recall and his substitution by Cecil Rhodes.

IV

This is not the end of the Rev. Mackenzie, but one may understand now why the Dutch hated him. Why, however, did Rhodes hate him?

The reason may be found partly in that very sentence which contains the much-quoted expression, Imperial factor—"We want to get rid of the Imperial factor in this question, and to deal with it jointly with the Transvaal"—and partly in his distrust of the combination of religion with politics, in so far, at least, as it applied, not to the political predicant, but to the political missionary.

Rhodes, whether as a matter of prudence or predilection, perhaps of both, was, in those days, an adherent of the Cape Dutch. "I have great sympathy with them; they have needs and experiences which we are all, I sincerely think, apt to overlook. I help them as far as I can instead of opposing them.

67

Is not that the better way? It pleases them and it pleases me.
. . . As for minor measures which I have supported, if men
like to put blue ribbons on their cattle when they send them
to market, why shouldn't they?"

Why, indeed? There is an undertone of cynicism in the last
sentence which is not without its suggestiveness. But, in fact,
in the whole style of diplomacy which this quotation embodies
Rhodes was the pupil of Hofmeyr. One might call it the art
of seductive leadership.

They became friends, Rhodes and Hofmeyr; they worked
together. As Rhodes was successfully pushing his way northwards Hofmeyr said to him: "You have got hold of the interior. Now be generous. Let us down gently."

"I will not let you down," said Rhodes. "I will take you
with me."

Yet what Rhodes did ultimately do was precisely, as Hofmeyr felt, to let them down, and not in Hofmeyr's meaning of
the term. For twelve years Rhodes and Hofmeyr worked together in amity, even in community; through Rhodes Hofmeyr
learnt to forget the distrust of the British which had caused
him, after the Shepstone annexation, to throw over his ideal
of union; and when an older, stronger passion led Rhodes to
betray their long association in the Jameson Raid, Hofmeyr
compared himself with a dishonoured husband. And that, indeed, was his position. He had been wronged, charmed back to
belief, and wronged again.

There was even a time when a leader of that Bond whose
motto had been "A united South Africa under one flag—but
not under England," came and asked Rhodes to throw in his
lot with theirs. Rhodes himself tells the story. The emissary
said: " 'Mr. Rhodes, we want a United South Africa,' and

I said, 'So do I.' . . . He said: 'There is nothing in the way.' And I said: 'No, there is nothing in the way—we are one!' . . . 'And we will take you as our leader,' he said. 'Only one thing. We must, of course, be independent of the rest of the world.' " "You take me," said Rhodes, "for either a rogue or a fool. I would be a rogue to forfeit all my history and tradition, and I would be a fool because I would be hated by my own countrymen and mistrusted by yours."

That seems, really, to define Rhodes' attitude towards the Dutch. He was prepared to work with them, he was prepared to admit, as he said, that men under republican institutions had republican feelings, he was prepared to unite with them, but—"May my right hand wither if I forget thee, O Jerusalem"—there was something nearer his heart than Africa, and that was England. He did not want the Imperial factor, it is true, but it was in the spirit of a soldier who, in the midst of hostilities, resents the ignorant interference of those at home. That is not to say he won't fight to the uttermost.

"I believe," said Rhodes, "in a United States of South Africa, but as a portion of the British Empire."

"No grander future can belong to any statesman than that of dealing with the complicated questions of South Africa and the enormous expansion that lies before us in the dark interior. With that I believe my life to be connected."

"If I forfeit my flag, what have I left? If you take away my flag, you take away everything."

"I believe, with all the enthusiasm bred in the soul of an inventor, it is not self-glorification I desire, but the wish to live to register my patent for the benefit of those who, I think, are the greatest people the world has ever seen."

Nevertheless

"It is the amateur meddling of irresponsible and ill-advised persons in England that makes every resident in the Republics, English as well as Dutch, rejoice in their independence, and converts many a colonist from an Imperialist into a Republican."

"The principle must be recognized in the Old Country that people born and bred in this colony, and descended from those who existed in this country many generations ago, are much better capable of dealing with the various matters that arise than people who have to dictate from some thousands of miles away."

v

Here we have, then, not only an explanation of Rhodes' attitude towards the Dutch, and, again, towards the Imperial factor, but we approach also the reason for his dislike of missionaries.

He felt himself British, but he wanted, first, to work together with the Dutch, since he recognized a union of the two white nations to be the destiny of South Africa, and he wanted, second, no misguided interference in his plans—neither the interference of those whose kingdom was narrowly England, nor of those whose kingdom was narrowly Heaven.

If it was, in short, a question of taking sides on matters affecting the natives, he was rather with the Dutch of South Africa than with the English of England.

Rhodes had spent his young manhood in Kimberley. There he had seen thousands of savages—men but newly arisen from the earth—working like mules, like oxen, under their white masters. They were away from their kraals, their laws, the things that were good and natural to them. Such social and spiritual qualities as they had could not be apparent in those strange conditions. Take a liberal Englishman today, just come from overseas full of sympathy and indignation on behalf of the native, and show him a mine: the natives, naked, sweating on the stopes; the natives, crowding, dust-brown, into skips with buns in their hands; the natives, herded in their lodgings, their concrete bunks one over the other; the natives, blanketed, flat-faced, dark, shouting, swarming—and watch that Englishman's face. It will show, not tenderness or brotherhood, but a sort of awakening, an awe, an apprehension. Here is not what he had imagined. The native is too frighteningly different. . . .

Next to the ugliness of Kimberley the thing that most impressed Trollope on the Diamond Fields was this strange way the native was being civilized by the mines: "One is tempted sometimes to say that nothing is done by religion, and very little by philanthropy. But love of money works very fast. . . ."

Yet even Trollope understood—and, if he did not endorse, he did not deprecate—the Boer point of view: "This savage! This something more, but very little more, than a monkey!" The words are Trollope's.

It was not till many years later that Rhodes struck the word "white" from his election cry, and admitted the common rights of every civilized man, whatever his colour.

But that was after his fall, after the Dutch would have no more of him, when he had nothing to lose from the Dutch and something to gain from the natives; it was in the days of his struggling to rise again, of his sorrow and perhaps, who knows? of his greater sympathy with those who had had to abandon hope, not before entering hell, but even before entering life. It was expediency, it may have been (how often is not expediency the father of principle!) also something risen above its begetting.

The thing, then, for which Rhodes' name stands in South Africa—this equal-rights idea—was not at all at the root of his political life. In his early days, in those eighteen-eighties, he differentiated most determinedly between "every white man" and "every civilized man"; he followed, not the missionary, but the Boer, tradition; he felt it necessary to link with the Boer tradition, and he said:

"I will lay down my own policy on this native question. Either you have to receive them on an equal footing as citizens, or to call them a subject race. I have made up my mind that there must be class legislation, that there must be Pass Laws and Peace Preservation Acts, and that we have to treat natives, where they are in a state of barbarism, in a different way to ourselves. We are to be lords over them. These are my politics on native affairs, and these are the politics of South Africa. . . . The native is to be treated as a child and denied the franchise; he is to be denied liquor also. . . . If I cannot keep my position in the country as an Englishman on the European vote, I wish to be cleared out, for I am not going to the native vote for support. . . . We must adopt a system of despotism, such as works so well in India, in our relations with the barbarians of South Africa."

The sense of superiority the present has over the past is due, in part, to the way Time so mischievously shows up the poor old past. There is Rhodes' remark about the despotism that works so well in India. There is his contemptuous, "I am not going to the native vote for support." There is a further remark

72

he now proceeds to make—namely, that the natives will, without question, be given the franchise when the missionaries turn out men capable of administering the telegraph and postal system, of carpentering and managing machinery. Is there, alas, anything more exasperating to the present-day South African than the fact that the native wants to do work which is reserved to the white man?

In this very speech, ironically enough, Rhodes congratulates himself that, by good luck rather than discrimination, he has nothing to recant on the Native Question, since, he confesses, it was as "a rabid jingo" he came down to the House; and he goes on to deride "the extreme philosophic sympathy of those who wish to endow the native at once with the privileges it has taken the European eighteen hundred years to acquire." Only in the matter of drink, he says, have the missionaries any right to interfere. Refuse drink to the natives, and what further need is there for missionaries? The franchise is not their business. "Let the missionaries be taught a lesson!"

Rhodes made this speech after the Bechuanaland trouble and it was the Bechuanaland trouble that inspired it. It was of the Rev. John Mackenzie he was thinking when he said, "Let the missionaries be taught a lesson."

VI

For the Rev. John Mackenzie, a prisoner of the Lord, was not the man to abandon a duty. After his recall he went about Cape Town denouncing (1) Kruger, (2) Rhodes, (3) Hofmeyr. He spoke also, as Rhodes himself was doing, of a fourth enemy, Bismarck—Germany was coming to South Africa.

And were they, he demanded, to let the Dutch take Bechua-

73

naland, to let the Cape take it, or the Germans? These people who considered only themselves, and not at all the natives? There was one country alone that could be relied upon to do her duty to the natives without any thought of personal advantage, and that was England.

He spoke with that passion England herself has for subject races, and which is so moving and comic, both together. For a nation need be little more than humble, and England not only pities it, not only likes it, but, indeed, admires it.

While Mackenzie was fulminating in Cape Town, Rhodes was in Bechuanaland trying to smooth down the question marks and notes of exclamation that had raised themselves over the soil of Bechuanaland like hairs on the back of a defiant, apprehensive dog.

It has been said that Rhodes was overbearing and ruthless, and overbearing and ruthless he was. But he could be all things when he had an object to achieve. He could be reasonable. He could be conciliatory. He could be sympathetic. Persuasiveness —a simple, confiding, colloquial, explanatory, and yet bluff man-to-mannishness was, as he knew himself, one of his most successful attitudes.

"You can't resist him," said Barnato, the Jew, as he yielded to him.

"We had a talk," said Hofmeyr, the secretive Boer, "and were friends ever afterwards."

"You have come back to us again," said the Matabele, whom he had despoiled of their country, "and now all things are clear and we are your children."

"Stay and work with me," begged Chinese Gordon in Basutoland, and afterwards asked him to come along and help to "smash the Mahdi." Rhodes did not go, and, too late, was sorry for it. Yet in time, so far from "smashing" the Mahdi, he was to say that he did not "propose to fight the Mahdi, but to deal with him." Whereupon "squaring the Mahdi"—the idea of bribery—became an amused catchword to be employed against Rhodes. And a story is told of how Parnell complained to Rhodes that the priests were against him, and Rhodes said, "Can't you square the Pope?"

And in fact Rhodes was not above bribery; he was not above anything that could help his plans. But precisely in this Mahdi business, he seems to have been relying on charms other than those of money, since, "I have never," he goes on to say, "met anyone in my life whom it was not as easy to deal with as to fight."

He was not altogether accurate. He did have one or two failures in his "dealings." He even failed now in Bechuanaland.

He began brilliantly.

He went first (it is a story he tells over and over again) to van Niekerk, the Administrator of Stellaland, with whom he had been able to negotiate before, and he found him not less pliable this time. But van Niekerk had a lieutenant, an enormous backvelder called "Groot"—that is, "Big" Adrian de la Rey, and de la Rey would have none of him. He lived up to his ogre reputation. "Blood must flow," he roared. Rhodes, the Giant-killer, six feet tall himself, smiled at him. "Give me my breakfast," he said. "Then we can talk about blood." And he stayed with de la Rey, he says, a week, became godfather to his grandchild, and made a settlement, the chief feature of which was the cancellation of everything done by Mackenzie.

This is the Rhodes who, unmaddened by the gods, might have altered history by dealing with Kruger. He said so him-

75

self. For there was that in Rhodes which there never was in Milner, as he reveals himself in his *Letters*. How could Milner, so lonely, academic, and withdrawn, so barricaded in his literary gentlemanliness, so unable to vary himself with a variable humanity—how could such a fruit of nineteenth-century bureaucracy meet a biblical patriarch?

Kruger had had three months' schooling in his life. He had read the Bible and no other book. He was married at seventeen, a widower at twenty-one, remarried twice, and the father of sixteen children. Early in the morning, on the stoep of his little iron-roofed house in Pretoria (not much better than Rhodes' iron-roofed house in Kimberley), facing his Dopper Church, he sat among his people, drinking coffee, smoking his pipe, spitting at large, talking as if he were Abraham of the Bible. This is how he established diplomatic relations with Moshesh, the leader of the Basutos. Kruger said to him:

"If you are so devout, how do you come to have more than one wife?"

"It is true. I have just about two hundred. Still, that is not half so many as Solomon had."

"But surely you know that, since Christ's time, and according to the New Testament, a man may have only one wife."

"Well—well, what shall I say to you? . . . It is just human nature." . . .

And this is how, Solomon-like, Kruger decided a dispute between two brothers about an inheritance of land: Let one brother, he said, divide the land, and let the other have first choice.

With such a man, as with Groot Adrian, Rhodes might have parleyed. To him, too, he could have said, "Let us have breakfast, and then we can talk about blood." Kruger would have liked that. He lived instead to say of Rhodes, "This man was the curse of South Africa."

VII

It was actually during the Bechuanaland affair Rhodes first met Kruger. Why could he not now talk pleasantly about blood and breakfast?

The answer is that he did not come alone, and others did the talking.

CHAPTER ، 8

THE FIRST STEP NORTH

WHEN Rhodes met Kruger, it was in the company of General (he was now General) Warren, and the Rev. John Mackenzie.

It was through Rhodes himself Warren was in Bechuanaland. Things had not gone in Bechuanaland as Rhodes had expected. The exhilarating success with van Niekerk and de la Rey had been the end of success. And though it might seem that he achieved in Bechuanaland what he desired, which was Bechuanaland itself for England and a path to the North, he achieved it according to the Rev. John Mackenzie's plans and not his own. He had said, "We want to get rid of the Imperial factor on this question, and to deal with it ourselves, jointly with the Transvaal." He had not been long in Bechuanaland before he was asking for Imperial intervention.

For, even while he was attempting to "deal" in Goshenland as he had dealt in Stellaland, things were happening—too many and too soon. The Goshenlanders were fighting again with the natives, they were hoisting, not the English, but the Transvaal, flag—the Germans were coming down the West Coast of Africa. Time was, as ever, against Rhodes. He could not wait to parley. He could not see the Germans combining

with the Boers to block England's way to the North. He had
to do the quickest thing, and he asked for that General Warren
to be sent whom he knew from his Kimberley days.

II

Things had never been the same in South Africa since the
finding of diamonds. Before that it had been a poor, lonely
place where the troubled of the world could come for sanctuary. Who else wanted it? No one of any worldliness. There
was room for all the superfluous, the hunted, the misfitting.

Diamonds had made South Africa known to the world. The
explorer Stanley had made the centre of Africa known. And
now everything was different. No more was it an old earthy
life of lands, herds, children, savages, a life untouched by the
dreams and desires of civilization. From the ends of the earth
journeyed the fortune-hunters. To the ends of the earth went
their stories of this rich land waiting to be taken, simply waiting meekly to be taken.

The takers came.

The English—of the Cape or England—took Griqualand
West as a reward and protected several native territories as a
duty. The King of the Belgians said the Congo was his personal estate. The French, in the Congo, too, wanted the Niger
and ran off with Madagascar. The Portuguese said all the
country from Angola on the West Coast to Mozambique on the
East Coast was theirs—it had been, they said, for centuries.
Things were going on in North Africa, West Africa, East
Africa.

In South Africa the Boers, not long in their own republics,
had the two little new republics in Bechuanaland; they had

79

also ridden out—three hundred odd of them—and got themselves a chunk of Zululand. By treaty they were not allowed to interfere with the natives. But the invaders of Zululand did as the Goshen and Stellalanders had done—they gave up their burgher rights and ceased thus to be bound by national treaties.

And suddenly here was Bismarck, too. He had hitherto been like Gladstone, he had not wanted colonies, finding he had trouble enough at home. But Stanley had been lecturing in Germany; conferences had sat, now here, now there, on the dividing up of Africa; German missionaries had asked him for the protection England would not give them on the West Coast; his merchants were avid for markets; Karl Peters was running about Germany selling concessions he had picked up from the East Coast Kaffirs for this, for that, for nothing; the concessionaries were offering to colonize in the old way with charters. Bismarck was in it too.

Even while Rhodes was struggling against Boers and blacks in Bechuanaland, the Germans were coming to the West Coast. Before the trouble was over in Bechuanaland, they were coming, led by Karl Peters, to the East Coast.

And Rhodes, crying: "Beware! Germany!" sent for Warren.

III

Warren arrived with four thousand men, British and Colonial, and, also, to Rhodes' astonishment and unspeakable chagrin, with the Rev. John Mackenzie, who had won him from under Rhodes' nose. Now not only he and Rhodes, but also Mackenzie, went to negotiate with Kruger. Before them, for the sake of frightfulness, rode two hundred dragoons.

That made everything wrong from the beginning. There

was the biblical patriarch with his half-dozen or so Boers, and there was the clanking general asserting in advance that there was to be no nonsense. As if this were not enough, he must needs bring with him the very missionary of missionaries. He might as well have brought Satan.

In days to come Rhodes was to have the experience and self-confidence to believe that in warfare the wisdom of a civilian might be better than the training of a soldier. When he was about to break his way Northwards he asked an Imperial officer how many men he would need and what it would cost. Two thousand five hundred men, said the officer, and a quarter of a million of money. So Rhodes found himself a young man of twenty-three who offered to do it, and did do it, with a tenth of the men suggested by the soldier, and a third of the money. When things were bad in Mashonaland for lack of money, he dismissed all the seven hundred guardian police except forty, and created volunteers. He was told he would need ten thousand men to take Matabeleland, and he took it (so he said, but his figures were not quite accurate) with nine hundred. He drove into Pondoland with eight cream-coloured horses, eight policemen, and some machine-guns, and so annexed it. His emissaries walked into savage kraals with a piece of paper and a few hundred pounds, and walked out with a kingdom. When the Matabele rose in revolt he joined a military column as a kind of associate general, and his weapon was a hunting-crop. He found Matabeleland full of soldiers and fighting. He left the soldiers camped behind him, and, with a few friends and revolvers, went out to settle matters through talk. During the Boer War he undertook to teach the various generals their business, and, while he was besieged in Kimber-

81

ley, competed with the maddened commanding officer in defending it, so that he was almost court-martialled for his pains.

The failure of the Jameson Raid was more significant than any of his successes, but it was the only failure in Rhodes' system of aggression, and one might choose to regard it as an exception.

The longer he lived, indeed, the less grew his respect for formal soldiering. But in those early Bechuanaland days he had not yet the experience, the arrogance, the material for comparison, which ultimately led him to the opinion that he could run a war better than any professional fighting-man.

At the negotiations with Kruger—the atmosphere being military—he submitted to Warren's authority and allowed him to make the terms. Mackenzie prompted Warren. Kruger departed from the meeting, humiliated and hostile. "Rhodes," he reports, scathingly, "pretended to be on my side." He refused to believe in the sincerity of Rhodes' conversion from "Don't part with an inch of territory to Transvaal" to "We want to get rid of the Imperial factor on this question, and to deal with it jointly with the Transvaal." But in fact Rhodes was sincere. There is no doubting his abhorrence, at the moment, of the Imperial factor. . . .

Warren, still inspired by Mackenzie, declared martial law over Bechuanaland; sent forth the fiat that no Boer was to own land in the country; brought a murder charge, never substantiated, against Rhodes' ally, the Administrator of Stellaland; disowned Rhodes' promises; told Rhodes he was a danger to peace; and, having well displayed his four thousand soldiers to the casual, ununiformed Boers, declared a British Protectorate over the whole of Bechuanaland.

He did his work without the firing of a shot. And so far,

very good. But the result of Warren's brisk and ruthless efficiency was such a passion against England that Warren had to be recalled. And what Rhodes said in Parliament, after he had resigned his deputy-commissionership in Bechuanaland, was this: "I remember," he said, "when a youngster, reading in my English history of the supremacy of my country and its annexations, and that there were two cardinal axioms: that the word of the nation, when once pledged, was never broken, and that, when a man accepted the citizenship of the British Empire, there was no distinction of races. It has been my misfortune in one year to meet with the breach of the one and the proposed breach of the other."

But what Kruger said was this: "That young man," he said, "is going to cause me trouble."

And he meant, most strangely, not the faulty Warren, but the virtuous Rhodes.

CHAPTER , 9

RHODES FOUNDS HIS GOLDFIELDS
COMPANY

I

THE trouble Rhodes was to cause Kruger, granted he did cause it, had another parent—Nature. Under Kruger's earth lay that which was to continue what Kimberley had begun —the civilizing of South Africa, the breaking of all that Kruger stood for and of Kruger himself—an old system of life and an old man who fought for that system. In the very year after Kruger's meeting with Warren, Mackenzie, and Rhodes, gold was found on the Witwatersrand—the Ridge of the White Waters.

It had been found before in South Africa, thousands of years before, some say, in Rhodesia; but for practical, immediate purposes it had been found in the 'sixties—where of all places? In the Tati district, over the top end of Bechuanaland, to finish off the irony of the finding of diamonds at the bottom end. A desert in the middle, and then, for the Lord's fun, on one side diamonds, and on the other gold.

Then it was found here and there in the Transvaal.

Now, something over twenty years after the first modern discovery, it was found on the Rand, and the history of Rhodes leads neatly from the year 1885 to the year 1886.

The city of Johannesburg dates from the year 1886. In that year the reef was struck, and a people whose habit it was to escape from civilization had civilization ineluctably thrust upon them. The Boers had fled from France and from Holland to the Cape. They had fled from the Cape to Natal and the Orange Free State and the Transvaal. During two hundred years and over they had lived more primitively than the people of the Bible. For the people of the Bible—even those who, like the Boers, had sojourned in the wilderness and drunk the bitter waters and quenched their thirst at Elim—the people of Moses had begun to civilize themselves in the desert.

There they had been given laws. There had been set to work in wood and gold (cherubim and candlesticks and bowls like almonds with a knop and a flower); in fine-twined linen and blue and purple and scarlet; in ramskins dyed and badger skins; in breastplates set with jewels; in perfumes, after the art of the apothecary, tempered together, pure and holy.

The Boers did none of these things in their desert. They wandered with their flocks, according to the season, from high-veld to low-veld. They lived in tents or in houses of corrugated iron and mud. They rode, slack in seat, long in stirrup, on shaggy horses. Their literature was the Bible—the Old Testament rather than the New. They saw no newspapers. They heard no news. Europe was breathlessly changing, and they were unaware of it. They had the freedom and security, the dignity and strength, the lordliness and hospitality—the narrowness, the evasiveness, the idleness, the ignorance, of solitude. To this very day there are Boers who live like those Boers of pre-gold days. But not so many. The telegraph, the train, the newspaper, the motor-car, have reached them—undone and remade them.

The world was desperate for gold in those 'eighties. There were Englishmen who, early in 1886, said that all the labour troubles were due to a shortage of gold; because it was so rare, and the sovereign so precious, wages were getting lower and lower, and there was again talk of bimetallism as the only remedy.

Nobody thought much of the gold that lately had been found in South Africa. It was considered nothing to the gold of Australia.

And in this very year, for the economic convenience of all the world, the gold-reefs of the Rand were dramatically uncovered.

Now what had happened in Kimberley happened also in Johannesburg. The Boers sold their gold-laden land as they had sold their diamond-laden land, and trekked away. The adventurers came from the ends of Africa and the earth—the traders, the gamblers, the outlaws, the thousands of natives; the miners, mostly Cornishmen; the engineers, mostly Americans; the financiers, mostly Jews. From Kimberley itself the adventurers came. Everyone in Kimberley was gambling on news from the Rand—men, women, miners, shopkeepers, clerks, in houses, in hotels, in the Kimberley Club, in the streets: would they strike the reef in that shaft or in that shaft? Brokers shouted their prices like bookies during a race. Champagne was the drink. Cigarettes were lighted (probably not often, but they tell such things) with bank-notes. . . .

The Boers who had not trekked too far away sold milk and vegetables to the new population on the Rand. They sold chickens, sheep, oxen, and horses—tough wanderers like themselves over the earth. They chopped the wood of the veld, loaded it on their waggons, and brought it to town—the family under the hood of the waggon, the father or eldest son, tall and brown and bearded, walking with a long whip, the sjambok, beside the oxen. That was what the Boers got out of the finding of gold. They did not attempt to work the gold themselves. There had been a time when their laws, holding it to be a source of wickedness, had forbidden the working of gold. They did not open shops and sell their goods to the easy-buying, excited, reckless crowds. They were not shopkeepers by disposition. They are not now.

In Pretoria, Kruger, behind him his council, his Volksraad, arose, like Joshua, and told the sun to stand still. He arose, big and stout, in his black frock-coat and his black trousers and his black top-hat and his ceremonial green sash, with his little sore, pouched eyes, and his clean-shaven, snapped-to mouth and his straggly beard that fringed his jaw from ear to ear, and the hand from which he had himself hacked the crushed thumb, and tried to stop time and the planets from revolving. . . .

What could he do? He could make it more and more difficult for the foreigners to vote—to have any say in his Government. He could penalize them by granting monopolies to particular people. He could put taxes on their food. He could give the posts in his service purely to Dutchmen, either the Dutchmen of the Republics, or, where a higher standard was needed than might be found among a people so recently wanderers in the desert, the Dutchmen of Holland. The Dutchmen of the Cape or Natal, being English subjects, he regarded as practically traitors: they were not eligible. "He has made an administrative scheme," said Rhodes in Parliament, "the essence of which is that no South African may have a part in it."

Rhodes was on the Rand now, with Beit and Barnato and the others who had founded their fortunes in Kimberley, and he warned Kruger concerning his treatment of the Uitlanders. Kruger remembered what his rival for the Presidency had said, "This gold will cause our country to be soaked in blood." And he told Rhodes that he had heard all those stories before. "I am here," he said, "to protect my burghers as well as the Rand people. I know what I have to do, and I will do what I think right."

The complainants resentfully went on making money.

III

It was Beit who made most. Rhodes, his deepest attention elsewhere, was persuaded by his general manager at de Beers— an American—that the handling of the ore must prove too costly for profitable working; and by the time he was wiser the best things were gone and one of the bigger gold-mining properties he might have had was bought by Beit, shortly to become his associate in the amalgamation of de Beers. And although Rhodes did eventually buy here and there against rivals and found the Goldfields Company, later the Consolidated Goldfields of South Africa, perhaps he himself expressed best the reason why he never became in gold what he became in diamonds: he could not feel gold as he felt diamonds. "I cannot," he said, "calculate the *power* in these claims."

He had not, moreover, a mind free for such calculation. To begin with, he was much perturbed by the illness of his young friend Pickering, and threw up certain important negotiations in order to hurry to his death-bed. And then his thoughts could not be solidly on gold, since they were also on politics: on questions of Boer and Briton and Union; since they were also on Bechuanaland—on questions of natives, missionaries, Germans; since they were also on millions of square miles reaching northwards as far as Egypt—he had just set his foot on the beginnings of those miles in Bechuanaland; since they were supremely, at the moment, on the controlling of all the diamond mines of South Africa and all the diamonds of the world.

CHAPTER ˙ 10

RHODES AMALGAMATES THE
DIAMOND MINES

I

H E WAS, indeed, taking advantage of the gold-rush
to buy the diamond shares of those who were forsaking
the chances of Kimberley for those on the Rand. For fifteen
years he and Barney Barnato had competed against one another in the race for wealth and power, and now the battle
was at its climax.

Barney Barnato, whose real name was Barnett Isaacs, had
come to South Africa in the year Rhodes had returned, for
the first time, from Africa to England to enter Oxford. Their
ships passed one another on the Atlantic. As Cecil Rhodes had
followed his brother Herbert to Kimberley, so was Barnett
Isaacs following his brother Harry. He brought with him not,
like Rhodes, a Greek lexicon and some classics, but forty boxes
of bad cigars to sell.

Both the brothers called themselves Barnato. The name
suited their music-hall turn of mind. They loved the theatre.
When Barney arrived in Kimberley in 1873 he found Harry
making his living by showmanship as much as by anything
else, and he was doing it under the name of Barnato; it was
actually Harry, and not Barney, who derived the name of

Barnato from Barnett. Barney, it is said, knew all Henry Irving's parts, and even played lead, at amateur performances, in "Othello," "Macbeth," and "The Merchant of Venice."

He was eighteen in the year he came to Kimberley. Rhodes, too, had arrived in Kimberley at the age of eighteen. He had arrived with a Greek lexicon where Barnato had arrived with those bad cigars. He had gone to Oxford, and Barnato to Jews' Free School. His father was a country clergyman, and Barnato's a Whitechapel shopkeeper.

But Bishop Stortford or Whitechapel, the sons were both natural tradesmen.

"There is nothing this country produces," said Barnato in later years, "that I have not traded in, from diamonds and gold right away through wool and mealies to garden vegetables."

With the money he got for his cigars, he went—as it was called—kopje-walloping. That is to say, he walked from claim to claim, carrying in his pocket a borrowed diamond scale, buying such diamonds as he could afford, and selling them to the regular diamond dealers. Rhodes was now not only a digger, but an ice-cream vendor, a water-pumper, a storekeeper, and an Oxford undergraduate.

Presently Barney and his brother were both digging for diamonds and selling them. At night they visited the bars, talked, and listened.

Barney was not altogether unpopular. He was vulgar, but he was generous. He spoke—as one might expect, but he had a straight blue eye. Wearing a checked suit, a buttonhole, a pince-nez, and a waxed moustache, he does not, in his photographs, make a very distinguished figure, but his brow is good, and the expression is keen and rather decent. What went on in that stiff-shirted bosom that it was not enough for him to play the magnate in London, he must needs belong to the Kimberley Club? Why, after even that triumph, could he not be happy? Eight years later he leapt from a liner and drowned himself.

The game as to who should eventually amalgamate the diamond mines of Kimberley was played out between these two, Rhodes and Barnato. Others had once been in it also. "What is your game?" said Rhodes to Alfred Beit. "I am going to control the whole diamond output before I am much older," said Beit. "That's funny," said Rhodes. "I have made up my mind to do the same. We had better join hands."

And so they did. And so, too, this and that opposition was wiped out until there were left in just Rhodes and Barnato and their respective adherents.

II

This is why, control of the market apart, the diamond mines of Kimberley had to be amalgamated, whether under Rhodes or Barnato or anyone else:

The digging at Kimberley had begun by being a simple matter of a man coming with a few tools and working his ground with a few Kaffirs. But Rhodes had barely arrived in Kimberley when things were already complicated. Too many men were working in too small a space. Claims of thirty-one feet square were divided into four and even into eight parts. The best of them had risen in value from one hundred to four thousand pounds. Every inch of soil was valuable. When first the hard bottom of the yellow ground was struck, claims were hurriedly sold to unsuspecting buyers because this hard bottom, it was thought, was the end of diamonds. It was then found that the real mine was the hard blue ground, and not the soft overflow of yellow ground. And more and more did the mines of Kimberley become inverted Manhattans where men had to extend themselves by sinking instead of by rising.

They sank in narrow vertical shafts that left a minimum of space between one man's working and the next. Across these grudged intersections had to go the carts and mules that moved the ground for sifting, washing, sorting. The natives had to sidle past the procession of carts, they had to walk precariously along the crumbling, unrailed edges—for that matter, so had the diggers.

Presently not only mules and carts, but natives and the precious earth itself, were tumbling into the shafts. Another year or so and accidents to people and animals, the falling of reef, the flooding of the claims with water, had not only forced the consolidation of claims, it had made necessary a Mining Board.

Soon the mines were open quarries bolstered up by timber. Roads and mules were gone. On iron ropes, stretched taut from the rim of a mine to the working floor below ran buckets bringing the earth up, tipping themselves over, depositing the earth where it was to be worked, righting themselves again, running down empty on another set of ropes.

Over each mine was a web of iron ropes on which scudded buckets rising and descending. Down below, deep down in the great open bowl, worked thousands of black men and their masters, each antlike group in a separate pit, at a separate mound of earth. Their shouting, chanting, commanding voices, the clank of their picks and shovels, rose from the depths, a mere distant humming. The buckets, whizzing and whining along the wires, made play on what was become a gigantic instrument of music. It was a distant chorus accompanied by a string band. . . .

Another few years and the Mining Board had spent over two million pounds in maintaining the mines, it was in debt, and could not get its overdraft renewed. Now, for every load of diamondiferous ground brought to the surface four or five loads of cumbering earth had to be removed. The pits were anything up to four hundred feet deep, and below the pits themselves shafts and tunnels led the way to the even more valuable blue ground that had recently been discovered.

The falls of débris grew ever larger. Once a fall of five million tons stopped the work of a mine for six months. Another fall killed eighteen people. The rain that comes so seldom to Kimberley could come in flooding storms. . . .

One of the possessions of Rhodes and his partners in their early days was a six-horsepower steam-engine, bought by Rhodes, with which they pumped water and made ice-cream. It was the only engine on the spot when in that year a thunderstorm burst over Kimberley and a mine was flooded. Rhodes contracted to pump out the water. A friend warned him to have a secure place into which to run the water, or it would flow back into the mine. Rhodes did better. He had a clause inserted in the contract holding the mine-management responsible for storing the pumped-out water. What followed was that the dam made by the mine people burst; the water ran back into the pit. Another contract followed, at twice, it is said, the amount of the first, and this was Rhodes' first substantial business undertaking. Why the mine should have paid Rhodes double for pumping the water a second time is not clear. However, that is the story.

There were, naturally, setbacks in Rhodes' fortune-making.

In 1876 he was writing to Rudd from his father's vicarage: "I suppose our affair at de Beers looks bad. Don't be dispirited. If ever you were in a good thing that will give you a good income, that will." And he and his partners had to lose the chance of buying the whole of de Beers mine because they lacked six thousand pounds to make up the price asked for it. Yet he was still an undergraduate at Oxford when the three partners had grown to six; they called themselves the de Beers Mining Company; they had a capital of two hundred thousand pounds; they were buying at competitive prices the claims they had once lacked the money to buy at a bargain.

It was not till 1887 that, in devious ways, with great effort, at enormous cost, Rhodes finally possessed his de Beers Mine.

Meanwhile Barney Barnato was acquiring the mine called the Kimberley Mine. The de Beers Mine and the Kimberley Mine were the most important two of the four mines on the Diamond Fields.

III

These were the steps by which the two men rose, side by side, towards power over diamonds:

There were the little beginnings: Rhodes' ice-cream-selling and water-pumping; Barnato's cigar-selling and kopje-walloping.

In 1876, the year Rhodes was encouraging Rudd, from England, to go on, despite the depression, buying de Beers claims, Barnato had three thousand pounds and bought with his money four claims at the Kimberley Mine. Out of these claims he made as much as eighteen hundred pounds in a week.

In 1880, the year in which Rhodes stood for Parliament and

floated the de Beers Mining Company with a capital of two hundred thousand pounds, Barnato floated the Barnato Diamond Company with a capital of one hundred and fifteen thousand pounds.

By 1885 Rhodes was worth fifty thousand pounds a year, and Barnato was richer still. He owned not only a great block in the Kimberley Mine, he owned also most of the share capital of the Oriental Company, whose claims were in the de Beers Mine.

Now Rhodes, estimating that three-quarters of a million pounds' worth of diamonds was stolen every year by the native mine-workers of Kimberley, compounded his natives. They were housed by de Beers, fed by de Beers, served by de Beers, searched by de Beers. To this day a native mine-worker is not seen in the streets of Kimberley, and the shops of Kimberley are not the wealthier for the presence of natives in the town.

Never again, after the amalgamation of the mines and the general adoption of the compound system, did the illicit diamond-buyer so easily chance a fortune, or seven years on the Cape Town breakwater, by buying the diamonds the natives stole; or the chiefs of the North receive from their tribesmen the old tribute of pretty stones, which are still sought for by adventurers. The mines retrieved the diamonds that were hidden in the pepper-corn hair, between the hard-skinned toes, in the mouths, in the ears, in the noses, and, for that matter, in the bowels, of the mine-workers. Purgatives were one means of searching them, and are today.

By 1888, de Beers Company, which, shortly after its formation, had paid a dividend of three per cent on its capital of two hundred thousand, was paying a dividend of twenty-five per cent on a capital of two and a third millions. And Rhodes was calculating that one might sell four million pounds' worth of diamonds for engagement rings alone.

But how to keep up the fashion and price of diamonds? How not to make them too common, too cheap?

For what Rhodes was doing at de Beers Mine, Barnato was doing at the Kimberley—he was absorbing lesser companies, buying up all the shares he could. His only great obstacle at the Kimberley Mine was the presence of a concern called the French Company.

Rhodes and Barnato competed with one another in the selling of diamonds and the buying of shares. The price of diamonds went down, yet the price of shares went up.

Both men felt that this underselling, this outbuying, must not go on. Both wanted control.

The crux, as Rhodes would have expressed it, was the French Company. It all depended on who could buy out the French Company.

Rhodes did so. He was associated now in this business with the Hamburg Jew, Alfred Beit. Beit had made his first money in Kimberley by letting a dozen corrugated-iron offices on the edge of a mine for eighteen hundred pounds a month. For twelve or thirteen years he made this money, and then he sold the ground for two hundred and sixty thousand pounds. In the meantime he had bought and sold diamonds, bought and sold claims. He was richer even than Rhodes.

The path from one Jew to another is an easy one. Rhodes went to England to see Lord Rothschild, and Lord Rothschild approved of him.

Within a few days, as Rhodes described it in a subsequent speech, he had three-quarters of a million pounds. He then used, he said in the same speech, the following arguments to Barnato: "You can go and offer three hundred thousand pounds more than we do for the French, but we will offer another three hundred thousand on that; you can go on and bid for the benefit of the French shareholders *ad infinitum*, because we shall have it in the end." . . .

They did have it in the end. The French Company took one million four hundred thousand pounds for their shares. The money was raised by an issue of de Beers shares at fifteen pounds. The shares rose to twenty-two, and Rhodes made an incidental profit of one hundred thousand pounds on the deal. The French Company's holdings in the Kimberley Mine amounted to a fifth of all the shares in the mine, and that fifth was Rhodes' buttoned boot opportunely thrust into the nervously opened door of Barnato's tight-shut house.

Rhodes now said, in effect, to Barnato, "Do you invite me in or do I force my way in?" In other words, he suggested amalgamation, and, failing amalgamation, war. Barnato rejected amalgamation, he rejected Rhodes' valuation of his mine, and it was war.

Barnato did not yet know Rhodes' single-minded tenacity. "You must never abandon a position" was one of those maxims of Rhodes' that are so useful when things go well of themselves.

He went about buying Kimberley Central shares wherever he could get them, at whatever price. He asked Beit to find him two million pounds for the purpose of these dealings, and Beit, interested by now, as he said, in the sport of the thing, found it. Barnato, greatly troubled, bought against Rhodes.

The shares went up and up. The time came when Rhodes

felt he could speak to Barnato. Later, in the presence of Barnato, he repeated their conversation to his shareholders. ("These are facts, I can assure you, although Mr. Barnato may shake his head and smile.")

"I said to him: 'Well, how are you getting on now?'

"He replied, 'Why, you've bought a million pounds' worth of Centrals.'

"I said: 'Yes, and we'll buy another million pounds' worth. And now,' I said further to him, 'I'll tell you what you will find out presently, and that is you'll be left alone in the Central Company. . . . Your leading shareholders are patting you on the back and backing you up, but selling out round the corner all the time.' "

They were selling to Rhodes. Rhodes' shareholders were standing firm, but Barnato's were undermining their leader.

Rhodes was undermining their leader in his own way. He was "dealing" with Barnato. Nearly every day he had Barnato and his nephew, Woolf Joel, to lunch or dine with him at the Kimberley Club, the sacred, the, to them, unattainable Kimberley Club. An attempt was made to put through a rule that no Kimberley resident, who was not a member, should be allowed to take more than one meal a month at the Club. But Rhodes himself arranged for the defeat of that motion, and the arguments, the blandishments, the threats went on. He hypnotized, he wore out, Barnato.

Barnato sold his shares to Rhodes. With two-thirds of the shares Rhodes found himself in control of the Kimberley Mine. He already—his company—had control of de Beers Mine, and Barnato's Oriental Company in that mine now fell under him, too. He said to his shareholders, "There is no desire on

our part to do what might be termed an American corner."
But that exactly was his desire. He wanted to control the diamonds of the world, and he did. He possessed himself of all
the diamond mines of Kimberley; he bought the last independent holding (through searchlight and despatch-rider) during the Kimberley siege. He drew in such outside mines as
mattered. No American trust, no trust in the world, had such
power over any commodity as Rhodes now had over diamonds.

The game was completely with Rhodes. His magnetized
shareholders offered him a bonus of ten thousand guineas for
his work, but he said no, he had enjoyed the game. And so,
said Beit, demurely refusing an equal gift, had he. Ten thousand guineas! Were people still thinking in thousands?

Barnato, one may assume, had not so much enjoyed the
game. On the other hand, he was, through Rhodes—call it
influence—elected a member of the Kimberley Club, and he
became a director of the amalgamated companies. Indeed, a
life governor. For, "Your crowd will never leave me in,"
Barnato had feared. "They will turn me out in a year or two."
And, "We'll make you a life governor," the inspired Rhodes
had reassured him.

In this way originated the life governorships of de Beers.
Four governors were eventually appointed—Rhodes, Barnato,
Beit, and another of Rhodes' partners. They became entitled,
between them, to a fourth of the profits exceeding one million
four hundred and forty thousand pounds in any one year. A
few years after Barnato's death, and three months after
Rhodes' death, the rights of the life governors were bought by
de Beers Consolidated Company for three million pounds'
worth of its shares.

The final round in the game took place at Dr. Jameson's cottage, Rhodes and Beit on one side, and Barnato and Woolf Joel on the other. They met to decide the terms of the trust deed of the amalgamation.

It was a game played in millions, but the oldest of the players, Rhodes and Beit, were only thirty-five. They had, all four of them, risen young to wealth and power. They were destined, all four, to die within eighteen years. The two losers in the game were indeed dead—and by violence—within eight years. Barney Barnato, as has been mentioned, drowned himself. Woolf Joel was shot dead in Johannesburg by an international blackmailer.

And were they, all these young millionaires, of those natural geniuses of trade whom Nature herself, in Emerson's words, appoints to be her Ministers of Commerce? Might one take it they would have made millions in, say, Finland? Were all the South African millionaires that came to fruition in the eighteen-eighties and eighteen-nineties such natural geniuses of trade? Strange, if so, that the breed should suddenly have arisen and suddenly have died out. . . .

It was during this night session Rhodes sprang on Barnato an idea new to him: the surplus funds of the company were to be available for enterprises not necessarily connected with diamonds; such enterprises as, for instance, Imperial expansion.

Barnato persisted that his business was diamonds.

There was another maxim Rhodes had: "If you have an idea, and it is a good idea, if you will only stick to it you will come out all right."

Such proverbs have been put better. Rhodes, however, had

made the discovery for himself. It was, as he always expressed it, one of the things he had learnt in his life. It had that power and sanctity.

He clung to his point. Towards dawn, when Barnato was exhausted and bewildered, Rhodes suddenly threw into the scale an argument whose weight overpowered Barnato. He offered Barnato a seat in the Cape Parliament.

It was now Barnato made the remark that some people had a fancy for this, and some for that, and Rhodes had a fancy for making an empire, and he supposed he, Barnato, would have to give in to him. "He tied me up as he ties up everybody," he explained, apologetically. "You can't resist him. You must be with him." And the time came when Rhodes, needing money for his Imperial schemes, could get it from Barnato and from nobody else.

But there were Kimberley Central shareholders who had not spent a night in Jameson's cottage, listening to Rhodes. Nor had anyone offered them seats in the Cape Parliament. They persisted in the belief that the business of a diamond company was diamonds. They objected to the amalgamation of Kimberley Central with de Beers, and took their objection to court, saying that the trust deed of their company permitted them to unite only with "similar" companies, and pointing out how far from "similar" was this new company Rhodes was projecting.

The case came before de Villiers, Chief Justice of the Cape and destined twenty years later to preside over the negotiations that led to the consummation of the most immediate of Rhodes' dreams—the union of the states of South Africa. He now upheld the objectors. "Diamond-mining," he said, "forms an insignificant portion of the powers which may be exercised by the company. . . . The powers of the company are as extensive as those of any company that has ever existed."

He suggested, however, a way out of the difficulty. Rhodes and Barnato took it. They liquidated the Kimberley Central Company, bought its assets for £5,338,650, passed a cheque for that amount (the biggest cheque yet written), and nothing now stood in the way of the amalgamation of the two mines.

Presently the other two mines in Kimberley, the du Toits Pan and the Bultfontein, tired of struggling against the continual falls of reef and the incoming tide that was Rhodes, also sold out to him. He added whatever other mines of significance had as yet been discovered in South Africa. He controlled now all the diamonds in South Africa, except those found along the Vaal River—that is to say, ninety per cent of the diamonds in the world.

He could keep down working-expenses, compound the natives, regulate the world diamond market. He could devote money made out of diamonds to spreading the British Empire.

The trust deed of the de Beers Company is the marriage contract of Rhodes' dream and his business, and the legitimizing of their offspring—Rhodes' North. The trust deed of his Goldfields Company similarly provides for his Imperial plans.

It was after the amalgamation of the diamond mines Rhodes made a speech a tenth as long as a long novel, explaining to his shareholders all the complications of buying out Barnato and amalgamating the mines, and did not refer to a note. He dealt with the holdings in the mines, the number of claims, the loads of ground, the carats per load. He described the borrowings of moneys, the floating of companies, the securing of control, the amalgamating of mines. He discussed the working-costs, the regulating of the industry, and the returns on capital.

Here is a sample of the speech:

"Now at fourteen shillings per carat, producing nine thousand loads per diem yielding eleven thousand carats, only claiming a carat and a quarter per load, we should obtain seven thousand seven hundred pounds per diem, which would cost us eight shillings per load (our return of the cost of work) —not counting savings that may occur in the future. The cost would therefore be three thousand six hundred pounds per diem, and we should therefore make a daily profit of four thousand pounds, or one million two hundred thousand pounds per annum of three hundred working-days." . . . And so on.

It is not interesting as oratory, but it is interesting to think a man can make a speech of nine thousand such words without looking at a note.

The million and two hundred thousand pounds a year was only a beginning, but the town of Kimberley did not profit by the profit of de Beers. The diamond-buyers outside the ring were left with only the river diggers to depend on. The shop-keepers of Kimberley lost the trade of all the native workers. Business fell to a point where it was no longer necessary for Kimberley to have a three-judge court; one judge sufficed to deal with the cases not only of Kimberley, but of the districts around.

The population went down. Kimberley ceased to have any other hold on existence than its diamonds. Rhodes could do with Kimberley as he chose. It was the thrall of de Beers. A revolutionary body, called the Knights of Labour, blamed for all Kimberley's troubles "the existence and domination of one great monopoly, one giant corporation, as well as the overweening greed and ambition of one wealthy, over-estimated, disappointing politician."

To which Rhodes, the over-estimated and disappointing politician, at this date not only chairman of de Beers and the Consolidated Goldfields and managing director of the Chartered Company, but also Prime Minister of the Cape, replied—indifferently, yet rightly, and therefore all the more maddeningly—that, but for the amalgamation, the diamond trade would have been ruined by cut-throat competition, and, with it, Kimberley.

He was at the flood. Whose little broom could sweep him back? He could afford to be, as he chose, as it suited him, either liberal, romantic, genial, persuasive and conciliatory, or, in other moods, morose, overbearing, cynical, mad against opposition, crude to the point of clownishness in his humour. Not only could he do nothing wrong, what he did became right, it was his duty to do what he wanted. He felt himself a god—nothing less. It was the year 1890. It was that year in which, crowning all his other triumphs, Rhodes' pioneers planted the British flag in the land that was soon to be called Rhodesia.

CHAPTER ' 11

LOBENGULA, SON OF MOSELIKATZE

I

IT WILL be remembered that the Cape leads to Bechuanaland, and that after Bechuanaland, on the way North, come,
first, Matabeleland and Mashonaland, and then everything else
in Africa up to Egypt.

Now, since 1885, Bechuanaland, the Suez Canal to the interior, as Rhodes expressed it, was under British protection. He
believed ("I have not these scruples!") "that the natives were
bound gradually to come under the control of the Europeans."
He had money from gold and diamonds. Over a country of
nearly half a million square miles, a country larger than
France, Germany, and the Low Countries combined, ruled, as,
later, in remorse, Rhodes called him, "a naked old savage."

Rhodes was ready to go North.

II

Lobengula (He That Drives Like the Wind) was the son
of Moselikatze (The Pathway of Blood).

Moselikatze was a Zulu; once he had been the headman of
the armies of the terrible Chaka, and his favourite. But then
that had happened to him which was destined to happen to his

own sons, which had happened also to Chaka, which was not unknown among the favourites of white rulers, which threatens the sons that rival the heads of the ape families: he had become too popular for the liking of his chief; he had seemed to menace Chaka's authority; Chaka had frowned on him—in terror of his life Moselikatze had escaped from Zululand, taking with him his followers.

They made their way over Africa in the manner taught them by Chaka. The time was about 1826. Over the Drakensberg they swarmed and into Basutoland, where they were defeated and where they were given their new name of Matabele—Amandibile (The People with the Long Shields).

They turned then north, harried and harrying, "eating up" the Hottentots and Bushmen they met on their path, so that within ten years there was not one left in the country they had passed through; "washing their spears" in the blood of the Griquas; wiping out small bands of the Boers who were trekking away at that time from the British of the Cape, but being eventually driven farther north still by those Boers.

They wandered on. They met Chaka's brother Dingaan, the Vulture, that one after whom Dingaan's Day is named in memory of his treachery and due punishment. With him there was bloody, indecisive fighting, which ended in a further escaping northwards—into the country, this time of the Bechuana.

The Bechuana they overcame. Not a tribe of the Bechuana escaped the spears of Moselikatze's warriors, except the weakest of them, the Batlapin. On behalf of the Batlapin, a missionary, Dr. Moffat, the father-in-law of Livingstone, came to intercede. To something in Moselikatze he was able to appeal —to his vanity or his humour or his admiration or his chivalry. Moselikatze waved a knightly black hand. The white man was the lord of this contemptible tribe. Then let that tribe be. The other Bechuana tribes, the powerful ones, might be eaten up. This wretchedest of them—since the white man wished it, and he liked the white man—should be saved.

Moselikatze remained the friend of Moffat and, through him, of England.

But still there was no end to the pilgrimage. Again the Matabele could not stay where they had conquered. They wanted to rest, but so did the Boers, and while they were neighbours to one another, there could be no rest. The Boers, among them Kruger, came with their guns, and northwards ever fled the Matabele.

But now, at last, excepting only a little business with a people they named, in contempt, the Amaswina, the Mashona (the Unclean Ones)—now, taking the Mashona into vassalage, they found sanctuary. For thirteen years they had fought, won, lost, fled. In 1839, between the Limpopo and the Zambesi Rivers, they settled down to make themselves a home; they extended that home by the practice of annual raids, and they agreeably called their principal settlement Gebulawayo (the Place of Killing).

III

Moselikatze was about as old as his century and he lived to rule his Matabele another thirty years. He governed in the way of his forefathers. This is the way he governed:

He had an advisory body of *indunas,* that is, headmen, and a Royal Council of relatives. The chief adviser was the court priest. Without him the king could not act.

The theory of government was that the land, rain, and sun

belonged to everyone, that none should have more of these things than the next, and each as much as he needed.

The country was divided into provinces. The provinces were divided into districts. Each district had a number of towns. Over the provinces ruled the greater *indunas*, over the districts the lesser *indunas*, over the towns the least *indunas*. Subjects had to obey their chiefs, wives their husbands, children their mothers. Moselikatze's three hundred wives were distributed over his kingdom and acted as additional chiefs. He travelled from one to the other, superintending thus his kingdom. Every male adult was a soldier. War prisoners became slaves. There were executions for witchcraft. There were ceremonial dances. There was rain-making. . . .

One uses the word royal. One uses the word court priest. One speaks of provinces, districts, towns. It sounds very grand. It sounds well organized to the point of profundity. One might take an example from Moselikatze. . . . In fact, a Matabele town was simply a kraal, a corral, a collection of huts and cattle-folds, looking something like a group of wasps' nests or anthills; the royal residence was a larger hut; and Moselikatze, a fine enough warrior, as his son Lobengula, "a naked old savage."

Europeans cannot imagine a native monarch. As King Edward once expressed it, when he insisted on a Fiji royalty being treated like the other crowned heads at a public ceremony, the man was either a king or merely a nigger. If he was merely a nigger, what was he doing there at all? If he was a king, he was a king and must be treated as a king.

After Rhodes took Matabeleland from Lobengula, he sent Lobengula's sons to a native school. When one of them wanted to go North with him, Rhodes said: "Now, if you come up with me, I must have no nonsense about your being a king. You will have to help wash the plates and clean my boots. You understand?" "I understand, sir," said the son of Lobengula, quite agreeably.

Another time Rhodes asked him what he would like to do when he left school. "Whatever sir likes," said the boy. Rhodes suggested he might care to be his valet. The boy wanted to know what that was. Rhodes explained, and Lobengula's son considered it a good career.

And it sounds ironic and tragic, does it not? and cruel of Rhodes—the enslaved son of the great conquered, bound to the chariot wheel, and so forth.

But the truth is, a native feels that a white man, because he is a white man, is his superior. The sons of native chiefs work complacently in European households—without any sense of calamity. As far as Rhodes and Lobengula's sons were concerned, the case against Rhodes may be dismissed shortly. They loved Rhodes and delighted to serve him. There is today a Rhodes Lobengula.

It is not, even humanly speaking, so easy to judge what the rights are of an uncivilized people in a civilized world.

IV

Take this question of their right to live as they choose to live. There are Europeans who think the natives should live as their forefathers lived—that is, on great uncultivated tracts of land, eating, drinking, and being merry, for tomorrow, fighting, they died. Yet Europeans themselves have not that privilege. Who, indeed, in these frightening days when people press against one another for air, for living, for life—in this hard, tight, crowded, anguished world—dare claim a lovely laziness in the sun? To come upon a land empty, or to be spawned there, is no longer sufficient title to perpetual possession of a great part of the only planet the human race can inhabit. Nor are Life, Liberty, and the Pursuit of Happiness unqualified birthrights. They are not rights at all. No contract yields them. Who can enforce them? Are they not rather grudged benefits—too often withdrawn in the very act of bestowal? The land, sun, rain, may, in truth, as Moselikatze held, be the inheritance of every man, but there is a condition in the Divine Will: man has to till the ground from whence he was taken; he may not rest lazily on the unbroken earth because his fathers did so; he must embellish or fructify it for the world. These are no longer the times when "the care of the house and family, the management of the land and cattle, were delegated to the old and infirm, to women and slaves. The lazy warrior, destitute of every art that might employ his leisure hours, consumed his days and nights in the animal gratifications of sleep and food. . . . The same extent of ground which at present maintains, in ease and plenty, a million of husbandmen and artificers, was unable to supply an hundred thousand lazy warriors with the simple necessaries of life. . . . (They) carried with them what they most valued, their arms, their cattle, and their women, cheerfully abandoned the vast silence of their woods for the unbounded hopes of plunder and conquest. . . ."

It is true Gibbon is here writing, not of Moselikatze's Kaffirs —though this life was exactly theirs—but of the Early Germans. Yet still less today than those centuries ago may one live like Gibbon's Old Germans. And, as Rhodes' world was ahead of the Kaffirs, that befell them which has befallen other nations outstripped in civilization by their neighbours—for instance, the fellow-tribesmen of the Druids, with whom Rhodes used to compare them; for instance, all the nations against whom Julius Cæsar, another millionaire somewhat given to irregularity, once strove. In almost the same way, indeed, as Rhodes was presently to overcome the Matabele, did Cæsar (the details quite matching) overcome those German tribes, the Usipetes and Tencteri. . . .

Now the Amandabile, who called themselves Izulu (Children of the Stars), are the servants of the servants of the white men. They wander over the lands that were theirs, naked and hungry and bewildered. Their meed of civilization is the work too hard, mean, stupid, and shameful for their masters.

V

The white man's penetration into the land of the Matabele began in the old peaceful way.

First came the missionary Moffat, the friend of Moselikatze, and other missionaries. Then came traders, bartering, for ivory or cattle, guns and wine and beads and blankets. Then came sportsmen, allowed, for the gift of a gun, to shoot elephant, buffalo, hippo, rhino, lion, leopard, and deer.

Then came the discovery of the Tati goldfields, and the concession-hunters.

Moselikatze died, and Lobengula, his son by an inferior wife (two elder and more dangerous sons having been liquidated), succeeded to Matabeleland, Mashonaland, the secret of the rain, the missionaries, traders, witch-doctors, slave-raiders, sportsmen, and concession-hunters. He succeeded to a war against civilization. The year was 1870.

CHAPTER ˌ 12

THE CONCESSION-HUNTERS

I

LOBENGULA was not, as he has been called, the last of the great black chiefs. The last of the great black chiefs, the Bechuana Khama, his neighbour and enemy, was a greater than he, and Khama, very ancient, died only a year or two ago. But Lobengula was the last to make a stand for black independence.

He was a large, big-bellied man, shiny with fat, very erect. He wore over his forehead his leather ring of majesty, and, suspended from his loins, a sporran of blue monkey-skin. Before him strode his *m'bongo*, his praisemaker: "Behold, the great elephant, he comes! When he walks, the earth trembles! When he opens his mouth, the heavens roar!" He was gouty with the champagne poured into him by concession-hunters— champagne enough, as it was said, to float a man-of-war. His signature was a cross, and the stamp of his authority an elephant. The seal is in Rhodes' house today.

Before Lobengula, on the throne of his bath-chair, or the still more elevated throne of his waggon, under his Tree of Justice, or within the sacred, smelly precincts of his goat-kraal, appeared his young men, creeping towards him on their bellies, calling him "Eater of Men!" "Stabber of Heaven!" "Thunderer!" complaining of boredom, desirous of marriage, and demanding, therefore, a blood bath for their spears . . . came concession-hunters of all nations, wanting the right to trade, to dig, to settle; and missionaries preaching the Christian virtues.

In this atmosphere Lobengula tried to keep harmony. The young men must not kill—not too much. The concession-hunters must not take—not too much. The missionaries must not convert—not too much. To everyone he gave a little for the sake of peace, a little, as warily, as indefinitely, as he dared. By the time Rhodes had a place in Parliament and his de Beers and his Goldfields; by the time Britain had her protectorate over Bechuanaland; by the time the stage was thus set for Rhodes' march north—Lobengula was a man standing against a wall in which stuck the knives thrown all around him by expert jugglers.

II

The Matabele had been the enemies of the Boers as they had both trekked north, but then, says Kruger, peace had been made. "Lobengula was even on very good terms with the Boers . . . who hunted in his territories." And, in 1887, says Kruger, Lobengula sent one of his principal *indunas* to Pretoria, asking for a Boer consul to be appointed in Matabeleland.

Kruger was trying, at the moment, to make a deal with the Swazis, who lay between him and his nearest port, Delagoa Bay. But he was prepared to expand in any direction. In response to Lobengula's request, then, he sent the proposed consul to Matabeleland with the draft of a treaty by which Lobengula was to place his country under Boer protection.

Lobengula agreed verbally to the treaty, but, before definitely signing, asked for time to consult his *indunas*. While they were considering, Kruger's emissary went to meet his wife, who was on her way to join him. He was killed by Bechuana, and "there is no doubt whatever," says Kruger, "that the murder was due to the instigation of Cecil Rhodes and his clique."

Kruger's Memoirs were dictated immediately after the Boer War, and they are not weakened by excessive restraint, nor is proof offered of their statements. Rhodes' connection with the murder is not established. It may be said, however, that fate was on Rhodes' side in the matter of inconvenient emissaries. They did have a tendency to vanish from his path.

The effrontery now of Kruger roused Rhodes to utmost indignation. That anyone else, and a poor man, too, should want to expand as he himself wanted to expand! "When I remember," he exploded a year later in the House, "that Paul Kruger had not a sixpence in his treasury when his object was to expand his country over the whole northern interior, when I see him sitting in Pretoria with Bechuanaland gone, and other lands around him gone from his grasp . . . I pity the man. When I see a man starting and continuing with one object, and utterly failing in that object, I cannot help pitying him. I know very well that he has been willing to sacrifice anything to gain that object of his. If you think it out, it has been a most remarkable thing that, not content with recovering his country, he wished to obtain the whole interior for a population of his own. And he has been defeated in his object."

It was a remarkable thing, and Rhodes was, of course, the man who defeated Kruger. But the word "pity" need not be taken as expressing literally the emotion that inflamed Rhodes when, in these days, he thought about Kruger. It was Kruger's very mission north that, like the German descent south, fired Rhodes to vehement action.

He needed for this action the assistance of the High Commissioner, Sir Hercules Robinson, and to him, when he heard the news of Kruger, he hurried.

III

He saw Sir Hercules Robinson on Christmas Day of 1887, and on Boxing Day a communication was sent to the Deputy Commissioner of Bechuanaland.

And who was the Deputy Commissioner of Bechuanaland? None other, most happily, than Rhodes' old Kimberley friend, Sir Sidney Shippard, that one nominated in his first will as co-heir of the fortune not yet made, but destined to Britainize the world.

And who, again, should Shippard's Assistant Commissioner be but a son of that Dr. Moffat, the missionary loved and favoured by Moselikatze?

This Moffat was now at Lobengula's kraal. And to him, through Shippard, a message was sent to find out how negotiations stood between Lobengula and the Transvaal, and instructing him to get in ahead of the Boers.

He did so. An agreement was signed between Lobengula and the Queen of England by which Lobengula undertook not to sell, alienate, or cede any part of the Amandibile country without the previous knowledge and sanction of the High Commissioner for South Africa.

When the Portuguese consul at Cape Town heard of this

treaty he said Lobengula's country had belonged to Portugal since the seventeenth century. It was part of the Kingdom of Monomatapa, he said. No one, however, was much agitated by this claim.

So now England not only had a protectorate over Bechuanaland; she had also, one might say, a protectorate over Matabeleland, and in the neighbourhood was still another tribe, the Barotse, wondering if friendship with England might not be a thing one ought to have. The anxious communications of the various chiefs with one another and their English overlords make pathetic reading.

To Shippard, fearing that England might favour Lobengula above him, writes the chief Khama: "I fought Lobengula when he had his father's great warriors from Natal, and drove him back, and he never came again. . . . Yet I fear Lobengula less than I fear brandy. . . . I dread the white man's drink more than all the assegais of the Matabele, which kill men's bodies, and it is quickly over."

And to Khama writes Lewanika, Chief of the Barotse: "I understand that you are now under the protection of the Queen of the English people. I do not know what it means. But they say there are soldiers living at your place, and some headman sent by the Queen to take care of you and protect you from the Matabele. Tell me all as a friend. Are you happy and quite satisfied? Are the ways of the white man burdensome to you? Tell me all. I am anxious that you should tell me very plainly, your friend, because I have a great desire to be received like you under the protection of so great a ruler as the Queen of England."

Well, civilization must march, and it is certainly wrong to

lie idle on one's back in the sun when one isn't washing one's spear in somebody's blood—yet, linked to the fate of the natives, do not these letters read something like enquiries from a prospective bride of Bluebeard's?

IV

But further than this arrangement with Lobengula Sir Hercules Robinson dared not go. He could not, on his own responsibility, do what the impetuous Rhodes urged him to do and annex Lobengula's country. England was not, at the moment, in the mood for further expansion. Rhodes, accordingly, decided to annex it himself.

He began by joining the horde of concession-hunters. The Moffat treaty was not yet through when he and Beit sent an old hunter to Lobengula's kraal to try for gold-mining rights. The hunter became ill, and returned empty-handed. And what happened next was that Rhodes, now in England, heard that two allied companies, the Bechuanaland Exploration Company and the Exploring Company, had the ear of Lord Knutsford at the Colonial Office, and, vehemently protesting to the Colonial Office his own nobler intentions and superior claims (thirteen millions to play about with as against their "beggarly fifty thousand"), he hurried back to South Africa to forestall them at Lobengula's court.

This time he sent three delegates to Lobengula—his old partner, Rudd; one Rochfort Maguire, an Oxford friend and a fellow of All Souls; and Thompson, his compound manager at de Beers, who understood native languages. They joined the rabble of questing courtiers around Lobengula.

Men who saw it say that the court of Lobengula was a remarkable sight. There was the wide empty land under the poignant blue sky; and the huts like great nests of wasps; and the naked black men and women and children; and the fat, shiny black chief himself, sitting on his royal waggon or his royal bath-chair, his leather ring round his head, his big belly full of champagne, his thick gouty legs firmly apart, his monkey-skin dangling between his legs.

In his court were both black witch-doctors and white missionaries. Traders came and went. Hunters came and went. Month after month, year in, year out, he entertained and held at bay hordes of pleading, protesting, demanding, threatening, quarrelling adventurers from every country of Europe. They buzzed about him like the suitors of Penelope. And what did they all want? To flay him of his skin. Nothing else. Why, particularly in this year 1888, were they circling in such numbers about his bewildered head?

The answer is the gold in the Transvaal.

Consider again the map of South Africa. In the Transvaal we have the Witwatersrand; on the borders of Bechuanaland and Matabeleland, Tati; not far away, Bulawayo; and, farther up, that part of Mashonaland destined to hold Salisbury. And the idea was that, in a line like the bend of a bow, there ran a streak of gold. Each concession-hunter hoped to get, at the cost of a few rifles, a horse or a bull, a waggon or two, a hundred pounds or so, a piece of land as large, say, as England (merely as large as England? Why not as large as the whole of Lobengula's territories or perhaps the half of Europe?) and full of gold.

Imagine the tearing rivalry.

Rhodes' party arrived towards the end of September, and settled down to work in the goat-kraal. Accompanied in everything by the smell of goat, they ate beef, drank beer, watched dances, praised Lobengula, begged, offered, threatened. They had, as their most urgent competitors, an ex-soldier called Maund, the representative of those companies whose request for a charter had spurred on Rhodes; and a group of men sent up by a relation of Beit's called Lippert. But there were dozens of others, some of whom Rhodes' people bought off, and some of whom, in one way or another, they warded off. Concerning one small syndicate there will presently be a story to tell.

Lobengula's young men could bear none of the adventurers, and it was only Lobengula himself who stood between the adventurers and extermination. Either because he regarded himself as their host and, for that reason, their protector, or because he was nervous of what might happen if a white man were harmed in his kraal, he protected those whose object it was to undo him. "The Ama-Kiwa," he said, "are my guests, and you shall not touch them. If you want to fight white men, go to Kimberley and see what they will do to you."

They wandered about the goat-kraal, unharmed.

The Rhodes men had made little headway when there arrived ("by one of those curious chances," says a chronicler, "which occur more often in fiction than in history") Sir Sidney Shippard. By another curious chance there arrived also, leaving Bechuanaland to look after itself, his assistant, Moffat. And by a third curious chance, Lobengula's favourite missionary, Helm. A fortnight later the Rudd-Rhodes group had their concession. On October 30, 1888, Lobengula signed a document giving Rudd and his associates—for a consideration of a hundred pounds a month, a thousand Martini-Henry rifles, a hundred thousand cartridges, and (sudden inspiration of Rhodes') an armed steamboat on the Zambesi—"complete and exclusive charge over all metals and minerals in my kingdom, principalities, and dominions, together with full power to do all things that they may deem necessary to win and procure the same and to collect and enjoy the profits and revenues, if any, derivable from the said metals and minerals." . . . "And whereas," continues the document, "I have been much molested of late by divers persons seeking and desiring to obtain grants and concessions of land and mining rights in my territories . . ." now, therefore, in short, the Rudd-Rhodes group is given power to exclude rivals, and Lobengula undertakes to help them in this exclusion. The missionary Helm wrote out the concession, explained it to Lobengula, and witnessed it.

The matter thus settled, Rudd, leaving his companions behind him to look after Lobengula and keep away rivals—which they duly did—set out for Kimberley, and, after nearly dying of thirst on the way and being rescued by the escort of the always opportune Shippard, duly brought Rhodes his concession.

A month or so later Sir Hercules Robinson posted it to London with a commendation of Rudd as a gentleman of character and financial standing who would "check the inroad of adventurers as well as secure the cautious development of the country with a proper consideration for the feelings and prejudices of the natives," and Rudd added that he was quite prepared to delay operations until he had won the confidence of the Matabele people.

Lord Knutsford at the Colonial Office had not received his copy of the Rudd Concession, with the High Commissioner's endorsement, before there was talk in the City and in Parliament. "Do you think," he cabled to Sir Hercules Robinson, "that there is any danger of complications arising from these rifles?"

Sir Hercules Robinson, answering uneasily that, whatever his opinion, it seemed useless to veto the guns since they could be brought in through other countries, referred him to the more experienced judgment of Sir Sidney Shippard. And Sir Sidney Shippard gave it. He gave the arguments for and against firearms, and his own reasoned conclusions on these arguments.

The Rev. C. D. Helm of the London Missionary Society, he said, favoured the giving of rifles "because the substitution of long-range rifles for the stabbing assegai would tend to diminish the loss of life in the Matabele raids and thus prove a distinct gain to the cause of humanity."

The Bishop of Bloemfontein, on the other hand (he admitted), and a second London missionary opposed the giving of rifles "on account of the increased facilities likely to be thus afforded for their cruel raids, the atrocity of which appears to be above question."

There was also, said Sir Sidney Shippard, gravely, another point to consider. Khama feared the advantage firearms would give Lobengula over him. This point, however, he reassured the Colonial Secretary, would be settled by Mr. Rudd's also giving Khama arms and ammunitions, and "the relative position of the chiefs would thus remain unchanged."

As to the question whether rifles should or should not be given at all—"I agree," said Sir Sidney Shippard, speaking, as he says, solely from the humanitarian point of view—"I agree with the Rev. C. D. Helm in thinking that the gradual substitution of the rifle for the stabbing assegai will directly tend to diminish instead of increasing bloodshed and loss of life. . . . The use of firearms in modern warfare has notoriously diminished the loss of life. . . . It will, in my opinion, be sound policy for us to furnish Lobengula with the means of maintaining his authority."

The Colonial Office, to whom, no doubt, the whole business of the concession already seemed so fairy-like that to associate human realities with it would have been not merely absurd, but even indecorous, did not dispute Sir Sidney's opinion that it was in the interests of humanity Rhodes proposed to give firearms to Lobengula.

It might here be recalled that Rhodes' first speech in Parliament dealt with the disarming of natives on which, failing, the Cape had spent four millions, and that Rhodes was against the disarming.

A year after Rhodes got the charter which was founded on the concession, Jameson was arrested for running guns to another native tribe with the same humanitarian motives. At present, however, Rhodes had still to get his charter. Indeed, he had still to make safe his concession.

CHAPTER ، 13

RHODES TAKES HIS NORTH

I

THERE are some who say that Lobengula, who had for so long, by means direct and indirect, maintained a whole skin against the onslaught of the vultures, could not have known what he was about when he signed away everything for so paltry a return, and he himself said that he never did do it—he never did sign away his whole kingdom. "They asked me," are the words of a letter to the Queen of England, the authenticity of which was disputed by Rhodes and others—"they asked me for a place to dig for gold and said they would give me certain things for the right to do so. I told them to bring vhat they would give, and I would then show them what I would give. A document was written and presented to me for signature. I asked what it contained, and was told that in it were my words and the words of these men. I put my hand to it. About three months afterwards I heard from other sources that I had given by that document the right to all the minerals in my country."

The other sources were at the kraal of Lobengula. They were the baffled rivals. There were some who advised him to send to the Queen of England for help, and there were some who said how could he make treaties with a Queen of England

and respectfully consider her envoys when there was no Queen of England—such a being simply did not exist?

At the end of February, 1889, there presented itself, accordingly, at the Colonial Office, a deputation from Lobengula. It consisted of two *indunas*, Maund of the Exploring Companies, Selous, the hunter, who had a sort of concession himself, and Colenbrander, the interpreter, a well-known link between black and white. The three white men, now proceeding against Rhodes, were all destined to serve him.

"Lobengula," said the deputation, "desires to know that there is a queen. Some of the people who come to his land tell him there is a queen and some tell him there is not.

"Lobengula can only find out the truth by sending eyes to see whether there is a queen.

"The *indunas* are his eyes.

"Lobengula desires, if there is a queen, to ask her to advise and help him, as he is much troubled by white men who come to the country to dig gold.

"There is no one with him whom he can trust, and he asks that the Queen will send some one from herself."

He was addressing Victoria as one monarch another, and he had no doubt that, as he was approached in his goat-kraal, so was Victoria in hers. And, indeed, the *indunas* did see her, the eyes of Lobengula were made assured of the existence of the Queen of England.

She now, through the medium of Lord Knutsford, informed Lobengula that he might trust her representative, the High Commissioner. She wished Lobengula, she said, to understand directly that Englishmen who had gone to Matabeleland to ask leave to dig for stones had not gone with the Queen's authority, and that he should not believe statements made by them or any of them to that effect.

She advised Lobengula not to grant hastily concessions of land or leave to dig, but to consider all applications very carefully.

"It is not wise," she wrote, "to put too much power into the hands of men who come first, and to exclude other deserving men. A king gives a stranger an ox, not his whole herd of cattle, otherwise what would other strangers have to eat?"

A more important question might have been what would the king himself, if he gave away his whole herd of cattle, have to eat?

Little enough, very soon, but for the grace of Rhodes.

While the eyes of Lobengula were being shown the sights of London, while the chairman of the Aborigines Protection Society was hoping that "Englishmen and Matabeles would meet together in the valleys of the Limpopo as they had that day in Westminster," Rhodes, now in England to get his charter, was explaining his ideas, convincing doubters, buying out rivals, claimants, and blackmailers. These were, he said, a worse trouble than the Boers, the Portuguese, or the natives. But he paid anything to anybody. He would have no obstacles. He found against him his old enemy, Mackenzie, and simultaneously Bradlaugh and Labouchere; the Aborigines Protection Society and also the London Chamber of Commerce; finally, and most interestingly, considering the future, Albert (afterwards Earl) Grey, the Duke of Fife, who was the Prince of Wales' son-in-law, and Joseph Chamberlain.

The Irish members did not trouble Rhodes. He had donated ten thousand pounds to the Irish Party funds—not for the reason that he wanted them to do anything for him, but since "in Mr. Parnell's cause . . . I believe lies the key of the Federal System, on the basis of perfect Home Rule in every part of the Empire."

W. T. Stead, whose friendship with Rhodes began during this period, says the date of Rhodes' letter to Parnell, June 19, 1888, is sufficient to prove the absurdity of the superstition that Rhodes had bought Irish support for his charter by a gift of ten thousand pounds. At that time, says Stead, no application had yet been made for a charter, nor had Rhodes obtained his mineral concession. . . . At that time, however, Rhodes was already trying for the concession; he had already made up his mind to oust the Bechuanaland Exploration Company and the Exploring Company, who had applied to the Colonial Office for a charter; he had already demanded first consideration of the Office, and arranged to send the Rudd group north. . . . Leave it, then, that Rhodes was opportunely in sympathy with the Irish Party.

But his most urgent problem was that prior application, just mentioned, for a charter to exploit the countries of Lobengula and Khama. There was nothing for it but to do with these people what he had done with Barnato, and amalgamate. A month after his arrival in England, the names of Rhodes, Rudd, and Beit were added to those of the signatories of the two Exploring Companies.

The amalgamation called itself the Central Search Association.

II

A month before his arrival in England there had taken place a company meeting at which a strange story was told.

This is what the Wood, Chapman, and Francis Syndicate, an affair that operated, not like Rhodes, in millions, but in hundreds, reported to their shareholders:

For a rental of a hundred pounds a year they had a concession from Lobengula over certain territory concerning which there was a dispute between Khama and Lobengula. Under the leadership of Wood, they were on their way, with waggons, oxen, machinery, and experts, to take up their concession, when, sixty miles from the king's kraal, they were held up by messengers of Khama, who had been warned that they were a military expedition about to invade his territory.

While they were arguing and explaining, there arrived the party of Sir Sidney Shippard, who told them that Shippard was coming to them with an important letter from Lobengula. They waited for Shippard.

He appeared, and did not show them any letter, but advised them, since the country was in a dangerous state, to return, under his protection, to Bechuanaland.

They did so, abandoning their enterprise, and found themselves in Khama's country.

They now discovered the real reason for their interception. It was nothing, says the report, but a device to get them into territory where Shippard had jurisdiction. For no sooner were they in Bechuanaland than they found themselves hailed before Khama, his son, two missionaries, and the Bishop of Bloemfontein, and charged with attempting to stir up hostilities between the Transvaal and England, and also between Lobengula and Khama.

Wood, a justice of the peace, a member of the Cape Parliament, a volunteer colonel, and a man, says the report, of unblemished character, vehemently repudiated the charges and demanded the evidence against him.

No evidence was forthcoming, but he was asked to bind himself and his syndicate, under penalty of two thousand pounds, not to enter, without the consent of the High Commissioner, the territory in dispute between Khama and Lobengula.

Since Wood, while submitting, under protest, on his own behalf, refused to do so on behalf of his syndicate, he was now sent, by ox-waggon, to Mafeking, the capital, a distance of three hundred miles; and there court proceedings were taken against him, as a result of which he was forbidden access to Lobengula's territory until the dispute between Khama and Lobengula was settled. . . .

The committee recorded their "most solemn and emphatic protest against the insult and indignity offered to Mr. Wood by the Bechuanaland authorities."

III

It will be seen that the concession was needing some care. There was Lobengula impugning the document itself and sending his *indunas*, his eyes, to see the Queen. There were the balked, conspiring rival claimants at his kraal, and still others trying to come in. There were the natives crying that they had been betrayed. Thompson and Maguire, who had been left behind to attend to Lobengula while other business was going forward, and who had once been so favoured that Lobengula had given Maguire a Matabele regiment—an *impi*—to keep out certain rivals, now lived at the kraal in peril of their lives. They had nothing between them and the maddened natives but the protection of their host, Lobengula himself.

In this pass there went up to Matabeleland Dr. Jameson—Leander Starr Jameson—Dr. Jim.

Jameson was a friend to Rhodes of ten years' standing, a Scot, a member of a family as large as that of Rhodes', and exactly Rhodes' age. He had come to Kimberley for the reason Rhodes had come to Kimberley—because he had a weak lung. He was a good surgeon, a man of charm, and a gambler. He was little and thin and insignificant, where Rhodes was big and burly and outstanding. He was bald and dark, where Rhodes was curly-haired and blond. He had wide-set, urgent black eyes, where Rhodes had eyes close-set, thick-lidded, and blue-grey. His imagination danced him into danger, where Rhodes' imagination tortured him into it. He had a nonchalant, I-suppose-I-must-do-this manner and a scheming, I-mean-to-do-this brain. A Robin Hood atmosphere attaches to him. He was a chivalrous sort of highwayman. His subordinates adored him. As many people in South Africa love him as detest him. He served Rhodes, ruined him, and was forgiven. He committed the most imprudent and devastating deed in South African history and became a Prime Minister. With Beit and Rhodes he created Rhodesia.

Strange to think of these three men, these three sickly bachelors, all born in the same year, an Englishman, a Scot, and a German Jew, making this great, untamed country the work of their lives. Rhodes had tubercular lungs and an aneurism of the aorta. Jameson had tubercular lungs, hæmorrhoids and gall-stones. Beit had dangerously unquiet nerves. They were nothing like Rhodes' ideal Englishman. No one would ever have chosen them to be Rhodes Scholars. They had not been

130

leaders or sportsmen at school. They were leaders now, but not for those particular qualities of character that are demanded in a Rhodes Scholar. Students they never became. Sportsmen they never became. Team sports one need not consider in mature men, but Rhodes rode horses all his life, he rode every morning, he rode everywhere—and he never could ride. He shot game, and could not shoot. He played cards, and could not play. Jameson's form of sport was solo whist, and he was not even, they say, a good player. He could lose a thousand pounds a night, fifteen hundred, a block of houses, at solo whist. Beit, for some whim, had a racing stable in Germany, but never saw one of his horses.

On the contrary, they were all lovers, in one form or the other, of the arts—or at least they loved beauty.

And these men had to be Empire-builders! They had to go North! . . . Or was it that Rhodes had to build Empires and go North, and they after him?

It must have been that. Jameson was an adventurer, and so other curious things might have happened to him. But how many men think of sallying forth to take three-quarters of a million square miles of land? Beit was a brilliant financier, and he was prepared to yield his money to Rhodes' ideas. But would he have left money for railways and bridges in Rhodesia without Rhodes? . . .

With Jameson, to see Lobengula, went one of those hangers-on Rhodes' wealth and achievements were in these days alluring, another Kimberley doctor, Rutherfoord Harris. Harris, an extremely energetic man, hung on to Rhodes' coat-tails till he pulled them off.

It was Jameson's mission to use his well-known charm on Lobengula.

He found Thompson and Maguire still there, and Lobengula guarding, but refusing to use, the rifles he had been paid for his concession—they were not used till four years later.

Jameson told Maguire to go to England and enlighten Rhodes, out of his first-hand knowledge, concerning the claims that were being made on him. He relieved Lobengula of gout and ophthalmia, and won over to Rhodes some of those concession-hunters hanging round still, balked of their prey. He half-persuaded Lobengula that no wrong had been done him. Then he left.

The next thing that happened was the return of the *indunas* from England. With Maguire gone, with Jameson gone, with Thompson alone remaining to haunt the kraal like a ghost waiting for the stroke of twelve, with the encouragement of the Aborigines Protection Society and the Queen of England's Biblical advice to give a stranger an ox but not a whole herd, Lobengula now gathered himself together to renew his protests against the Rudd Concession.

"I am thankful," he wrote, "for the Queen's word. I have heard Her Majesty's message. The messengers have spoken as my mouth. They have been very well treated.

"The white people are troubling me much about gold. If the Queen hears that I have given away the whole country, it is not so. I have no one in my country who knows how to write. I do not understand where the dispute is, because I have no knowledge of writing."

The letter was sent to the Queen through Sir Sidney Shippard. About the same time Maund also wrote to England. Maund's letter took forty-seven days to arrive, and Lobengula's, through Sir Sidney Shippard, a hundred days.

But the letter alone was not enough to satisfy the inflamed

Matabele. They knew now that they had been betrayed; they had seen the fruitless return of the envoys, with their present to Lobengula of a picture of the Queen; they doubted if any letters could help them. A terrible council meeting was held of *indunas* and white men and Lobengula.

Lobengula handed to Helm, the missionary who had written out and endorsed it, a copy of the concession.

"Read that paper," he said. "Tell me faithfully if I have given away any of the land of the Matabele."

"Yes, King," answered Helm, "you have. How can white men dig for gold without land?"

"If gold is found anywhere in the country, can the white man occupy the land and dig for it?"

"Yes, King."

"If gold is in my garden, can they come and dig for it?"

"Yes, King."

"If gold is in my royal kraal, can they enter and dig?"

"Yes, King."

"Lochi," said Lobengula to his chief counsellor, "you have done this, you have blinded my eyes, you have closed my ears, you have betrayed the Matabele nation."

Lochi had no reply to make. His advice may have been wrong, but there is no proof that it was treacherous.

"I am a dead man," he said as he left the council meeting.

And a dead man he was. There came warriors of the king's regiment and made away with him, his family, and his adherents.

Thompson, seeing the reddened eyes, leapt on a horse and did not halt until he arrived at Tati, a hundred miles away.

On October 29th, just one day less than a year after the

signing of the concession, Rhodes received the Royal assent to his charter.

On November 18th arrived Lobengula's letter, written on August 10th and entrusted to Shippard.

Lobengula might now send as many eyes, and write as many letters to the Queen as he wished.

On the Board of the new Chartered Company, whose chairman was the Duke of Abercorn, were its original enemies, Albert Grey and the Duke of Fife. Amalgamated with it were not only various companies of Rhodes', and the two Exploring Companies, and a decrepit company, associated with missions and called the African Lakes Corporation, whose home, far away north, Rhodes hoped to reach one day, but also that company Maguire had driven off with an *impi*, and the Wood, Chapman, and Francis Syndicate which, not long ago, had recorded its "most solemn and emphatic protest against the insult and indignity offered to it by the Bechuanaland authorities."

CHAPTER · 14

THE PIONEERS OCCUPY MASHONALAND

I

THE new Chartered Company took the title of the British South Africa Company. It had as predecessors among such companies anything from the Hanseatic League, which established German trading rights in England in the thirteenth century, to the Hudson Bay Company, which exists today. There had been English Merchant Adventurers; English charters over Russia and Turkey; English, Dutch and French East India Companies. America had been colonized by charter. Recent chartered companies existed in Borneo, Nigeria, and East Africa. The concessions of Karl Peters had just been similarly blessed by Germany.

The petitioners had asked for railway, telegraph, colonizing, trade, and mineral rights over a region bounded south, west, and east by British Bechuanaland, the Portuguese territories, and the Transvaal, but bounded north not at all.

The charter, with certain stipulations mainly affecting the natives, was granted in terms of the petition. The tenure of the charter was for twenty-five years—or less if the company misbehaved itself.

The capital of the Chartered Company was a million shares of one pound each. Five hundred thousand of these shares were distributed among Chartered directors and their supporters at three shillings, the rest of the money to be paid when called for. The remaining shares were kept for contingencies. Towards this issue de Beers subscribed two hundred thousand pounds. . . .

The right Great Britain had to grant a charter over Lobengula's dominions was that of the protectorate implied in the Moffat Treaty of February, 1888.

The right Rhodes had by the Rudd-Rhodes Concession was that of digging in Lobengula's land for minerals. Could one dig for minerals if one had not the land in which they might lie? Was not Rhodes' position something like that of Shylock when Portia told him to tarry a little:

> "This bond doth give thee here no jot of blood;
> The words expressly are 'a pound of flesh' "?

II

But Rhodes was far from being the man to tarry. Lord Knutsford had not yet dipped pen in ink to tell Lobengula of the charter when the twelve young men, known as Rhodes' Apostles, were sent northwards to spy out the land and prepare themselves for escorting a pioneer column.

To Barotseland went one, seeking on behalf of Rhodes a concession from its chief, that Lewanika who had once asked Khama to tell him, as a friend, if he found the ways of the white man burdensome. To another man was delegated the work of constructing a telegraph line for which poles and wire had already, months before, been ordered. To consult with Rhodes in Kimberley came those whose work it would be to build railways; to acquire for him such territories as were not yet absorbed by white men; to fit out columns of pioneers, police, and labouring natives; to guide such columns.

In Lobengula's goat-kraal sat Moffat, now the accredited representative of the Queen, and once again Jameson, keeping the chief sweet. "I want to see Rhodes," protested Lobengula. "Let Rhodes come," he demanded. But Rhodes was doing other things.

It took Jameson four months to work out of Lobengula a promise of safe passage through his lands for the pioneers. And in the end it was not so much a promise as a frightened denial that there was no promise. "I never refused the road to you or your *impi*," he said to the threatening Jameson, and with that Jameson returned to Kimberley, and on that Rhodes built his preparations.

A young man called Frank Johnson, with him two partners, tendered, for the sum of £88,285 10s., to select and equip an expedition to Mashonaland, to provide transport and build a road, and to do it in nine months. The hunter Selous was engaged to guide the expedition. As those who had once been Rhodes' strongest opponents were on the directorate of the Chartered Company, so were Johnson and Selous, among the earliest concessionaries over Mashona and Matabeleland, now his servants.

In June Rhodes received Imperial sanction to his occupation of Mashonaland; and immediately the hundred and seventy-nine pioneers engaged by Johnson, accompanied by three hundred police with more in the rear (Bechuanaland police and the company's own police), set off from their base on the border of Bechuanaland along a road opening out before them, as Selous selected it and the natives cut it.

Jameson accompanied the column. He had ceased to be

interested in his practice as a doctor. He was given over to
Rhodes.

III

They had hardly started when there was trouble. For the
two *indunas* who were to show them the permitted road had
not appeared, and Selous, with whom Lobengula had a feud
on account of some hunting misdemeanour, now ventured to
cross over into Matabeleland to look for them. There was a
prompt and ironical warning from Lobengula: "Has the king
killed any white men, that an *impi* is collecting on his border?
Or have the white men lost anything they are looking for?"

Jameson hastened once more to Bulawayo to work his charms
on Lobengula. With him went an interpreter.

They arrived at the king's kraal before dawn, and found
Lobengula asleep, wrapped in his karosses. Lobengula threw
off his karosses, stood in his naked fury before Jameson, and
denounced Selous' trespass. "Who told Selous he could make
that road?" he raged.

He would not hear Jameson. He went to his women's quarters, where Jameson could not follow him.

Later in the day Jameson tracked him to his goat-kraal. He
was sacrificing. Around him were his witch-doctors. Jameson
and his interpreter walked up to him. The appalled witch-
doctors closed in round the white men. The king stood motion-
less. Across the cordon of witch-doctors the wide-set, urgent
eyes of the small white man met the protruding, reddened eyes
of the big-bellied savage. "The king told *me* I might make
that road," Jameson answered his question of the early morning. "Did the king lie?"

138

There was, as Jameson tells the story, a long silence. Then Lobengula waved the witch-doctors back to their places. "The king never lies," he said, turned his back on Jameson, and went on with his sacrificing.

"I thank the king," said Jameson; but Lobengula did not look up, he said no other word, and Jameson returned to his column.

The expedition was not again interrupted. The enemies of Lobengula took possession of his land, and he stood between the pioneers and his fuming warriors. He had given his promise of the road, and he kept it. Not a man was harmed on the journey through Mashonaland. . . . Waggons were dragged by rope across streams infested with crocodile; they broke on the granite kopjes; the oxen who drew them on the four-hundred-and-sixty-mile trek became thin and weak. Roads were cut through marshy, timbered valleys. Unaccustomed white faces sweated in the winter sun. Unaccustomed white hands grew calloused by pick and shovel. Scouts patrolled. Laagers were nightly made. The pilgrimage was a grand idea, it read spectacularly—here was dangerous living! Actually it was so uneventful, it was, beyond anything, tedious. The pioneers took a month to reach the lucky pass called Providential that led to the clear plateau, four thousand feet above sea-level, and another month to hoist the Union Jack at a spot they named Salisbury. . . . But no Matabele touched a man, nor was a life lost.

When the news came of the founding of Salisbury, Chartered shares were for the first time sold on the open market; they rose magnificently, and five thousand new shareholders bought them. They were not to discover until a year later that the Rudd Concession was not theirs, and only could be theirs at a high price.

It was to Mashonaland rather than to the more convenient Matabeleland Rhodes sent his pioneers because he knew he had no right to the land and preferred to argue the matter, if necessary, with the humble Mashona rather than with the arrogant Matabele. They say the Mashona hid behind the great rocks when they saw the white men; they were lured out with difficulty to exchange their poor grain and animals for beads and tobacco.

The pioneers were paid seven and six a day, they were each given, like the Boer invaders of Stellaland and Zululand, three thousand morgen of land, and also the right to peg out fifteen claims in any one place. They had read books by explorers saying there were miles of quartz reef in which one could actually see the glinting gold.

After them, along the road they had cut, trailed the waggons and Scotch carts of would-be miners, tradesmen, and land-owners. The first private waggon to arrive at Salisbury carried whisky, and nothing else.

The dry winter season ended; spring came, and the heaviest rains in memory; Salisbury was a swamp; mosquitoes and malaria arrived; there were no drugs, food, or doctors; for two and a half months posts dared not cross the swollen rivers; only companies were allowed to mine, and of the vendors' scrip of these companies the Chartered Company was to get half (but, indeed, hardly anyone found gold); the lands allotted to the pioneers were miserable—the pioneers, like the children of Israel, cried, "Moreover, thou hast not brought us into a land that floweth with milk and honey."

But where was Rhodes? Why was he not comforting his people?

It was not for lack of wishing it Rhodes was far from them. The romance of his life was begun. His dream was reality. He could not have loved more this soil to which he had no title than any Matabele born of it, and he was eager to do for it what a Matabele could not even imagine. He called it My North. He called it his Thought. He gave his name to it as if, indeed, it were born of him. But now he could not be with his pioneers because he was busy elsewhere safeguarding their land, and he had just taken office as Prime Minister of the Cape.

CHAPTER · 15

RHODES PRIME MINISTER OF THE CAPE

I

H E DID, six weeks after their outspan at Salisbury, make an attempt to get to the pioneers. But by that time the rains were over the land; the new High Commissioner, Sir Henry Loch, was with him, a man not so easily led as the last one; Sir Henry Loch refused to risk his life and his Prime Minister's in crossing swollen rivers; they turned back. It was not till a year after the founding of Salisbury that Rhodes, laden with gifts, plans, and words, came to cheer his struggling pioneers.

Sir Henry Loch, indeed, had not wanted Rhodes to be Prime Minister. This was how it had happened:

On the very day the charter was signed Rhodes had made a railway agreement with the Cape. The Cape was to build a railway from Kimberley through Southern Bechuanaland, and thence the Chartered Company was to continue it. Even while Rhodes' men were journeying to Lobengula in 1888 to get the concession, he was speaking in the House about a line from Kimberley to Mafeking. During the whole of the 1889 session Rhodes had not once been seen in Parliament. But when, in June, 1890, he heard the government was about to abandon the Kimberley line for a line nearer the farms of the Bond members, he gave the pioneers, just ready then to start north, his blessing, waved them good-bye, and hastened to Cape Town. That railway should go, as had been arranged, not eastwards, but in the direction of all good railways—which is to say, northwards! "Your Hinterland," points Rhodes' statue from Cape Town, "is there!"

Once again the government was under the leadership of the man, Sir Gordon Sprigg, whom, in his first year, he had defeated on a question of railways, and who was destined to be four times Prime Minister of the Cape without having ever led his party, election-wise, into power. Once again, on a question of railways, Rhodes defeated him. Sir Henry Loch offered the premiership to Sauer, the leader of the Opposition, one of those country attorneys who in South Africa, as in America, achieve political distinction. Supporting Sauer and not to be allured by Chartered shares were John X. Merriman, a man like a knife—true, long, shining, sharp, and narrow, later himself to be Prime Minister of the Cape; and James Rose Innes, a future Chief Justice of the Union. They were, however, the three of them, held to be negrophilists. Sauer had not, accordingly, the Bond support. Rhodes had that support and Sauer suggested that Loch send for him. It was with reluctance Loch, who feared Rhodes' heel, did so, but Rhodes first asked Hofmeyr either to form a Cabinet or to take a place in his. Hofmeyr preferred to work as a private member. Thus Rhodes became Prime Minister. The three negrophilists served under him.

That railway could now go north.

And then he wanted the British crown colony of Bechuanaland to come to the Cape, and the Protectorate to the Chartered Company. And then there were new annexations to be made secure, and others to be put through. And then there was a deal to be arranged with Kruger that Kruger might turn his eyes towards the edge rather than the middle of Africa.

These were the immediate things. But perennially, and most urgently now that Rhodes had Mashonaland, there was the question of Union.

He was such a Prime Minister as had not happened before in South Africa and was not likely to happen again—a fervent Englishman who had the unanimous support of the Cape Dutch; a taker of native lands under whom lovers of natives, such as Sauer, Innes, and Merriman were proud to serve; a man of thirty-seven who was the Old Man to older men; a man who had the applause of England and the ear of the world; a man of gold and diamonds and lands and dreams; a man of magic who could not, it seemed, go wrong. One began to feel about Rhodes that there might be such a thing as luck, even such a thing as repeated luck, but that this long-continued luck, this run of luck, was something more than accident. It was a man's happy relationship with the gods; his belief in them, theirs in him. How could Rhodes doubt his gods? They had given him good fortune so often, they must intend his success. This confidence animated Rhodes and those who followed him. He could not go wrong because he felt he could not go wrong. With the exhilarated discovery that he had the goodwill of the gods came the faith of the healer and the Midas touch. "It is good to have a Minister with luck," he exultantly told the people of the Cape.

Now among all the other things he was doing, he was prepared to do his duty to this colony. But that duty was only a part of his larger duties, which were, not like the Cape, bounded by the Orange River, nor yet by the Limpopo, nor further by the Zambesi or the Congo or even the Nile. He was back again to 1877, to his young manhood, to the days when, in his first will, he had wanted "the colonization by British subjects of all lands where the means of livelihood are attainable by energy, labour, and enterprise, and especially the occupation by British settlers of the entire continent of Africa, the Holy Land, the valley of the Euphrates, the islands of Cyprus and Candia, the whole of South America, the islands of the Pacific not heretofore possessed by Great Britain, the whole of the Malay Archipelago, the seaboard of China and Japan, the ultimate recovery of the United States of America as an integral part of the British Empire . . . the foundation of so great a power as to hereafter render wars impossible and promote the best interests of humanity."

But, indeed, that early vision had never left him. "When I find myself in uncongenial company," he came to tell Lord Rosebery, "or when people are playing their games or when I am alone in a railway carriage, I think of my great idea. . . . It is the pleasantest companion I have." At every step forward in his fortunes, in anticipation of that step or in realization of it, his idea, his vision, was revived. Did he enter Parliament? A new will was made. Did he consolidate his Goldfields and de Beers? A new will was made. Did he take Mashonaland and become Prime Minister? A new will was made. And again Matabeleland? A new will was made. And certainly, as the years passed, he no longer spoke in terms so flamboyant as those of his early twenties; he substituted English-speaking peoples for actual Britons; he came to realize his limitations and reduced his scheme to a mere beginning of it, the scholarships; but yet the thought behind each successive will remained the same—the world for England, England for the world.

This very year, in England about his charter, he had formed

145

a friendship with W. T. Stead, and they had talked about his schemes, and he not long after wrote Stead an open letter speaking of a "Union with America and universal peace, I mean after one hundred years, and a secret society organized like Loyola's, supported by the accumulated wealth of those whose aspiration is a desire to do something. . . . They are calling the new country Rhodesia. . . . I find I am human and should like to be living after my death; still, perhaps if that name is coupled with the object of England everywhere, and united, the name may convey the discovery of an idea which ultimately led to the cessation of all wars, and to one language throughout the world, the patent being the gradual absorption of wealth and humane minds of the higher order to the object. . . ."

Now with his own hand he had made his beginning with Africa; it was not merely that, through his urgency, Warren had planted the British flag in Bechuanaland, since that remained, after all, merely a country for natives; he himself, with his own schemes, his own money, his own pioneers, had begun that "colonization by British subjects of a land where the means of livelihood were obtainable by energy, labour and enterprise." And soon he would have the other lands around it.

Barotseland, indeed, he had already snatched from under the noses of Germany and Portugal. On June 27, 1890, on the very day the pioneers crossed the Bechuana border into Matabeleland, his envoy received, for two thousand pounds a year, a concession of the mineral and trading rights over Lewanika's dominion—a concession of the Barotse country, Rhodes called it, "which I may tell you is over two hundred thousand square miles in extent."

On September 13th, the day after the pioneers hoisted the

146

Union Jack at Salisbury, he acquired for one hundred pounds a year a concession over Manicaland to do most things that could enter the mind of a human being—about fifty main activities are specified. The chief of Manicaland complained to the Portuguese that he had signed the concession under duress, and they intervened. Fruitlessly. In Manicaland, too, arrived Rhodes' pioneers.

A few days later he made, for five hundred pounds a year, a similar bargain with the chief of Gazaland; but when, next year, Jameson, having walked seven hundred miles, arrived, half-starving and full of fever, to take up the concession, the Portuguese again intervened, this time with success. Jameson was arrested for gun-running, and the territory was eventually assigned, by agreement with England, to the Portuguese.

Yet, at least, Rhodes saw to it that his pioneers should get their goods through the Portuguese harbour of Beira. He saw to it by the simple method of sending a young man there with goods and thus discovering in practice what would happen. But he might be fired on, he might lose his life, people protested. "Not a bit," said Rhodes, cheerfully. "They will only hit him in the leg. No, my dear fellow, they will only hit him in the leg."

The Portuguese fired blank shot at the young man (his name was Willoughby, and he was to share many enterprises with Rhodes and Jameson); Britain protested, and Rhodes got his route.

In 1891, Hofmeyr himself opposed the Boers in their attempt to establish a separate republic in Matabeleland.

The concessions and assets of the Lake Company, below the Congo, were bought by Rhodes in 1893.

Matabeleland was also, as will be seen, taken in 1893.

And the Orange Free State? And the Transvaal? Not so loud. Not so fast. Let us leave the Free State and Transvaal to their own destiny. Yet could one possibly avoid thinking of them?

II

For what was Rhodes working now? For his own greater power or the greater power of England?

It does not matter. The primary purpose, not merely of an artist, but of any man, is to express himself. If the world benefits, good for the world. Least of all is an artist entitled to complain of a doer's egoism, since his own activity is, of its very nature, nothing but egoism. Grant that Rhodes had a personal ambition: it is also a fact that throughout his manhood his unfaltering purpose was, to a degree ludicrous in any but a successful man, the enlargement of England for what he believed to be the benefit of the world. He came to the Cape Parliament with the idea of an All-British South Africa, perhaps of an All-British Africa. He died with that idea. His actions declare it and a hundred of his speeches pronounce it.

He spoke of it in Parliament, in election speeches, to his friends, his shareholders, and his settlers.

"I believe," he said, "in a United South Africa, but as a portion of the British Empire."

"I am not going to say that you could make a United States of South Africa to the Zambesi tomorrow, but I do say that this thing could be done gradually by promoting the means to the end."

148

"We should state by our policy that we are prepared to take the administration right through to the Zambesi."

"I would abolish the system of independent states antagonistic to ourselves, south of the Zambesi."

"My plan is gradually to assimilate the territory south of the Zambesi."

"If you were to sleep for five and twenty years, you might find a gentleman called your Prime Minister sitting in Cape Town and controlling the whole, not only to the Zambesi, but to Lake Tanganyika."

"The future is clear—we shall be one."

"It is not a question of race. It is a question whether we are to be united or not."

"We human atoms may divide this country, but Nature does not, and the Almighty does not."

"I have not faltered in my greater thoughts—the closer union of this country."

"I will not change my policy. I must make it all one, and whether you, the fathers, are for or against me, I know that your children will be with me."

"I am sometimes told my ideas are too big. 'Yes,' I answer, 'they would be too big if I were living on a small island—say, Cyprus or St. Helena; but we must remember that we are living on the fringe of a continent. Our history is only beginning, and therefore big ideas are essential to progress.' "

"We must try to keep the continent together. . . . If we were to go up in a balloon, how ridiculous it would appear to you to see all these divided states, divided tariffs, divided people."

"When the thought came to get through the continent it was a mad thought, it was the idea of a lunatic. . . . It is now not the question of the lunacy of the project; it is merely a question of the years it will take to complete."

"It has fallen to few to be the author, so to speak, of a huge new country."

"Sir Hercules Robinson said, 'But where will you stop?'

" 'I will stop,' I replied, 'where the country has not yet been claimed.' . . .

" 'Well,' said Sir Hercules Robinson, 'I think you should be satisfied with the Zambesi as a boundary.'

"I replied: 'Let us take a piece of notepaper, and let us measure from the blockhouse (on Table Mountain) to the Vaal River; that is the individual effort of the people. Now,' I said, 'let us measure what you have done in your temporary existence. Then we will finish up with measuring my imaginations.' "

His imaginations were not only boundless, but constant. ("I can state to you that I shall never abandon my object." "You can accept from me tonight what I think now, what I thought nine years ago, and what shall be my thought in the future.") The quotations here given are taken from speeches ranging over practically the whole period of his parliamentary career, and they are given, all but the last, chronologically.

It may be recalled that the first land mentioned in his first will is "the entire continent of Africa."

III

And was this moral of Rhodes? Was he "a valuable instrument for the cheap extension of empire," or was he, as Harcourt suggested, merely a recrudescence of the ancient privateer? Could he himself defend his attitude?

He gloried in it. In his mind was the future thought of Spengler: "A man may lay hands on the treasure of the world with a good conscience, not to say as a matter of course . . . if only he feels himself to be the engine of a mission. When he feels so, the idea of private property can scarcely be said to exist as far as he is concerned."

The natives of Africa, in their rags, their servitude, their hopelessness, are today a spectacle that only use makes natural and bearable. Yet, if one looked down from Olympus ("We are to be lords over them") with the eyes of Rhodes, could one say that monarchs prepared to sell the rights of their countries for anything from one hundred to two thousand pounds a year were entitled to possess those countries? . . . But they did not understand. If they did not understand, were they, in these days of understanding, so entitled? . . . But they could not help themselves. If tens of thousands of people were unable to help themselves against a few white men, should they not be governed by those white men? "These," said Rhodes, "are my politics on native affairs, and these are the politics of South Africa. Treat the natives as a subject people as long as they continue in a state of barbarism."

These were also the politics of Aristotle, who said that Barbarians were by nature slaves; and they were the politics of law and the world.

The charter of Raleigh, the first English colonizer, allowed him to take "any remote barbarous and heathen lands not possessed by any Christian prince or people." No state, that is, but a Christian state, had international rights, human rights. Now that the Turks, the Japs, and the Chinese wear trousers and can shoot, they too have become human. And savages under League mandates are, at least officially, human.

But in Rhodes' own time only the General Act of Brussels of 1885 stood between the European exploiter and the African exploited. The African had, one might say, a local existence, he had no international existence. The first taker of a savage land was as much entitled to that land as if its inhabitants were animals. Their desires and demands were a baying to the moon. The concessions a man might get from them were no more than evidence that he was the first European comer. Not the Christian principle of the equality of man, in which Nietzsche saw the survival of the weakest—degeneration and death; but the old Teutonic principle he revived, the Dostoevskian (one might infer, as Rhodes did, the Darwinian) principle of the God-made inequality of man, was the international law.

> "Rich old white man
> Owns the world.
> Gimme yo' shoes
> To shine.
> Yes, sir!"

These are the words of Langston Hughes, an American Negro.

Only the pity of individuals stood between the African native and his white master. Rhodes' way was the way of the world. His world. Raleigh's world. Cæsar's world. The world of the old Teutons. . . . Our own world (but it is ever the habit of the present to patronize the past) seems more imaginative. Rhodes was in many respects a precursor of our world, and he, too, was more imaginative. It was his great quality—imagination. He did what he did, but he knew some pain over the means. He had begun by feeling about the natives what was felt in his time and situation. He came, in the manner of

152

his race, to care for whom he had conquered. He was ashamed of what he had done to "that naked old savage," Lobengula. He had said once: "I have no native policy. I could not afford to say I have. I am a beginner at these things." He ended by pleading that the natives might be helped to use their "human minds."

But that it was magnificently right of him to make the world English, and thus something on the way to perfection, he never doubted. It was sad about the natives, but there were sublimer things than Christian pity. Rhodes did not know it, but he was a Nietzschean.

CHAPTER · 16

RHODES THIS SORT OF MAN AND THAT

I

THE astounding thing about Rhodes is not his genius for money-making, nor yet the unashamed opulence of his imagination, nor even the amazing union of the two ("I have tried to combine the commercial with the imaginative"), but the fact that, with a mind playing in millions, with the dream of an edifice rising to the clouds, he was prepared to manipulate units and, until he felt Time beating him, patiently to lay brick on brick. "It took me twenty years," he told the Bond, "to amalgamate the diamond mines. . . . That amalgamation was done in detail, step by step . . . and so your Union must be done in detail."

He was now, after five years' neglect of his parliamentary work, in Cape Town instead of in Salisbury, partly because he needed to win the Bond's sympathy to his Chartered Company and, through that sympathy, their help; partly because he believed, as he always said, that the future of South Africa rested with the Cape ("I have undertaken that northern development as a Cape Colonist. If there was anything that induced me to take the position of Prime Minister, it was the fact that I was resolved in my mind that we should extend to the Zambesi"); and partly because one could pull strings better from Cape Town than from Salisbury.

154

He had already, before coming down, offered de Villiers, the Chief Justice of the Cape, a seat on the Chartered Board. "The Board," he had suavely explained, "is, of course, not one in the sense of boards of ordinary land or gold companies. . . . It will really legislate, be a sort of permanent executive for the territory." He had also offered Hofmeyr a seat. He wanted the Dutch support. He had asked Johnson to enrol Boers in his pioneer column. His Charterland never ceased to cry out for Boers. He wanted them with him.

But de Villiers and Hofmeyr, friendly though they were with Rhodes these days, had refused his invitation. The best Rhodes had been able to do was to offer favours to Bond members. Did Rhodes stoop to bribery? Let us say, in the words of Dostoevsky's Raskolnikov, he stooped to pick up power.

The stories of how Rhodes tempted men are numerous and, considering their sources, not to be questioned. He distributed offices, advantages, and shares. He would do this sort of thing: If an influential man was against him in an election, he would say, "What does he do?"

"He sells produce."

"Buy a thousand sacks of mealies from him."

He was, after the election of 1898, charged by the opposing candidate with bribery. His constituency, it may be recalled, was the diamond-digging district of Barkly West. There was a digging area along the Vaal River much thought of by the diggers, but owned by de Beers, who, in their policy of restricting the diamond output, had hitherto refused to allow digging on it. It was announced, on the eve of the election, that this area would be opened to the public. The opposing candidate considered the announcement a bribe. The matter was heard by a special court of five judges. They held that, as the promise was not conditional on the votes of the electors, it was not a bribe. But Rhodes was warned, and he did not get his costs in the case. It was after this finding he maintained in the House that not a single charge of bribery had been proved against him.

When Chartered shares stood at something like four pounds he offered them at par to various members whose complaisance he desired. "But I am with you," said one of them, who tells the story. "I am with you. I don't want the shares." And he adds how, at one time, Rhodes owned a number of horses whom he called by the names of the men who had included, in the charge they made Rhodes for those horses, the price of their principles.

Rhodes used to show people the horses with sardonic amusement. They were among the things he did not trouble to disguise. "He occasionally blurted out truths," said Harcourt to Wilfrid Blunt, "other rogues would hide. He boasted how he bought up everybody by putting them into good things on the Stock Exchange."

They say politics at the Cape were pure before Rhodes' time. However, no one seems to have protested much against his methods until after the Jameson Raid. . . .

II

When Rhodes went to England at the end of this year of 1891 to arrange for the inclusion in his charter of still more territories, he was not only, as on his last visit, chairman of de Beers and the Goldfields, he was also managing director of the Chartered Company (he was, really, the Chartered Company) and Prime Minister of the Cape. He was Rhodes, the Empire-builder. He was the new hero, the Kipling hero, the carrier, for England, of "the white man's burden." They compared him—Rosebery compared him—he compared himself—with the Elizabethan adventurers.

Why not rather with Clive and Warren Hastings? But those men got into trouble, did they not? And then they weren't exactly colonizers; they didn't, like Raleigh, go and discover new lands for Englishmen to live in. Raleigh was the man; he was Rhodes' spiritual ancestor. He had been before him at Oriel. Like Rhodes, he had received a patent to colonize, to trade, to mine, in lands that were not Christian. He had sent men out to explore for him. He had induced settlers to go to his American colonies. Those settlers had had the same difficulties as Rhodes' settlers—sickness, the natives, the climate, the land. They had complained—like Rhodes' settlers, like Moses' settlers, like all the pioneers whose children afterwards take the credit for their ancestors' fortitude. But there, after two and a half centuries, Virginia and the colonies of Raleigh's time persisted. Rhodes' colonies would do the same.

It is true Raleigh had not found his El Dorado in either North or South America any more than Rhodes was to find a greater Rand in either North or South Rhodesia. And—stay!—did not Raleigh, too, have trouble, really most serious trouble? For that matter, did not Cæsar and Alexander have trouble no less serious?

But the description attached to Rhodes was Elizabethan adventurer.

And where, moreover, could he have a successor? As he said himself, the world was all parcelled out. There were only the stars left. He used to look at them longingly, says Stead. And by this Stead does not mean that Rhodes was brooding on the vastness of the universe, and what is man, and so on. No, according to Stead, he could not bear the fact that they were beyond his grasp. "These stars that you see overhead at night, these vast worlds which we can never reach! I would annex the planets if I could. I often think of that. It makes me sad to see them so clear and yet so far away." Such are the preposterous words Stead puts into Rhodes' mouth (how patient is paper!). We are to believe Rhodes seriously spoke them. . . .

England prepared to treat him as a hero. He had left England twenty years before, a sickly boy voyaging to South Africa to take up a grant of land. He was met now, on his arrival home, by a political duke and an international millionaire—Abercorn and Rothschild—both prepared to dance to his piping. The Prince of Wales told him to name his own day for lunch—the Prince of Wales was the father-in-law of the Duke of Fife, another dancer to Rhodes' tune. Queen Victoria had him to dinner and asked him if it was true he was a woman-hater. To which Rhodes is supposed to have answered, but it is not highly probable that he did, "How can I hate a sex to which Your Majesty belongs?" And she said, "What are you engaged on at present, Mr. Rhodes?" And he returned, "I am doing my best to enlarge Your Majesty's dominions." And Lord Salisbury, the Prime Minister, arranged a great dinner for him: he was bound to do something like that for an empire-builder. And, more significant than anything else, the sacred mailboat was delayed overnight that Rhodes might attend this dinner. Was not Rhodes practically South Africa?

To business men and politicians he came as a wizard. The Barings had recently crashed; there was an urgent shortage of bullion in England, and no one yet realized the magnitude of

158

the Rand. Here was a man who had in his pocket the key to the gold of Ophir. Chartered shares went up to three pounds fifteen shillings, and five thousand investors bought them.

Society was entranced by Rhodes. Sir Richard Burton, the Elizabethan adventurer immediately before him, the last but one, then, of Elizabethan adventurers, had just died, and the title was vacant. Rhodes filled it. He inherited, too, the enthusiasm lately bestowed on Stanley, the lion of the summer. Stanley had lectured. He had written a book called *In Darkest Africa*, which General Booth had capped by writing a book called *In Darkest England*. He had received the D.C.L. of Oxford, and the LL.D. of Cambridge, despite a certain questioning these days of his words and doings. He had even, for all his fifty years, successfully married. . . .

But what was Stanley, the henchman of the King of the Belgians, the inspirer of Bismarck, to Rhodes? Rhodes was not, like Stanley, international; he was national—he wanted everything for England. He had no need to lecture for money; he was a millionaire. Where Stanley did not even bear the name of his father, Rhodes was of worthy English family. He was thirteen years younger than Stanley. He was the most eligible bachelor in the world.

He could not, it is true, be described as a person exactly light in hand. For all his physical impressiveness, he was clumsy, restless, ill dressed, and nervous of speech. He talked too much about ideas. He was not easy with women. He did not care for women. They were—well, women, the adjuncts of a more interesting sex. He had the feeling about women of small boys who do not like girls to interfere in their games. Yet a man who could write to a woman: "I wanted just to say to you one thing. Now do not be annoyed. You always make

159

me feel that you are my exact idea of an Englishwoman"—
such a man could not have been quite without the notion of
how to make himself attractive. It was not to Rhodes, an ab-
stract Elizabethan, but to Rhodes, a very concrete Victorian,
that women, in these days, began to offer themselves in marriage. They wrote from all over the world, saying how much
better he would do if he were married. They wrote sometimes,
if they already had husbands, merely in worship.

Rhodes not only neglected to answer these letters, he seldom
even saw them. His secretaries opened and read all letters
written to him, even those marked "Private," "Confidential,"
and "Strictly Confidential." Rhodes did not agree that he
would do better married. He used to say he was too busy to
marry. It got about (as Queen Victoria herself had heard—
and it did not make him unpopular) that he was a woman-
hater.

"As regards Rhodes' relations with women generally," says
one of his secretaries, "he led an absolutely innocent, open,
and simple life. . . . I knew exactly what he did and where
he was. He very rarely went out at night, and when he did go
out, it was to attend a public function . . . invariably accompanied by one or some of his friends. When at Groote Schuur"
(the house Rhodes was presently to build himself) "he never
went to the play, and very seldom to private parties, probably
not more than once or twice in twelve months. . . . There
were very few nights that he had not guests to dinner. After
dinner he invariably played bridge until he felt sleepy, and
usually left us abruptly for his room."

Could one have better testimony than this to Rhodes' mo-
nastic purity?

The same secretary declares he only once saw Rhodes drink

too much, and that was during his negotiations with the Mata-bele on the Matoppos. He became then "talkative and jolly," but "he went to bed quietly and climbed up his waggon un-assisted."

Another secretary says, rather less agreeably, that Rhodes was not an habitual drunkard. He says Rhodes drank cham-pagne in a tumbler, sometimes champagne and stout in the forenoon, and after dinner five or six liqueurs.

Rhodes himself told one of his biographers that under the stress of worry he had sometimes taken liquor between meals. "But I mean to do so no more." And this same biographer says he only once saw him excited by drink.

Sir Herbert Baker says: "I can add my strong testimony in repudiation of suggestions of Rhodes' insobriety. He was apt to eat and drink with an absent-minded carelessness, but al-though he would sit at table absorbed in talk often to a very late hour, he drank moderately, and little or nothing after dinner."

The stories of Rhodes' insobriety, which are here refuted, are strongly current in South Africa, and they seem to be unjust. Rhodes, as his heart more and more troubled him, as that aneurism grew larger and larger, developed the swollen purpled face which is characteristic not only of alcoholic excess, but of a sick heart's embarrassment. He did, of course, demand the stimulation of drink. Men, in those early Kimberley days, exciting, dull, nerve-racking, hot, bleak, were for ever drinking. Rhodes, in his de Beers negotiations, was always discussing some terrific matter over a drink. "My wealth, my life, my dreams, were formed here in Kimberley," he said. And also his habits. His friends drank. His brother Herbert drank. He did learn to drink. There were times when he felt he needed drink. But even those who say so say, too, that he was no drunkard. Whether Rhodes drank more or less heavily, more or less than most men who had never been diggers, it is clear that he drank not too much. He did the work of fifty men and he did it effectively. There is no record that either his work or his relations with people suffered through drink. His body may have done so, or it may not. He had, at one time, seven doctors among his personal friends, and Jameson was his most intimate friend. One might infer that those doctors, and particularly Jameson, would not have let Rhodes kill himself with drink. Rhodes was a passionate and, in many ways, an uncontrolled man. He had a wild, quick temper. He could let fly an arm at a servant, and then, as suddenly, repent. Servants of his, who speak of him with a sort of affectionate awe, tell how they used to edge away from him and towards a door when he was angry. But he knew his work depended on time. He placed his work above everything. He was bitterly, usuriously anxious to live. He knew he had not long. He would have hoarded his precarious life.

III

His ecstatic reception in England, the new ways of existence it revealed to him, the full realization it brought him of his place in the world, led to a sudden and complete change in Rhodes' manner of living.

In his twenty years in South Africa it had never before entered his mind that he ought to have a home. The house he shared with Jameson in Kimberley was one of the sights of the town. In a room smaller than a small dressing-room, on a truckle-bed hardly large enough to hold his big body, with

162

sheets and blankets of any description and sometimes not present at all, and (as one visitor saw it) with a gladstone bag for
a bolster—Rhodes dreamed of annexing, if not, as Stead says,
the planets in the heavens, at least the planet he dwelt on. In
Cape Town, when he was attending Parliament, he lived first
at a private hotel, and then in rooms over a bank. In Bulawayo he had a cottage something like his Kimberley cottage.
In the Matoppos, where he loved to go and brood, where he had
his greatest triumph, where he chose to be buried, he had a
few of those whitewashed huts that are shaped like the huts
of the natives and called rondavels. He bought farms among
the Drakenstein Mountains and saw there the lovely homes of
others, but again, for himself, wanted only a cottage. For himself, that was all he wanted to the end.

But on his return from England in 1891 he decided that a
man in his position had a social duty to the world, and that
meant a different sort of home.

As absorbedly as he had amalgamated de Beers and pushed
his way north he now gave himself to the business of building
a house, not pretentious, and yet fit for Rhodes, the Prime
Minister of the Cape, the managing director in South Africa
of the Chartered Company, the natural host of the country—
fit, in short, for Rhodes, the Empire-builder. . . .

Near the city of Cape Town, at the foot of the Devil's
Peak, were three large barns in which, until one hundred and
fifty years before, the Dutch East India Company had kept
their provisions. To each barn was attached the home of the
keeper of these stores. The largest of the buildings was called
de Groote Schuur, which means the Great Barn, and lately
the governors of the Cape had used it as their summer home.
Now it was in the market, and first Rhodes leased it, and then

he bought it. He bought with it also, in time, fifteen hundred acres of mountain land. And here his home was created.

He found the maker of that home within a year. An unproved young architect called Herbert Baker was going about the country speaking with admiration of the old Cape houses. To him Rhodes showed not only Groote Schuur, at present languishing under the name of The Grange, and itself disguised to match that name, but also a sketch of the house as once it had been; and to him he gave the work of bringing Groote Schuur back to its first self.

"He surprised me," says Baker, "by the absence of detail in his instructions. He merely gave me in a very few words his ideas, or his 'thoughts,' as he used to call them, and trusted to me for the rest."

That was Rhodes' way. He could trust people. As he had assigned to young Frank Johnson the contract for bringing his pioneers to Mashonaland, so now he assigned to young Herbert Baker the work of making his home. Nor did he often give his subordinates details. When he spoke of doing things in detail, step by step, he did not mean a niggling superintendence. "You must do this. You must think. Remember, you must think, think. You must use your brains." It was a policy that was bound to lead, now and then, to misfortune. For such misfortune Rhodes took responsibility. But some believe that if Rhodes had filled in his instructions better there would have been no Jameson Raid.

Now he left it to Baker not merely to make of Groote Schuur the house it once had been, but also to furnish it as those early Dutchmen had furnished it.

People smiled at this. It was, they thought, another of his schemes to win over the Bond. But here originated, in fact, one of Rhodes' truest benefits to South Africa—he brought back taste to the country.

It was a time when the shoddiest of Victorian furniture was being imported from England and housed in the most vulgar of dwellings. The clear lines of the old Cape architecture were not to be seen among the new, nor the clear shapes of the old Cape furniture, nor the strong hand-wrought fittings of metal. They returned to use and favour through Rhodes. "I like teak and whitewash. . . . I want the big and simple, barbaric, if you like," he told Baker. And together they found old Dutch furniture, or had new made after its style, old Dutch glass and Delft ware, and porcelains of the East brought to the Cape by servants of the Dutch and English East India Companies.

Yet even when the house was ready for Rhodes the Prime Minister, Rhodes the man could not bring himself to leave the old outbuilding from which he had watched Baker's progress. He could not be troubled to move from it until he was made to realize that it stood between Groote Schuur and a clear view of the mountain. Then he allowed them to pull it down.

He did not stay long in the renewed Groote Schuur. There came the Jameson Raid, and the hatred of those who had trusted him, and the falling away of his honours, and, in physical fact, the breaking of his heart; and, as in a Greek play —messenger following messenger with bad news—there came also one saying that his home was burnt down.

Then Groote Schuur was rebuilt by Baker as it is today.

CHAPTER ˒ 17

THE HOME RHODES BUILT

I

ONE may understand Rhodes from his house as much as from anything else.

In these days that house is the home, while Parliament sits, of the Prime Minister of the Union of South Africa. To the Prime Ministers of the Union Rhodes bequeathed it eight years before there was a Union and while Britons were still fighting Boers.

The house looks as it looked in Rhodes' time. It is maintained, and its grounds, with his money.

Groote Schuur is a house of two stories and, counting the kitchen quarters, thirty rooms; white; with gables and large, small-paned windows. The thatch that caused the first Groote Schuur to burn down, and that causes all the old Cape houses to burn down, is replaced, less attractively, by tiles. Over the entrance is a bronze relief showing the landing of van Riebeek.

A long row of white pillars supports the heavily beamed stoep which faces the mountain Rhodes loved. The floor of that stoep is, like the floor of the hall and the floors of de Hoogh's pictures, of black and white squares. On it stand the old chests, the green jars, and the weatherworn chairs of Rhodes.

All the rooms in the house are either teak-panelled or white-washed. They are teak-beamed, with great brass candelabra. They have cabinets filled with china. They have old pieces of brass and copper, and heavy chairs and heavy tables and heavy chests.

As Rhodes himself possessed no trinkets except a set of plain gold studs, not even a watch, so, in his house, too, there are few little delicate things. There are no little delicate chairs or tables. There is no piano. There are no paintings (but once there was a Reynolds). There are no rare editions. There is a spinet. There are some Gobelin tapestries, and some books on open shelves.

It is a man's house. And, in fact, Rhodes kept no women servants, and the maids of visitors had orders to remain as inconspicuous as possible. There are fifteen bedrooms and two bathrooms: one of which, in marble, with a terrific granite bath, was Rhodes' great pride. Few of the bedrooms have adequate mirrors. Rhodes' own room possesses no full-length mirror, no bookshelf, no bright picture, nothing soft. There is a large bed with an uncomfortable mattress. There are large cupboards. There is a large atlas. There is an old French map of South Africa. There are prints of Rameses, of Bartholomew Diaz discovering the Cape, of Napoleon's coronation. There is a model of the young Napoleon and of the sacred bird the Phœnicians were supposed to have left in Rhodesia. There are carvings of this sacred bird throughout the house.

The one sentimental thing in Rhodes' bedroom (though, again, everything in Rhodes' bedroom expresses his romantic sense) is a photograph of that wife of Moselikatze who in 1896 helped him to make touch with the Matabele. She hangs on the wall with her little senile eyes, like liquid slits in her old wrinkled face, and her breasts like empty sacks, and her skeleton hands—the only woman Rhodes cared to remember.

His bedroom is built so that one may see the mountain; so that one may watch, through a great crescent of windows, the brilliant massed flowers, rising step by step to the mountain, the hydrangeas climbing its slopes, the bare stems of the trees striping with black its purple shadows. Rhodes chose to look— not at the sea, not at this plain of water with waves moving like long grass in the wind; he chose to look at the mountain. He always chose to look at the mountains rather than the sea. When he marched up Africa it was not along its coast lines— the Portuguese could have those, he said—but along its central plateaus. He selected a mountain-top for his burial. Was it the illness that had brought him to Africa which turned him instinctively away from the sea and towards the highlands? Was his taste so grounded?

One can, indeed, from a ledge at Groote Schuur look towards where the Indian and Atlantic Oceans meet, and this immensity Rhodes could perhaps tolerate, he could feel himself moved by so great an amalgamation. "Come, let us walk up the mountain and see the two oceans." Are these not also Shelley's words on amalgamation? "See, the mountains kiss high heaven, and the waves clasp one another." . . . Amalgamation ("All things by a law divine in one another's being mingle") was the principle of Rhodes' life. And bigness. And so he used to take people up the mountain to see the union of the oceans. But the sea, as such, the wind on the wave, was not Rhodes' inspiration; it was never a part of, at least, this Englishman's being.

There were, in truth, times when Rhodes imagined himself not so much an Englishman as an ancient Roman. He felt a kinship with Hadrian, he thought he looked like Titus. He saw England the successor of Imperial Rome. His favourite work was Gibbon's *Decline and Fall*.

His Gibbon has this quotation from Tertullian, the Carthaginian, marked with four heavy marginal lines: "You are fond of spectacles . . . , expect the greatest of all spectacles, the last and eternal judgment of the universe. How shall I admire, how laugh, how rejoice, how exult, when I behold so many proud monarchs, and fancied gods, groaning in the lowest abyss of darkness; so many magistrates, who persecuted the name of the Lord, liquefying in fiercer fires than they ever kindled against the Christians; so many sage philosophers blistering in red-hot flames, with their deluded scholars; so many celebrated poets trembling before the tribunal, not of Minos, but of Christ; so many tragedians, more tuneful in the expression of their own sufferings; so many dancers . . . !"

Did Rhodes think to himself, awed, "Before me too lies this fate!" And, with such thunder in his ears, did he fail to notice Gibbon's consolatory little anti-climax, "But the humanity of the reader will permit me to draw a veil over the rest of this infernal description, which the zealous African pursues in a long variety of affected and unfeeling witticisms"?

There are no other markings of consequence in this copy of *The Decline and Fall*, but that Rhodes was impressed by Gibbon's work may be judged from this curious circumstance: he gave Hatchard's, the London booksellers, instructions to have all Gibbon's authorities collected and, if necessary, translated—and then typed, indexed, and uniformly bound for him. He suddenly woke up when Hatchard's had accumulated eight thousand pounds' worth of translations. At eight thousand pounds' worth, then, the typescripts, hospitably including in their list the *Lives* of the Cæsars, Horace, Ovid, Terence, Cicero, Martial, and other writers already available in English, abruptly end.

Even then those hundred and fifty substantial volumes take up more than half the space in the small room called Library. But there are books also in the billiard-room and study.

These books are mainly concerned with history (two hundred and fifty volumes), biography (one hundred and thirty volumes), and Africa (one hundred and seventy-five volumes). Not included in these books on Africa there are a number on Cape Colony, and fifty on Egypt. Among the biographies there are twenty *Lives of Napoleon*, a *Life of Alexander the Great*, and a series of the rulers of India. There are—these figures are given approximately—one hundred and thirty books listed under Classics, eighty under Social Science, seventy under Travel, sixty under Federation and Constitutional Government, and fifty under Geography. There are seventy books of reference. There are twenty-five novels, twenty-four books on art and science, seventeen (Shakespeare, Ruskin and so on) that fall under the heading Literature, nine on Architecture, and a few—Frazer's *Golden Bough* is one and Smiles' *Self-Help* is another—rather despairingly huddled together as Miscellaneous. There is no poetry.

The library is that of a conscious empire-maker, not of a reader.

And yet Rhodes saw himself not only an ancient Roman, he aspired to be a bit, too, of an ancient Greek. He was the Pericles of South Africa. And deliberately, since through Greek art "Pericles taught the lazy and indolent Athenians to believe in empire." So he said.

But he loved beauty for its own sake. He had the imagination. He had that poignant sense of the appropriate which is taste. And as his desire for the interior of Africa, rather than its coasts, flowed, one might assume, from his weak-lunged fear of the sea, so, too, was his taste a reflection of himself.

"Men," said Lord Milner, "are ruled by their foibles, and Rhodes' foible was size." Certainly Rhodes' foible was size. But one might also call it his principle and his wisdom. "There is no use in two dozen of anything. You should count in hundreds and thousands, not dozens. That is the only way to produce any effect or make any profit."

So, not only had he to possess a country three-quarters of a million square miles large; to give his name to that country; to dream in continents and nations; to control all the diamonds in Africa, and pay for that control with the biggest cheque yet written; to own and bequeath millions of money; to see two oceans from his garden; to rest in death on a View of the World . . . but, of the immediate, the homelike sort of things, the avenue to Government House in Bulawayo (when Bulawayo became his) had to be three miles long; the streets of Bulawayo had to be wide enough for a waggon and its span of oxen to turn about in; his Inyanga farm in Rhodesia had to be of a hundred thousand acres; the reservoir of his dam in the Matoppos had to hold fifty million gallons of water; he had to surround his town house with fifteen hundred acres, and to have a mountain in his garden; his fruit trees in the Cape had to be planted in batches of a hundred and fifty thousand, and he coveted the whole of the great Drakenstein Valley for a farm.

"How much do you want me to buy?" asked his farm manager.

"Buy it all!"

"All! . . . All the Drakenstein Valley! . . . It would cost a million!"

"I don't ask your advice. I want you to buy it. Buy it!"

The manager bought as much as the owners would sell him.

But Rhodes had other aspects than that of size in his taste as in himself. He wanted in his surroundings, as in his living, his dreams, his actions, his words, not only size, but also shape, weight, simplicity. When he asked Baker for the "big and simple—barbaric, if you like," he was anticipating merely his last words to his Rhodesians: "Think simply. Truth is ever simple." As Rhodes the man was ponderous in his body, his humour, his manner, his very hands, so even the tables and chairs in his house are hard to lift in their heavy fashioning from heavy South African woods. His bath is hewn out of a granite rock. His grave is hewn in a granite hill.

As he knew clearly what he wanted, and wanted it all his life, so he preferred to deal in what he called "globular sums," so the trees against his mountain have no softening lower branches, so he felt he could not, as he said, "possess the mountain he had bought" until it was cleared of its covering bush.

His very flowers had to grow in massed shape. Nor were they delicate little flowers. With the Imperialism of Disraeli he did not adopt, too, Disraeli's primrose (though who can say, really, whether Disraeli himself loved the primrose? An idle word in a queen's hearing, and for life a flamboyant Oriental is compelled—Heaven alone knows how tediously—to the pallid primrose). . . . In Rhodes' garden there are troops of canna, hydrangea, bougainvillea—strong, scentless flowers— marching in regular formation towards his mountain. And he loved the mountain shapes, sculpture, and architecture. He sent Baker to study the granite temple of Thebes and the Greek Doric of Pæstum and Athens, the Greek horses at St. Mark's, the sarcophagus of Alexander at Constantinople, that he might bring back from them a design for a monument to the siege of Kimberley, a classic bath for Kimberley, and a lion-house for Groote Schuur.

Only the siege monument was completed. When it came to the bath, the "nymphæum," he could not get the directors of de Beers to sanction the expenditure, and he was too ill to force that sanction. This bath, this temple, filled with mine water, was to have been in marble, and to have stood among lilies and papyrus; long avenues of orange trees, backed by larger trees, were to have led to it, and poignant meaning to have been given it by the desert on whose edge it rested. . . . One has to know Kimberley, a town where diamonds grow so much more readily than grass, to appreciate the sublimity and the folly of the idea.

The lion-house was to have been a part, Baker imagines, of "a great, colonnaded building which would give scale to and interpret the beauty of the mountain-side." There is a zoo at Groote Schuur, but the lion-house was not built.

A university, too, was to have risen from that mountain-side where the young would come, "Dutch and English, east and west, north and south, to get to know and like one another

173

and so make an united South Africa." Today a university exists, but it is not the university which Rhodes planned.

And then he built a house in his grounds ("Do not be mean" was his only instruction to Baker) where artists might dream. To this house Kipling used to come during the English winter. . . .

And the statue of van Riebeek had to mark the place where the first Dutch landed at Cape Town; a bronze over the entrance at Groote Schuur had to exhibit that landing. "It will be all one country now, and we must make this its most beautiful capital."

And on the granite hill where Rhodes meant to rest forever there were to rest, too, beneath a monument, the fallen in the Matabele War. Today this monument, like the university, stands—never seen by Rhodes. It stands, vulgarly neat, in the unmade world whose grandeur so gripped him that he knew at once, "I shall be buried here, facing north," and two years later came again in search of it, saying over and over: "I had to find my hill. I had to find it. It has stayed with me. . . ."

CHAPTER · 18

THE PEAK OF EXISTENCE

I

THE thing one fails to remember about Rhodes—so vehemently he lived—is that for a long time death was his daily companion. Not the death sanctimoniously evoked by "In the midst of life we are in death," nor the ironic death which, being of the essence of life, makes rottenness life's very fundament—but the real, immediate, frightening death that grimaces from the scaffold at a man condemned.

Rhodes had come out to South Africa because death was before him. He had fled back to South Africa from Oxford because its breath was in his very face. "You the same Rhodes, sir?" the doctor said who had once written him down as tubercular beyond recovery. "Impossible! According to my books you have been a corpse these ten years." . . . He had gone into the desert with Herbert because, from another place now, it was attacking him, not lungs this time, but heart. Following those three years during which he had founded himself in gold, amalgamated the Diamond Fields, taken Mashonaland and other northern lands, become Prime Minister of the Cape and been acclaimed the hero of his nation, there began a decade of the illness that brought his end.

He had come back from England resolved to live as befitted

an empire-builder. He had accomplished in this year of 1891 a score of things any one of which might have made a man significant for life. At the end of the year he fell from a horse and broke his collar-bone, he had also influenza, his heart could not bear the double strain—he worked henceforth knowing that his time was short and he must hurry. He thought he might live to be forty-five. He lived to be forty-eight.

It is said of Rhodes that he was not physically courageous. When he went shooting on the veld and there was fear of lions and other wild animals, he instinctively (it is said) chose to sleep surrounded by his companions, so that he might only be got at over their bodies. They tell that he did not like to be alone in a house at night, and that in the old Kimberley days frightening pranks (even of the ghostly sheet and pumpkin kind) were played on him.

Yet the very fact that Rhodes is thought of without pity, that it is hard to remember why he worked so hurriedly and acted so violently, that one accepts such working and such violence without the awed reflection, "It was a man fighting death did it!"—this, if nothing else, makes of Rhodes a creature of special courage. He does not arouse pity. He does not call for it. He does not feel it for himself. He wishes, certainly, for another ten years of life that he may go on with his work. He envies the man who "will see it all . . . and I shall not." He falls into the habit of repeating the story that "Rhodes has taken a country as big as Europe, and we shall get that, but he will get only six feet by four." He says to Lord Rosebery: "Everything in the world is too short. Life and fame and achievement, everything is too short." He says to Stead: "From the cradle to the grave, what is it? Three days at the seaside." He speaks of that "terrible time," the one unconquerable thing.

And, dying, he says: "So much to do. So little done." . . .
But these are not a coward's whimperings. They are the recognitions of Ecclesiastes: "For the living know that they shall die: but the dead know not anything, neither have they any more a reward, for the memory of them is forgotten.

"Also their love, and their hatred, and their envy, is now perished; neither have they any more a portion for ever of any thing that is done under the sun." . . .

But "Rhodes is dead," wrote Wilfrid Blunt, one of those who can love none only the aristocratic or the submerged. "Rhodes is dead. I did the rogue an injustice when I thought he might be shamming"; and "I would scourge him with his crown still on him," said Meredith. One could not believe that Rhodes might have suffered.

II

In this year of 1891, whose beginning saw his triumph in England, and whose end, Fate's warning that he was not to get far with his exultant work, Rhodes did the following things:

He obtained in England Imperial sanction for his further territories, "an arrangement of boundaries," he said, "which seemed almost impossible."

He said to the Prime Minister of England: "If you wish to retain the sentiment of the colonies, you must consider day by day how you can give the people some commercial advantage, and thus show them that the tie with England is of practical advantage to themselves." By which he meant preferential tariffs.

He donated five thousand pounds to the Liberal Party funds,

and this was later said to have been a bribe to them not to abandon Egypt, and an explanation of why Harcourt and Campbell Bannerman did not afterwards press Rhodes closer at the Raid Enquiry. . . . Rhodes accordingly published his correspondence with the party organizer. And it now appeared he had hoped, in giving the donation (for which he had been asked), that a Liberal Government would not evacuate Egypt; had been assured they would not; had eventually judged from speeches of Gladstone and Labouchere they might; and had then asked that his donation be diverted to charity. . . . The point, of course, was that Rhodes wanted to safeguard his project of a railway line to Egypt.

And although one may question whether the ten thousand pounds to the Irish Party was conceived in a spirit of simple friendship or in a spirit of friendship *for* friendship—that Rhodes ever imagined he could buy the Egyptian policy of the Liberal Party, from Gladstone and Rosebery downwards, for five thousand pounds is beyond sense. He did believe that every man had his price, but he also knew better what price. . . .

Now, when he came back from England hailed as the greatest of Englishmen, he proceeded to prove himself, in addition, the most essential of South Africans. He explained to the Bond that his sentiments were theirs—self-government and, "although you have not stated it," union. And to achieve union, he told these Dutchmen straightly, he would, for his part, "abolish that system of antagonistic states hostile to ourselves south of the Zambesi"—by which he meant the Dutch republics. Whereupon (say the biographers of Hofmeyr) the alliance between Rhodes and the Bond was so magically sealed that never, declared Hofmeyr, had they had "a Premier who, on most questions, had been more one heart and soul with our

Colonial Afrikanders than Mr. Rhodes. . . ." (Thundering and continuous applause.)

In this same speech Rhodes also announced that he had obtained "enormous subscriptions" to found a teaching university at the Cape. It was an idea Napoleon had had before him —to promote Imperial conformity through a national university. But Rhodes' inspiration came, as it happens, from Bloemfontein. He had there seen the warm feeling among the old students of a college, and had come away impressed with the discovery that "the period in your life when you indulge in friendships that are seldom broken is from eighteen to twenty-one." In Bloemfontein, then, was born, not only Rhodes' thought of bringing about South African union through a university, but also his plan to help world union through his Scholarships.

And he had the place for his university—the grounds of Groote Schuur, his home.

He had other ideas in this fruitful year of 1891. He had an idea that Pondoland might be annexed to the Cape, and an idea that he would like to run Bechuanaland if England would give him fifty thousand pounds a year for doing it. (But only a little while ago, when he was trying to get his charter, he had offered to *contribute* to the cost of administering Bechuanaland.)

He continued his railway through Bechuanaland to Mashonaland—which made Loch afraid the fifty thousand pounds would all be used on railways.

He continued his railway towards the Zambesi, and borrowed money for both these railways from de Beers, giving as security the possible—the mythical—diamonds of Mashonaland. However, he faithfully repaid the money. An accountant,

179

who speaks with authority, says that Rhodes' money dealings were always in strict order.

He arranged also, where others had failed, to connect the Cape railway through the Free State with Johannesburg; and this was the reason he was later so maddened by Kruger's discrimination against Cape imports.

And, though he now scotched a Dutch republic in Manicaland, he also considered lending Kruger, on behalf of the Cape, the money Kruger was seeking in Europe, and coming to a friendly customs relationship with him.

He thought one might perhaps buy up the whole of the Portuguese province of Lourenço Marquez.

To that end there were further negotiations with Kruger, and this, according to Kruger, is the conversation they had:

RHODES: We must work together. I know the Republic wants a seaport. You must have Delagoa Bay.

KRUGER: How can we work together there? The harbour belongs to the Portuguese, and they won't hand it over.

RHODES: Then we must simply take it.

KRUGER: I can't take away other people's property. If the Portuguese won't sell the harbour, I wouldn't take it even if you gave it to me, for ill-gotten gains are accursed.

Exit Rhodes.

In 1891, further, Rhodes passed a new Bank Act which restricted the issue of notes in the Cape and stabilized its finances; and he supported a new franchise—"A dual vote to property and intelligence," he called it. . . .

And—annexation, self-government, union, extension, tariffs, finance, franchise—there was something more to be done in that direction. In May, 1891, Rhodes wrote to the Prime Ministers of Canada and New South Wales.

This is his letter to Sir John Macdonald, the Prime Minister of Canada:

DEAR SIR,

I wish to write and congratulate you on winning the elections in Canada. I read your manifesto and I could understand the issue. If I might express a wish, it would be that we could meet before stern fate claims us. I might write pages, but I feel I know you and your politics as if we had been friends for years. The whole thing lies in the question, can we invent some tie with our mother country that will prevent separation? It must be a practical one, for future generations will not be born in England. The curse is that English politicians cannot see the future. They think they will always be the manufacturing mart of the world, but do not understand what protection coupled with reciprocal relations means. I have taken the liberty of writing to you, and if you honour me with an answer I will write again.

Yours,

C. J. RHODES.

P.S.—You might not know who I am, so I will say I am the Prime Minister of this Colony—that is, the Cape Colony.

If Rhodes was otherwise than sincere in this letter and even in the irresistible postscript, written at a time when the whole Empire was blaring his name, he was a literary artist. But stern fate did claim the man to whom it was addressed, and before ever he received it.

III

And was Rhodes (we are still in the year 1891) forgetting his North? What with donations, tariffs, federations, universities, railways, Bank Acts, northern annexations, southern annexations, eastern annexations, and closer unions with England, was Rhodes leaving his children unaided to their swamps, their mosquitoes, their tse-tse flies, their natives, their chagrins and their whiskies at ten and six the tot? Had he failed to notice that Chartered shares, which had risen to three pounds fifteen when he was in England, were run down now to twelve shillings and even ten shillings just because the settlers had not "in a race out from home and a race back" achieved a "quarter of a million of money"; because Chartered funds were being poured out like water and none were coming in; because Chartered shareholders had discovered that the Rudd Concession was not theirs unless they bought it, and who knew whether the whole Mashonaland affair might not be a bubble, seeing that even the Rudd Concession was a concession, not over the land itself, but merely over what lay below the land, and could one get below it if one had no right upon it?

The last trouble Rhodes had the opportunity of settling this year. And although he was prepared to argue that the power given the concessionaries "to do all things which they might deem necessary to defend their minerals" implied their right to establish industrial settlements and protecting forces—in short, all the rights—he really knew better. He wrote to Lord Salisbury that the Rudd Concession did not, in terms, purport to give more than mining rights, and that, therefore, "the Chartered Company had but an imperfect right, if any right at all," to grant land titles. And he was more than satisfied to pay stiffly for a power which, on paper at least, looked stronger than his arguments.

Among the concession-hunters at Lobengula's kraal Rhodes' people had found, in their own days of concession-hunting, the minions of one Lippert, a Transvaaler of German birth. And when Lobengula saw that all his mineral rights were definitely gone to Rhodes, he followed the policy of the Swazi king in dividing his assignments, and thus the power against him. To

Lippert, then, at a price of a thousand pounds down, and five hundred a year, he ceded, for a century, his land. Lippert, suggests Sir Percy Fitzpatrick, was the agent of Germany; but it does not seem likely, or he would not have sold his rights, as he did, to Rhodes.

Nor, in spite of the fact that he was Beit's cousin, did he sell to the Rhodes' group because they were dear to him. On the contrary, he and Beit were on bad terms. He sold for no other reason than that he got a high price, and Germany, one may presume, was not a partner in what was to Lippert a simple commercial affair.

So now Rhodes had the Lippert as well as the Rudd Concession. At last he possessed, it seemed, everything that once had been Lobengula's; not merely the secret treasure under his earth, but his earth itself.

Rhodes was never to know that the earth he still had not. He was barely dead when his settlers began to claim Rhodesia for the Rhodesians, and not for the Chartered Company. They had been prepared to sing "God save Rhodes." They had proved the followers he had dreamt of: even when his guiding was errant they had not deserted him. "Lay me there," he said of the Matoppos. "My Rhodesians would like it. They have never bitten me." "My Rhodesians," he called them, as he spoke too of "My North."

But, with Rhodes gone, they were not prepared to sing "God Save the Charter." There was nothing to them in being the subjects of a Chartered Company. And so other chartered companies, too, had found in their time. It was a more glamorous thing to rule, than to be ruled, for profit.

On the day the World War opened, on August 4 of 1914, His Majesty's Privy Council met to discover how far, by charter, conquest, and cession, the Chartered Company owned Rhodesia. The World War was all but over when it decided that, as to the Charter, it "gave the capacity to own and to grant land, but in itself granted none"; as to conquest, any conquest was, by constitutional practice, on behalf of the Crown; as to cession, the Lippert Concession was a personal contract and could not make of Herr Lippert (Beit was also, as *Punch* said when he died, called "Herr" in those war days) the owner of the entire kingdom "from the kraal of the king's wives to his father's grave," nor could it make of all Lobengula's subjects "sojourners on sufferance where they had ranged in arms—dependent on the good nature of this stranger from Johannesburg even for gardens in which to grow their mealies, and pasture on which to graze their cattle. The Lippert Concession," said the Privy Council, ascending abruptly from poesy to business, "may have some value as helping to explain how and why the Crown came to confer the administration of Southern Rhodesia upon the company, but as a title to unalienated land it is valueless."

Not the Chartered Company (and so much now for Elizabethan adventurings), not the company with the Lippert Concession, but the Crown, was the successor of Lobengula. And, considering the matter of sovereignty merely, Rhodes himself had admitted this: "The Charter must change, first, perhaps, to a system of Imperial Government, but finally to Self-Government." . . . "A change must occur from the Chartered system of government . . . to Self-Government, and from Self-Government to a system of union with the Cape Colony." What neither Rhodes nor anyone else realized, and what it took the Privy Council four years to decide, was that the Chartered Company would never be paid for this land which they believed they had acquired with the Lippert Concession. They controlled, it is true, the minerals, the railways, their own tremendous estates, and the land bank. They had shares in all the best mines and in numbers of subsidiary companies. They had rights and concessions. But precisely the land of Rhodesia they had not. And when, in due time, accounts came to be squared between the company and the Crown they were paid what it had cost them to run the country. This, they said, was something like eight millions. But the Privy Council decided it was more like five millions. . . . And so much they got.

In 1920 the Chartered shareholders received, after thirty years, their first dividend. It was sixpence.

IV

But when Rhodes went up to see his pioneers in that stupendous year of 1891 no one knew he had not everything—or, indeed, not anything, of the land he was selling, leasing, granting. He did not know it himself. He came like a god from Olympus, like all the gods from Olympus, the universal owner, the universal donor. He came with a passion for the country which overflowed on to all those who called it theirs. "I feel I ought to be with them," he said when they went through to Mashonaland, and he had to stay in Cape Town as Prime Minister. And if the Cape did not want him to be both their Prime Minister and the maker of the North, "there will be no happier man than myself, because I can then go and live with those young people who are developing our new territories. I know them well, and, believe me, the life is better than that of receiving deputations." . . .

He found, however, that the settlers themselves did not find

185

the life so enchanting. They complained because food and gold both were scarce, and because half their claims had to go to the company. And then they might not dig for diamonds since diamonds (if any) were secured to de Beers, and they could not get the best land, for the best land was reserved to the company—and it rained, and they had malaria, and the Mashona were lazy, and the Matabele were dangerous, and there were no roads or trains or telegraphs, and they were imprisoned in their loneliness.

Rhodes asked them if they were sure it was food and not liquor they meant. But then he regretted the taunt and promised that they should get their food sooner and cheaper. And it was this promise he fulfilled when he sent Willoughby to find out if the Portuguese would shoot an Englishman carrying goods through Beira—or, as he demurely explained it to his Chartered shareholders: "Unfortunately, some of our younger spirits went up and forced the route from Beira, and then we had the unfortunate dispute with the Portuguese, which, however, did bring about the happy result." . . .

As for the gold, did they think, he asked the settlers, that gold was to be picked up like gooseberries? The gold was there, and it must be found, and he would do what he could about the fifty-per-cent difficulty. And the telegraph was near Salisbury now, and the railway from the south was following, and even the sceptical Lord Rothschild had given him money for the railway from the east. He would get them also friendlier natives. (But in the end they preferred their own natives.) He would send them horses through Beira. (But the horses died, so eventually he sent donkeys.) And were any of them in want? There was his own pocket. Were they thinking of coming to Cape Town? had they friends joining them from England? There was his new home, Groote Schuur. Were they in despair and anxious to give up altogether? "Help this man home and charge to me," ran the notes the dispensers of his money were continually receiving; and from little banks in little northern villages came odd scraps of paper—notepaper, newspaper, blotting-paper, scrawled over in pencil and undated, that were the cheques of Rhodes to his needy settlers. He gave money. He lent money. One man repaid him four hundred pounds. "Look at this. He's paid me back. The bloody fool's paid me back. What did he want to pay me back for?" It was something unimaginable that anyone should pay Rhodes a debt.

He told the settlers, and he so clearly meant it, that he believed with all his mind and heart in the North that was theirs. Surely, he said to them later—but he said much the same to them now and always—surely to be here was "a happier thing than the deadly monotony of an English country town or the still deadlier monotony of a Karroo village. Here, at any rate, you have your share in the creation of a new country. . . . You have the proud satisfaction of knowing that you are civilizing a new part of the world. Those who fall in that creation fall sooner than they would in ordinary lives, but their lives are better and grander."

And to a friend he (later, too) said: "How glorious this is, and how lucky you are to be here! But why are you here? Because turnips did not pay in ——shire. Had they paid, you would have remained an average country gentleman and a fairly respectable member of Parliament. How much better to be here under the stars, thinking out great problems!" . . .

Is there anything harder to fake than a genuine enthusiasm? Even words on paper hide their faces and are without light or lift when their authors cry, "Lo, behold!" in unbelief.

187

But as it is hard to imitate enthusiasm, so is that enthusiasm powerful. Stronger than Rhodes' money was Rhodes' passion in the making of Rhodesia.

He had to go back now to Cape Town, but his settlers felt they could struggle on because he had been among them.

And then he had left with them his dearest possession, the fascinating Dr. Jameson. Jameson had just returned, full of malaria, from his concession-hunting in East Africa; he had, on his way back, managed to warn off a group of questing Transvaalers, he was their new administrator. "I am more indebted to him," said Rhodes, "than to any man in South Africa."

v

He said it to his shareholders in London. For he had not only his settlers to comfort, he had also his shareholders. There was another aspect to his North than the Imperial and romantic, there was the commercial; and he might be pondering great problems under the stars, but his shareholders, who had never seen those clear African stars, were not. They had bought Chartereds for anything up to four pounds, believing that here was the greatest gold-mining thing in history; and no new Rand had yet been discovered—nor ever would be, wrote Randolph Churchill from Charterland. Chartereds, in short, were running down so that eventually they touched ten shillings, and "the condemnation of the home papers could only," said Rhodes, "be compared to their previous sanguineness. They condemned the country as everything that was bad."

There were, in these days, people who spoke of South Sea Bubbles.

Many years later Rhodes told an election audience what had been his feelings in those uncertain days. He had just (as he described) had that accident which, followed by influenza, was to mark the beginning of his final decade. "I was in bed in Cape Town for a long time, and when I came to my senses I had always to be thinking of the condition of the country, the exhaustion of the funds subscribed for its development, and the reports of the failure of the country."

It was at the end of 1892 that Rhodes met his shareholders for the first time in London, and confessed with what good reason the papers had criticized and the shares had slumped. "I went round and met Dr. Jameson in the country. I found the position as follows: a discontented population of about fifteen hundred people and an expenditure of about two hundred and fifty thousand pounds a year on police"—and no returns.

And what was to be done about it? The whole expansion business was in danger—the dream of Rhodes' life. Who would continue to believe in him, who would follow him ever northwards, if he failed so in his very beginnings?

It was Jameson who found a plan—a Jameson sort of plan, simple and daring; questionable, perhaps; but, perhaps again, never to be questioned. He said to Rhodes: "Give me three thousand pounds a month and I'll pull through." Three thousand as against twenty thousand? But how could he? By what magic?

Well, magic is often the too obvious. One could save seventeen thousand pounds a month by the obvious process of not spending it. There were those seven hundred costly police they had in Mashonaland. Why need there be seven hundred? Bechuanaland was next door, able to support as many police as one could possibly want. Bechuanaland could not allow Mashonaland to get into trouble. It had a friendly administration, hardly deterred by reverence for the Colonial Office—as one may judge by Shippard's advice about the guns paid to Lobengula. The officer in charge of the police was the same Major Goold Adams who had intercepted the Wood, Chapman, and Francis Syndicate; who was later to intercept Lobengula's peace emissaries; and finally to become Governor of the Orange River Colony. Bechuanaland was being financed, not by a chartered company whose shareholders asked questions, but by an Imperial Government whose taxpayers did not. If more police were enrolled in Bechuanaland for the safety of Mashonaland, who would seriously trouble? Let the company then reduce its own force. Let it reduce its force from seven hundred—to, say, one hundred.

It was a plan. One might call it a gamble. But then, again, is that a gamble which is the only hope?

The Chartered force was reduced to one hundred. The Bechuanaland force was increased. Next year the Chartered force came down to forty; the settlers themselves were enrolled as volunteers; the country, it was discovered, could run very well on Jameson's charm and the three thousand pounds a month which Rhodes got from de Beers, his own pocket and Alfred Beit's. "What deficiency there was in the revenue I had personally to find."

And so the company's expenditure descended from two hundred and fifty thousand to thirty thousand a year. A little revenue—stamps, customs, licences—trickled in. The budget was balanced. Zambesia, as Rhodes called it, Charterland, as Jameson called it, Rhodesia, as newspapers were beginning to call it, was saved. . . .

The figures given here are from speeches of Rhodes. They are not quite accurate. Nor is eight hundred thousand square miles—he always spoke of eight hundred thousand square miles—exactly the size of the territory Rhodes acquired in the North. Seven hundred thousand would be nearer. Except in his specifically financial speeches Rhodes gave his figures—one might say descriptively, rather than mathematically. He used them to illustrate a situation with which he was dealing. As his picture, then, let those figures stand. . . .

If the British taxpayer did not know about the new Bechuanaland police—well, England was a very rich country; it was, despite the warnings of Labouchere, worth the money in Imperial pride that Zambesia should not collapse; it would have cost England more to take Rhodes' territories than it had cost Rhodes (he had, he said, given England "eight hundred thousand square miles without a sixpence of cost"); and, finally, as Othello, in a spasm of sense, remarks: "He that is robbed, not wanting what is stolen, let him not know't, and he's not robbed at all."

It was with a justified confidence, a feeling of mission, a consciousness that the whole Empire would hear him and he was not speaking only as a Chartered director to Chartered shareholders, but as a Briton to the British—it was in this exultant mood Rhodes met his first Chartered audience.

He had now fourteen thousand shareholders in his various companies. Before he died he had thirty thousand. Among those shareholders were women who had bought just a few Chartered shares that they might see his noble brow and his sensual mouth and hear the voice that could so incongruously, from that large frame, break into an ugly falsetto.

CHAPTER · 19

ENGLAND'S TRADE, ENGLAND'S LIFE,
IS THE WORLD!

I

IT WAS in this speech Rhodes talked about "squaring the Mahdi"; and the Gladstone policy of "scuttle"; and the fact that the British Isles could support only six million people; and the way other countries were shutting out British goods.

"Squaring the Mahdi" is one of the tags pinned on to Rhodes. It is supposed to be an example of how Rhodes thought bribery the best policy.

And, in fact, Rhodes was not (as has already been said here) incapable of distributing productive favours. There were times when he did feel that bribery, like mercy, blessing both giver and taker, was twice blessed. He did sometimes think that a little immorality was better than a lot of trouble. . . . Or perhaps he deliberately rejected morality. His mission may have seemed to him something beyond any current conceptions of right and wrong. The discovery of his patent, as he called it, for spreading England and unifying the world and so bringing about the millennium may have been his proven right where all other rights were merely the experimental rights which could be thrown away. He may have seen himself, like Napoleon, the servant not of morality, but of destiny. "I am not a man like other men," believed Napoleon. "The laws of morality and decorum could not be intended to apply to me."

"I like Rhodes," said Labouchere, his most persistent enemy. "An entirely honest, heavy person." He thought Rhodes (who called him "a cynical sybarite") a simple and direct man who deceived himself in perfect good faith.

But he was wrong. Rhodes may have been simple in that he had one clear object in life, but he did not deceive himself. He knew his deviousness. He could be sardonic about it. He had that cynicism which is the only humour a man with a purpose dare allow himself. He felt, at the same time, that his end, not merely justified, but authorized, his means. . . .

However, the point is not whether Rhodes was good or evil. He was not, as it happens, evil in the sense of being inhuman. He had imagination, and so he could be largely generous and warmly sympathetic and very pitiful. The objection to the idea that by "squaring the Mahdi" Rhodes meant bribery has nothing to do with his character. It has to do, like the five thousand pounds to the Liberal Party, with his intelligence. Rhodes was not a fool. It is not at all likely that to an ecstatic, hero-worshipping audience of Englishmen he would calmly suggest a system of bribery. The very context of the remark: "I do not propose to fight the Mahdi, but to deal with him. I have never met anyone in my life whom it was not as easy to deal with as to fight," indicates clearly that Rhodes hoped to apply to the Mahdi those methods he had applied to Groot Adrian de la Rey: "Blood must flow." "Give me my breakfast. Then we can talk about blood." . . .

The reason Rhodes hoped to deal with the Mahdi was also the reason he was talking about "scuttle," and England's smallness, and the cold, competitive world. Rhodes wanted to take his telegraph up to Egypt. He wanted the British flag to precede him. And here was Gladstone, with his new government, anxious "to retire from every portion of the globe." Rhodes had barely, eight months before, arrived in England when there was talk that they were preparing to scuttle out of Uganda— Uganda, whither he was taking his telegraph ("without any contribution from England"); Uganda, which was on his way to Egypt.

"Our burden is too great," Gladstone complained to him (Rhodes himself tells the story, now in this speech, and now in that. All Rhodes' little stories occur again and again in his speeches). "Our burden is too great. I cannot find the people to govern all our dependencies. We have too much, Mr. Rhodes, to do."

Rhodes denied that England's burden was too great. "If you will only take the countries, you will have the people capable of administration."

"But," protested Gladstone, "apart from increasing our obligations in every part of the world, what advantage do you see to the English race in the acquisition of new territory?"

"Mr. Gladstone," answered Rhodes, "the practical reason for the further acquisition of territory is that every power in the world, including our kinsmen the Americans, as soon as they take new territory, place hostile tariffs against British goods. . . . Great Britain is a very small island, not nearly the size of France, and she has not that wonderful wine industry, nor has she a continent like the Americans. Great Britain's position depends on her trade, and if we do not take and open up the dependencies of the world which are at present devoted to barbarism we shall shut out the world's trade."

As everyone knows today, Rhodes saw other than "practical reasons" why Britain ought to go out and take new territories. But these he did not now confide to Gladstone. He was not ashamed of the other reasons. He meant the world, in due time, to hear them. But just at the moment he had to talk to Gladstone as a Prime Minister to a Prime Minister; he could not be the young romantic. And it was to Stead, his new friend, he confided his dream of a cessation of all wars, of one language throughout the world, of a federation with America ("We could hold your federal parliament five years at Washington and five at London"), and of "the only feasible thing to carry out the idea—a secret society gradually absorbing the wealth of the world!" It was not really of a little frightened England Rhodes was thinking when he demanded the keeping of Uganda, but of a bold and spreading England. He still had in his mind the exhortation of Ruskin, "She must found colonies as fast and as far as she is able, formed of her most energetic and worthiest men; seizing any piece of fruitful waste ground she can set her foot on, and there teaching her colonists that their chief virtue is to be fidelity to their country and that their first aim is to be to advance the power of England by land and sea." . . . His words to Stead are no more than a recapitulation of his first will, made fifteen years before, to the purpose of "the foundation of so great a power as to hereafter render wars impossible, and to promote the best interests of humanity." They are the meaning of his last will and the plan behind his scholarships. He had, above everything, as Milner said, the foible of size. He wanted a big England—the biggest possible England—and the biggest possible was planet. "Some preliminary inspection of the planet would seem almost essential," he told Stead.

The contrast now between the littleness of England and the largeness of America and France was humiliating to him in exactly the same way as some people find it humiliating to have a smaller house than their associates. It had that personal flavour. It was not only to Gladstone he spoke of how much bigger those countries were than England, and of what England was to do about it. He could not bear the thought that England had once possessed America and today did not. "So low have we fallen!" he exclaims when Englishmen call it fortunate that England no longer had America. "What an awful thought it is," he writes to Stead, "that if we had not lost America . . . the peace of the world (would have been) secured for all Eternity!"

In the meantime, since that very America ("our kinsmen") placed hostile tariffs against Britain's goods, let Britain retaliate. "Being a Free Trader," he writes to Stead, "I believe until the world comes to its senses you should declare war with those who are trying to boycott your manufactures."

So much, too, he now told Gladstone. He did not, however, feel that this was the precise moment to add what he adds in his letter to Stead: "You might finish the war (the tariff war) by union with America and universal peace. I mean after a hundred years, and a secret society organized like Loyola's."

He felt, perhaps, that Gladstone was not the sort of man to whom one might confide one's admiration of Loyola.

III

Rhodes was something of a phrase-maker, and, although he did not invent the expression of a "war to end war," he said

196

that, as a Free Trader, he believed in tariffs, and, calling himself a Liberal, he derided the Liberal idea of a Little England.

And the principle of tariffs he linked to the principle of colonization. . . . Connecting which with Rhodes' native labour policy Sir William Harcourt remarked: "Mr. Rhodes is a reasonable man. He only wants two things—slavery and protection."

When Gladstone now, with what Rhodes described as "his bright intelligence," said he could not believe that hostile tariffs were shutting the world to England's trade and that he was sure the principle of Free Trade would, despite the temporary wrongness of other countries, prevail, Rhodes answered him to the tune of Grover Cleveland: "It is a condition which confronts us, not a theory." He told Gladstone that he wished he could agree with him, for he liked the logic of Free Trade. The trouble was, however, that practice did not square with logic.

Rhodes had wanted the enlargement of England before he discovered in the world's trade war a presentable reason for such enlargement. But he was sincere, too, in his belief that here, in colonization, lay England's only remedy against hostile tariffs.

He had this belief, as he admitted, from Hofmeyr. Hofmeyr, regretting that his "Utopian scheme" had not been "taken up by an abler delegate and one who is a greater master of the English language than I am," had, in 1887, put before the Colonial Conference in London the suggestion that a two-per-cent tariff against foreign goods throughout the Empire would promote closer union between its various parts, it would be no hardship to the poor, and the revenue might be devoted to the British navy.

A customs union between the South African states had always been one of Rhodes' most persistent schemes as an aid to federation. But it was not until he became Prime Minister that he began to apply himself to tariffs as an Imperial affair. Now, for the rest of his life ("being a Free Trader!") he demanded tariffs.

Here are some of the things Rhodes said about tariffs and colonial expansion:

"The classes can spend their money under any flag, but the poor masses . . . can only look to other countries in connection with what they produce. Instead of the world going all right, it is going all wrong for them. Cobden had his idea of Free Trade for all the world, but that idea has not been realized. The whole world can see that we can make the best goods in this country, and the countries of the world therefore establish against us, not protective tariffs, but prohibitive tariffs."

"The question of the day is the tariff question, and no one tells the people anything about it. . . . These islands can only support six millions out of their thirty-six millions. . . . We cannot afford to part with one inch of the world's surface which affords a free and open market to the manufactures of our countrymen."

"If the world as a whole hit on a prohibitive tariff against the mother country, what would occur? The land cannot provide for the support of forty millions, and they would be exactly in the position of a ship out of which the provender had been taken and yet the rats were left. The food having been exhausted, there would be only one solution, and that is, to eat themselves."

"The politics of the next hundred years are going to be tariffs and nothing else. We are no longer going to war for the amusement of royal families, as in the past. We mean business."

"I do not know why you should be interfering in all the countries of the world, unless it is because you have woke up to the fact that you cannot live unless you have the trade of the world."

"Free Trade principles have not prevailed. . . . The workmen find that although the Americans are exceedingly fond of them and are just now exchanging the most brotherly sentiments with them, yet they are shutting out their goods. The workmen also find that Russia, France, and Germany locally are doing the same, and the workmen see that if they do not look out they will have no place in the world to trade at all. And so the workmen have become Imperialist, and the Liberal Party are following."

"I went to the Thames with its endless factories. They were making goods—not for England, but for the world. . . . I went into a club and saw four hundred people standing about, and, for the sake of amusement, I asked what they were doing. I was told they were doing business, not with England, but with the world. There was not a single man who was not doing something with the world. The same thing applies to everything here. It must be brought home to you that your trade is the world, and your life is the world, and not England. That is why you must deal with these questions of expansion and retention of the world."

IV

Rhodes was a romantic, and a romantic keeps his balance by cynicism. He himself demanded English expansion and cohesion not merely because he believed the English to be "the greatest people the world has ever seen, whose fault is that they do not know their strength, their greatness, and their destiny," but also because he wanted this bigness for its own sake, he wanted to belong to a big nation. And then empire-making was his particular game. . . .

But he knew that other people craved solider satisfactions than the imaginative: "Sentiment rules the world, but how often does one's pocket rule sentiment." "You will always find that, dear as your friends are, when it comes to a matter of business, your friends do not regard you." He had said to Salisbury in 1891: "If you wish to retain the sentiment of the colonies, you must . . . show them that the tie with England is of practical advantage to themselves." To his shareholders he said: "You must show that it is to the benefit of the English people these expansions are made, because the man in the street . . . naturally asks, 'And where do I come in?'" Past his own dreams and desires, Rhodes knew that to the man in the street, whether in London or Cape Town, the question was this, "Where do I come in?" that London had no interest in Cape Town or Melbourne, nor Cape Town and Melbourne in one another, though, perhaps, a little in London. He believed a commonwealth of English-speaking nations could remake the world, but he had small faith in the "human atoms" that composed these nations or any other nations. He cared for them, not as individuals, but as parts in a whole of his designing.

v

Several of Rhodes' ideas about tariffs and colonial expansion he laid before this first meeting with his Chartered shareholders, and he did eventually get his way about Uganda. Harcourt had said: "It is not Egypt only they want us to swallow, but the whole of East Africa." Rosebery, however, had supported Rhodes. "He fought the whole Liberal Party . . . and it was a question of either remaining in Uganda or of parting with Lord Rosebery." It was also a question of England's future policy. Did she mean to go on expanding, or had the time come for contraction?

Now, at this meeting of November, 1892, Rhodes was asking, in advance of the retention of Uganda, as an inducement to its retention, that each one of his fourteen thousand shareholders should subscribe ten pounds towards the cost of his telegraph line to Uganda—not as a charitable contribution, but as a profit-earning business arrangement. And once this line was through "we should certainly not hear any more about the abandonment of that place." And, "I feel perfectly clear that when I get to Uganda I shall get through to Wady Halfa. I do not propose to fight the Mahdi, but to deal with him." Then, "If I do get the money to make the line to Uganda I shall get the money with which to extend the line to Egypt." . . .

Only the year before there had been talk of taking the Chartered Company to law because, on top of other disappointments, the shareholders had discovered that the Rudd Concession was not theirs, and only would be theirs at the price of a million Chartered shares, and the consequent halving in value of the first million.

Now they sat listening entranced to the imaginative assumptions of Rhodes. There was no longer an infuriated Mahdi, a wild resistant country, hostile natives, great expense, there was only the flowing talk of Rhodes. He made everything seem possible to the point of ease. They applauded him in ecstasy. They gave him their money and their devotion. They were Rhodes' humble subjects in the realm of his imagination. Is there a limit to imagination? It may stretch from the circle of a pinpoint to embrace the universe. Rhodes felt himself emperor of the universe.

VI

It was with a shock he woke to find himself once more on the brown earth. In his dreams he had been whizzing to the stars like a bucket on the wires of his own Kimberley mines, and suddenly clamour and commotion in Cape Town! What was it? A catering contract! One of his Cabinet Ministers, who was even now with him in England, had given a fifteen-year railway catering contract, without calling for tenders, to a friend. The powerful trinity of Innes, Merriman, and Sauer were wild about it. They cabled to Rhodes that either the offending Minister must go or they would.

But the man was actually his companion in England. Rhodes liked him. He had brains. Hofmeyr liked him. They used all to go riding together. And merely a little business about a catering contract. It was too bad to kick him out. Rhodes offered to cancel the contract. He did cancel the contract. Not good enough. He goes or we go.

In April, 1893, Rhodes returned to Cape Town and consulted Hofmeyr about what should be done. Said Hofmeyr, "Let them all go."

Rhodes' way of letting them all go was to resign. He offered to serve under Hofmeyr, and when Hofmeyr refused the responsibility, he offered to serve under the Chief Justice, de

Villiers. But even while de Villiers was debating whether he could, or could not, take the Premiership without Sauer in his Cabinet, Rhodes suddenly changed his mind about the whole affair. One morning, de Villiers, waiting to notify Rhodes of his acceptance, read in his newspaper that the Ministry had resigned and that Rhodes himself was forming a new Cabinet. The new Cabinet did not include the four Ministers who had caused the disruption in the old. It also did not include de Villiers. Nor was there any reason for Rhodes' action except just the reason that, after all, he wanted to remain Prime Minister—a Prime Minister unhampered by all these too-scrupulous people, who kept chanting "watch your step" when he wanted to leap or fly.

De Villiers wrote to Rhodes that he had prepared his address to the electors and made every preparation for a new way of life: "I was kept in suspense," he wrote, "from Monday morning to Wednesday morning, waiting for the interview which never came off." And he said afterwards that he bore Rhodes no ill-will over the matter. But if he did not, it was surprising.

Sauer also wrote to Rhodes:

My dear Rhodes,
    Only a word. The coming and going of Ministers must be, but our severance is to me a pain. I shall, however, look back to my association with you as one of the honours and pleasures of my life. . . .

It was a severance not only with Sauer and his companions, but with something a little too delicate for one whose spirit was against the delicate. Rhodes partly made good the loss by including in his Cabinet W. P. Schreiner, a man of their own kind and later to be Prime Minister. He still had Hofmeyr. But something went out of his life then which he never replaced, even though the procession of his triumphs was not yet ended. Henceforward Rhodes had around him his doctors— not too squeamish, as he said, when there was blood-letting to be done; except for Hofmeyr and Schreiner, he had about him men who did not, and could not, stay him. Stendhal says that one of the main reasons of Napoleon's fall was his taste for mediocrity in his entourage; he wanted instruments, not Ministers.

That was also one of the main reasons for Rhodes' fall.

The man who had lost the catering contract sued the government, and was awarded five thousand pounds damages.

CHAPTER ˙ 20

WHAT SHOULD OFFER ITSELF BUT MATABELELAND!

I

RHODES had first thought that by staying in the Cabinet without portfolio he could watch his interests from Cape Town and yet be free. But then, it seems, he had decided that to be Prime Minister unclogged by exigent subordinates might be better still. There was Kruger in the Transvaal, reëlected President now for the third time. There was Bechuanaland which he needed for his North. It could only be got at through the Cape. There was Lourenço Marquez, which he needed for his North. It could only be got at through the Cape. There was the North itself: three thousand pounds a month to find for Mashonaland—from his own pocket, de Beers, or some one else. How long could Jameson manage on charm and credit? How long would the Chartered shareholders wait for the new Rand in Mashonaland? And his railways—money for his railways. And his telegraphs—money for his telegraphs. And concessions he had to pay for, and countries he had undertaken to run. And Sir Henry Loch demanding stronger Imperial control over the Chartered Company. He could not go away. He had to stay in Cape Town and watch Kruger and watch Loch and watch Parliament and watch his opportunities and find moneys. His heart was in the North, but his head was needed in the Cape.

II

And out of the blue a piece of luck! Matabeleland! The solution to every problem! Matabeleland! Was the grass not good in Mashonaland? The grass of Matabeleland was good. Did the settlers' cattle not thrive? The cattle of the Matabele throve. Did one need labour? The Matabele were strong. Had the new Rand not appeared in Salisbury? Were shares dropping? Were funds low? Through Bulawayo ran the arc of gold that began in Johannesburg. Was there terror of savages? It was the Matabele, not the Mashona, one feared. . . . And the Cape to Cairo railway—it had to go through Matabeleland. Rhodes' territories—they needed Matabeleland. The root of the matter, the heart of the North, the answer to the settler, the answer to the savage, the answer to the shareholder, the answer to the creditor—it was Matabeleland.

And what should suddenly offer itself but Matabeleland!

III

As far back as 1890 Rhodes had said to people in Mashonaland who, in effect, had asked him what about it: "So long as the Matabele do not molest my people I cannot declare war upon them and deprive them of their country; but as soon as they interfere with our rights, I shall certainly end their game; I shall then ask your aid, and be very glad to get it, and when all is over I shall grant favours to those who assist me."

This is the report of Rhodes' companion at the time, his great admirer, a Bond Member of Parliament to whom he (naturally) offered a farm in Mashonaland.

IV

In those days—in 1890—Rhodes had not the Lippert Concession. He says, indeed, to the questers after Matabeleland, "You must remember I have only the right to dig for gold." For this reason, then, he had to conquer Matabeleland. But afterwards he had bought the Lippert Concession. So why could he not simply walk into Matabeleland? Why had he still to conquer it? And, on the other hand, if he had always meant to take it by conquest, why did he buy the expensive Lippert Concession?

The answer is that he had to satisfy both savages and shareholders of his right. Could he explain the concession to the spear-brandishing Matabele? Could he admit the necessity for a war of conquest to the conscience-burdened Englishmen? He had to have both arguments—a military argument for the Matabele, and a civil argument for the English. And, as to the military argument, there was an inquisitive world. One had to show a reason other than rich land, fat cattle, probable gold, northern pathways, and one's own intense acquisitiveness in order to satisfy this curious world. Even the fear of theft and murder was not enough. Pillage had to occur, killing had to occur, before one could say to a world that wanted a virtuous bad reason rather good reasons not so virtuous, "We were forced to make the war."

In 1892 the *Financial Times* said that the Chartered Company were doing "all in their power to provoke Lobengula."

207

Rhodes' luck northwards occurred in this very month of May that saw at the Cape the climax of the contract affair. A catering contract began Rhodes' political disruption. Five hundred yards of telegraph wire began his conquest of Matabeleland.

And it was not even the Matabele that carried off the five hundred yards of telegraph wire. The Mashona did it. It was the Mashona who had to be fined in cattle for the depredation. And they paid the cattle. But the cattle they paid were Lobengula's cattle which they had been herding in return for their milk. Only in special circumstances had any of Lobengula's subjects herds of their own. Nominally all the cattle of the nation were vested in the Chief, and to this very day descendants of those cattle are earmarked for the royal house of Lobengula. That was what the native commissioner said when Lobengula's grandson, Rhodes Lobengula, was charged, in 1931, with extorting cattle from the Matabele. And that was why the company considered all the cattle in the conquered territory theirs when they overcame Lobengula.

Now, in this May of 1893, on the company's demanding either the persons of the wire thieves, or else a fine of cattle, the cattle were so cheerfully yielded that something not quite regular might have been suspected. According to Kruger—but the words of Kruger about Rhodes need not be taken as unprejudiced—the company would not choose to suspect an irregularity. They would welcome Lobengula's inevitable action. For, of course, Lobengula could not allow his subjects, the Mashona, to give away his cattle as a fine. Nor could he allow them to steal the company's telegraph wire. Whatever anybody might say about Rudd and Lippert Concessions, although he had given the pioneers the road to Mashonaland and seen them settling there and trading and farming and mining and governing there, although he himself had pegged mining claims under the company, he was still the ruler of the Matabele and Mashona. They were his to command and punish. He was responsible for their actions. That, at least, was what he wanted to think. It was certainly what he wanted others to think.

These are Kruger's words: "It is affirmed in Africa that it was Rhodes, through his administrator, who informed Lobengula that the Mashona had stolen cattle, and that it was his duty to punish the raiders. Lobengula at once dispatched a band of his people, as was the custom in these cases, to revenge the robbery. Rhodes used this fact as an excuse to demand Lobengula's punishment on account of the massacre of the Mashona. Whether there be truth in this statement or not, one thing is certain, Rhodes had his way and his war."

And this is what Labouchere wrote in *Truth*: "Mashonaland was found to have no paying gold. The shares of the company were unsaleable rubbish. A pretext was therefore found for making war on Lobengula and seizing Matabeleland. . . . All the circumstances showed that the coup had been carefully prepared long beforehand. When the train had been laid, a quarrel was picked with the Matabele, who had entered Mashonaland at the company's request, and they were attacked and shot down by this same Jameson while doing their best to retire in obedience to his orders. Instantly the whole of the company's forces, all held in readiness, entered Matabeleland under the pretence that the Matabele and not the company were the aggressors. Lobengula's savages were mowed down by thousands with Maxims. Those who were taken prisoners were killed off to save trouble. The envoys sent by the king to try and make terms were barbarously murdered. The king himself fled, and died before he could be captured. His territory and the flocks and herds of his people were parcelled out among the company and the band of freebooters who had been collected by promises of loot. One million new shares were created by Jameson's principals and colleagues, and in the subsequent boom shares were unloaded on the British public at prices ranging up to eight pounds per share."

The truth is that many things did happen as Kruger and Labouchere say. And Rhodes did want Matabeleland, and Lobengula was driven into war, and his possessions were promised and parcelled out to the volunteers, and Chartered shares had gone terribly down, and after the war they did boom. But there seem to be also one or two reasons why Rhodes should not have wished war to happen as it happened and when it happened. The company's forces had just been reduced from seven hundred to forty. The company's funds were exhausted. However awkward, menacing, tantalizing, desirable Matabeleland might be, if Rhodes had really, as Labouchere says, planned the coup long beforehand he would not have prepared for it by disbanding practically all his trained forces. The probability is that, although Rhodes was not ready for war, he was still not going to lose the chance of making a war when that chance presented itself.

The name of Lobengula means "He That Drives Like the Wind," but some call it "Driven by the Wind." There was a wind of fate that, at this moment, drove him forwards and Rhodes behind him, over him, over his fallen body.

Here—denunciations, reasoning, explanations apart—are the things that happened to Lobengula in the year 1893.

There was the cutting of the telegraph wire, the seizure of
the cattle, Jameson's revelation to Lobengula that the cattle
were his, and the *impi* sent by Lobengula to punish the thieving
Mashona.

At the same time Lobengula also told Jameson and the
officer in command at Fort Victoria, where the trouble was,
that the white people were not to be alarmed. "I send you
warning that my *impis* will pass your way, but have orders not
to molest any white man." The messages—like other messages
of Lobengula—were not delivered in time. The settlers saw the
naked Matabele with their war plumes and their spears, burning the huts of the Mashona, killing the Mashona, carrying off
their women and children and beasts, carrying off also, the
company said, the cattle of the Europeans. It was too long
since the spears of the Matabele had had a blood-bath: a little
hasty surreptitious raid, always hampered by the idea that the
white men would come and interfere, an insignificant business
against some insignificant tribe, a little occasional jaunt from
which one returned with captive women and children—there
was hardly anything substantial and satisfying to one's manhood. . . . Here was an affair more like those of the good old
days when the Mashona were always available to wash the rust
from one's spears and to replenish with women one's needy
kraals. The excited Matabele overflowed the countryside. The
equally excited settlers and the no less excited police banded
themselves against the savages. The white women and children
were taken to safety. The terrified Mashona fled so that not
one, they say, was left on mine or farm.

Jameson ordered the return of the cattle stolen from the

Europeans and instructed the police at Victoria to drive the Matabele back over the border. What cattle? Which border? Lobengula demanded, suddenly again a king. "I am not aware," he wrote to Moffat, now the British Assistant Commissioner— "I am not aware that a boundary exists between Dr. Jameson and myself. Who gave him the boundary lines? Let him come forward and show me the man that pointed out to him these boundaries; I know nothing about them, and you, Mr. Moffat, you know very well that the white people have done this thing on purpose. This is not right; my people only came to punish the Amahole for stealing my cattle and cutting your wires. Do you think I would deliberately go and seize cattle from you? No, that is not right."

On the other hand, there are, against the affirmations of Kruger, Labouchere, and Lobengula that the war was deliberately prepared, these telegrams sent by Jameson: To Rutherfoord Harris: "The Victoria people have naturally got the jumps. Volunteers called out, rifles distributed, etc. . . . Will wire you when I hear the Matabele have all cleared." . . . To Loch: "At present this is merely a raid against the Makalakas round Victoria and not against whites. . . . I hope to get rid of the Matabele without trouble." To the police: " (War) from a financial point of view would throw the country back till God knows when. . . . I trust to your tact to get rid of the Matabele without any actual collision."

One may or may not choose to take these telegrams at their face value. Collision, however, was now unavoidable: if the Matabele no longer wanted it, the settlers did. They said they would never feel safe while these savages could come in and murder them at any moment. Which was true. Eager as they may have been for the gold and the herds and the soil of

Matabeleland, there was also the fact that civilized people and uncivilized people could not live side by side. Side by side? No, together. As Lobengula wrote to Moffat: "I am not aware that a boundary exists between Dr. Jameson and myself." The white people could not go on their lands or down their mines or into the veld without the fear that something might happen to their women or children or cattle or Mashona servants. Particularly the Mashona, whom the Matabele regarded as their natural sport and over whom Lobengula still chose to exercise his kingship.

Only Lobengula himself stood between his warriors and the whites. Whether in fear, diplomacy, or honour, Lobengula was anxious for peace. Since ever the first concession-hunter had come to his goat-kraal he had had to keep his young men tame. And what if one day he failed to keep them tame?

One might say, then the white people should have left the black their land. But sooner or later contiguity had to come. However much land the natives might have, eventually that land was bound to touch the land of the Europeans. And where that happened, trouble had to happen. Trouble was inherent in the plan that made the white people so and the black people so. The whites wanted war, but were not ready. The blacks wanted war, but did not understand. The Lord wanted war, and war befell.

VII

It was before Jameson had himself arrived at Victoria that he sent those telegrams saying the Victoria people had the jumps and he hoped to get rid of the Matabele without trouble, and a collision must be avoided. But when he came and saw how things were, he knew at once that here was the molestation of which Rhodes had so long ago spoken—if one chose, here was war.

He summoned the *indunas* of the Matabele. "If you have not gone when the sun is there," he said, pointing to the skies, "we shall drive you."

Said one *induna*, "We'll be driven."

Said another, "Where is the border?"

It was an hour and forty minutes by the sun that Jameson allowed them. The Matabele retired pell-mell. An officer and thirty-eight policemen, mounted, followed them for three miles. A shot was fired. The police said it was a Matabele fired the shot. The official report says a white sergeant fired it. The white men raised their guns. Thirty of the three hundred Matabele were killed, and a number were wounded. "The Matabele," continues the official report, "practically offered no resistance." No European was hurt.

From his kraal at Bulawayo Lobengula had, until this happening, tried still to keep his peace with the white men. He had tried to keep it for twenty years. In his goat-kraal he had played one concession-hunter against another, Boer against Briton, Briton against Portuguese, mineral right against land right, to keep the peace. He had given Jameson the road to keep the peace. For three years he had lived with Rhodes' settlers overrunning his lands, and kept the peace. He had sent his Matabele to punish the wire-thieving Mashona—and keep the peace. When his Matabele smelt blood and began to loot and murder he had ordered them back, offered to return the stolen cattle, and to make good any loss—all for peace.

But now—and even now only for the moment—his patience was gone. When he heard that his men, retreating in terror

214

according to Jameson's command, had been fired upon and so many killed and wounded, he rose in his indignation and withdrew his offer to return the cattle and pay damages; he said he wished he had allowed his soldiers to kill and burn and loot and revenge to the fulness of their hearts' desire; he demanded that his subjects, the guilty Mashona, whom the Europeans were protecting, be handed over to him for punishment; he told the Chartered Company that they had "come not only to dig the gold, but to rob me of my people and country as well"; he refused to accept their monthly subsidy of one hundred pounds under the Rudd Concession. "It is the price of my blood," he said.

He was to lose more blood without recompense. For already Jameson had wired to Rhodes asking if he might go into Matabeleland, and Rhodes, in Parliament when he received the message, had wired back: "Read Luke xiv, 31."

And Jameson had read Luke xiv, 31. "Or what king," Holy Writ had instructed him, "going to make war against another king sitteth not down first, and consulteth whether he be able with ten thousand to meet him that cometh against him with twenty thousand?"

The Maccabeans held justice with courage to equal a thousand men, but it has not been computed how much exactly courage alone is worth. Had Jameson justice with courage? At least he had courage.

He replied to Rhodes: "All right. I have read Luke xiv, 31."

And so much, then, for Lobengula's blood.

CHAPTER · 21

THE END OF LOBENGULA

I

LOBENGULA may not have wanted war, the Chartered shareholders may not have known how important to them was war, Rhodes and Jameson may not have been ready for war—there were those who had the desire for war and no doubts—the settlers.

It was now three years since the pioneers had taken the road to Mashonaland. The enthusiasm of adventure was past; daily unyielding travail, tedium, sickness, fear, were their present lot; hope was thinning, patience was going—the loaf risen too high in the heat had collapsed in the draught, their cake was dough; salvation offered itself only in the crushing of the Matabele, the freedom from their menace, the taking of their fat lands, their fat cattle, and their prophesied gold. If Lobengula was furious with the administration, so were they. If he had protests to make, so had they. They held meetings, threatened vengeance, authorized or no, against Lobengula, told Jameson if they were not allowed to "break up the Matabele power" they would leave the country.

Their demands reached the High Commissioner. "I cannot believe," he replied, "that there are any such fair-weather trekkers who, at the first breath of difficulty or danger, would think of leaving the country. Should, however, there be any such, then in my opinion the country would not suffer by their departure."

But the settlers were far beyond these schoolmasterly admonishings. Some of them were old soldiers. Many of them, since the disbanding of the police, were volunteers. They wanted war. "Go in and finish it," they demanded of Jameson.

On August 14, 1893, the day after Lobengula's refusal to take his monthly hundred pounds from the Chartered Company—"It is the price of my blood"—on August 14th Jameson signed an agreement with his settlers, which is known as the Victoria Agreement, promising land, gold, "loot," and other advantages to those of them who should follow him into Matabeleland. "Loot" is the word used in the document.

II

It was a secret document. The Colonial Office did not know of it. The High Commissioner did not know of it. He was still trying to keep peace between black and white.

Ten days after the Victoria Agreement Lobengula wrote another of his confiding letters to Queen Victoria.

He wrote, saying he was keeping her advice to tell her if there was trouble between him and the white men, and where was this boundary the white men spoke of, and how could white men say they had bought his country and the people in it? "Your Majesty," he wrote, "what I want to know from you is if people can be bought at any price. . . . Your Majesty, what I want to know from you is: Why do your people kill me? Do you kill me for following my stolen cattle which are seen in the possession of the Mashonas living in Mashona-land? I have called all white men living at or near Bulawayo to hear my words, showing clearly that I am not hiding any-thing from them when writing to Your Majesty."

The white men Lobengula meant that were living at or near Bulawayo were these: Colenbrander, once his own emissary to England to protest against the Rudd Concession, and now the agent of the Chartered Company; Colenbrander's wife; eight or ten traders; a missionary with his family. They were all of them, in these days, in danger of their lives. The pursued Matabele had returned from Mashonaland and recalled raiders from Barotseland. There had been months of terror, burning, looting, ravaging. Heads were on fire. And now, at last, white men had killed Matabele.

Past his fear, passion, and resentment Lobengula did this: he sent such white people, as chose to go, to a place of safety. He promised his protection to those who remained in his kraal.

That promise he honoured. Even while Jameson's volunteers were marching on Bulawayo, a guard of Lobengula's black men were keeping watch over the white traders in his kraal.

But what happened when, in response to Loch's invitation, Lobengula sent three envoys "to talk matters over so that there may be peace" was this:

III

The envoys reached, on October 18th, the camp of Major Goold Adams at Tati. He was here, with his police, to help the Chartered volunteers against the Matabele.

Already, a month ago, he had warned the High Commissioner that Jameson would "not be able to keep the Salisbury and Victoria people much longer inactive; they will either do something to bring on a row or will leave the country."

Since then Lobengula's *impi* had been mobilizing. Along the roads to Mashonaland were black scouts. Here and there—at a river or a pass—rested bodies of armed warriors. The witch-doctors were doctoring the roads.

For months the Europeans had been saying they would not wait to be butchered by the Matabele. From Lobengula's kraal, on the other hand, one Dawson, a white trader, wrote to the High Commissioner that Lobengula would fight only in self-defence. Lobengula and Jameson now communicated with one another through the High Commissioner. "I am obliged to watch both friend and enemy," wrote the High Commissioner to a lady in England, afraid that Lobengula would attack the settlers, afraid that the settlers would attack Lobengula, and that, whichever happened, he would be responsible. But from the High Commissioner, at last, because cattle had been stolen and shots fired, Jameson had sought and received permission "to take the necessary measures to clear the border of Matabele *impi*."

Which meant war.

His volunteers had long been more than ready. Rhodes had bought horses and supplies. Rhodes himself—Parliament prorogued—was hurrying northwards. Rhodes had sold, for what they would fetch, fifty thousand Chartered shares and arrogantly told the High Commissioner that "the company asked for nothing and wanted nothing." . . . "I felt," he later said, "that if there was a disaster, I was the only person to carry it through." But also he felt, without needing to say it, that, if there was not a disaster, he was the only person to make terms. Therefore he wanted his hands tied by no obligations.

In the Transvaal, against Kruger's protests, a Dutch Colonial in the company's service had collected men and horses and joined Goold Adams and his Bechuanaland police. They had, as guide, the hunter Selous, and, as a contribution from Lobengula's hereditary enemy, Khama, eighteen hundred Bechuanas. Each European force consisted of two hundred and twenty-five white men with their horses, field-guns, and attendant natives, and the Bechuanas brought their own equipment.

Now, since the High Commissioner's permission to Jameson to take necessary measures, Jameson's volunteers—white men with horses, guns, and natives—were marching on Bulawayo. They were accompanied by the Lord's benediction, a modern mace-bearer. The Bishop of Mashonaland (not, he says in his memoirs, as chaplain to the British force, "but as bishop of the country in which both contending parties lived) was with them.

So was Jameson. Jameson combined, in his own person, Administration, War Office, General Headquarters, Intelligence Department, Generalissimo, and everything else. Sir John Willoughby, whom Rhodes had once sent to force the trade route through Béira, and be shot in the leg if necessary, and whose horse (it was his great distinction) had once tied for first place in the Derby, was Jameson's military adviser and staff officer. He had hurried out from England for the fun. He had no definite commission.

While they went towards Bulawayo Goold Adams went towards Tati, that place where, in modern times, gold had first been found, and where men were still mining.

He arrived there four days before Lobengula's envoys.

The envoys were two *indunas* and Lobengula's brother. They had with them, as interpreter, the trader Dawson. They were travelling on horseback towards Cape Town "to talk matters over" with Loch "so that there might be peace." They had not heard that Goold Adams was in Tati.

It is said that Goold Adams knew nothing of their mission; that Dawson, without reporting to him, left the natives with a mine foreman and joined his own friends; and that Goold Adams, seeing some idle Matabele about, the escorts, he supposed, of Dawson, "took the obvious course" of arresting them. Why, without enquiry, it was so obviously his course to arrest these elderly Matabele, bewildered in a camp of three thousand armed men, white and black, is a puzzle not adequately explained by any partisan of Rhodes'. It is said that Goold Adams told them that, unless they attempted to escape, they would not be harmed. Well, they did attempt to escape and they were harmed. One *induna* was shot dead, the other was clubbed dead, Lobengula's brother eventually returned home.

One may believe that the death of these men was not intended. But, remembering how often missions and messages harmful to Rhodes' interests were intercepted, it seems not unreasonable to suppose that this particular mission, inconveniently attempting a peace when all was ready for war— men on the march, shareholders eager, money spent—was not held up merely by accident.

Nor did the Romans believe Cæsar's explanation of why he had seized the German leaders come to make terms with him, and then destroyed their hosts. Cato suggested that Cæsar should be thrown to the Germans themselves for punishment.

Even Labouchere did not go so far as this with Rhodes. He did not want Rhodes offered to the Matabele.

So much, however, for Lobengula's desire towards peace. Rhodes, in Kruger's words, had his way and his war.

v

It was a most neat and swift little war. Everything went like clockwork. The Matabele, using against Rhodes' troops, not only their spears, but also the old Lee-Metford rifles Rhodes had paid to Lobengula for the Rudd Concession, using them inexpertly, were swept down by the Maxims. There were two battles fought by the company's men, each on a river bank. In the first, on the Shangani River, the casualties of the Matabele were between five and six hundred, and a Matabele general, disabled by wounds, hanged himself from a tree. The casualties of the volunteers were one white trooper and one coloured driver killed, and six white men wounded. In the second, on the Inhembesi River, the crack Matabele regiments, the Ingubu and the Imbezu, were engaged, and also the regiment that had fought in the Shangani battle. The Imbezu lost, it is estimated, five hundred of their nine hundred men. "The Imbezu and Ingubu," reports Willoughby, "were practically annihilated. I cannot speak too highly of the pluck of these two regiments. I believe that no civilized troops could have withstood the terrific fire they did for at most half as long." The company lost four men killed, and seven wounded.

There was also a successful battle fought by Goold Adams' troops. And, after it was over, the Bechuana said they had small-pox and wanted to go home. At first, Goold Adams was rather perturbed about this, but already the company's troops were in Bulawayo, so it did not matter.

The company's troops arrived in Bulawayo on November 4th. As they approached they heard, they saw a Vesuvian explosion, a roaring and a smoking. They hurried to find Lobengula's kraal blown up by the cartridges whose Lee-Metfords no longer needed them, and Lobengula gone. The regiments were piped in by an old pipe-major of the Royal Scots, and on the Tree of Justice that still stood in the ashes of Lobengula's kraal was raised the Chartered Company's flag.

Three days later Jameson sent a letter to the flying Lobengula:

. . . To stop this useless slaughter you must at once come to see me at Bulawayo, where I will guarantee that your life will be safe and that you will be kindly treated. . . . I sign myself your former, and I hope your present friend, L. S. Jameson.

To which Lobengula, dependent now, in his flight, on a half-caste scribe, answered:

I have the honour to inform you that I have received your letter and have heard all what you has said, so I will come. But allowed me to ask you were are all my men wh. I have sent to the Cape? . . . And if I do come were will I get a house for me as all my houses is burn down, and also as soon as my men come which I have sent then I will come and you must please be so kind and sent me ink and pens and paper. I am, yours, etc, King Lobengula.

VI

Jameson waited three days for Lobengula and he did not come. He then sent a body of men to bring him in. For a fortnight they pursued him and he evaded them, but at last, on the Shangani, he held council with the *indunas* that remained to him. "Matabele! The white men will never cease following us while we have gold in our possession, for gold is what the white men prize above all things. Collect now all my gold . . . and carry it to the white men. Tell them they have beaten my regiments, killed my people, burnt my kraals, captured my cattle, and that I want peace."

The gold Lobengula had was a thousand sovereigns. Two messengers were deputed to carry it to the white men. How were they to approach those white men? They crept fearfully along beside one of the pursuing bands, and seeing, at last, two troopers detached from the main body, they quickly handed these troopers their gold, made their explanation, and vanished.

The mission had the fate usual to Lobengula's missions. The gold was never delivered by the troopers. They were charged with the theft of it, found guilty, and sentenced to fourteen years' imprisonment with hard labour. Two years later they appealed on the grounds that the evidence against them was insufficient and the sentence beyond the magistrate's jurisdiction. Their appeal was upheld, and they were released.

During the month of December various deputations of Matabele came into Bulawayo to ask for peace; and on December 19th Rhodes entered Bulawayo with a column he had joined on the march, bringing with him food, surgical aid, and horses.

He stood where Lobengula's kraal had stood, in its ashes, and addressed the conquerors of Matabeleland. One might now call them the conquerors of Matabeleland. He recapitulated to them, as characters do on a stage, their own history during the last few months, that a wider audience might know it, and he told them they had done with nine hundred men what it had been estimated would need ten thousand men.

This was not quite accurate, for there were also the troops under Goold Adams, the Bechuanas, the Cape Boys, and the friendly natives. Counting these (and why not? since all the Matabele were counted) there were really about four thousand men. However, Rhodes said nine hundred, and that is the number generally accepted.

He told them, too, that they had done the work without assistance from Her Majesty's Government—which again was not quite accurate, for the Bechuanaland police had been increased on account of the war, and four hundred of them were even now left behind to protect the country. Still, Her Majesty's Government had certainly not given him the spiritual support of enthusiasm, and there were actually Englishmen, said Rhodes, who had called them "freebooting marauders, bloodthirsty murderers, and so on. . . . It is such conduct," he indignantly commented, "that alienates colonists from the mother country. We ask for nothing, for neither men nor money, and still a certain portion vilify us. In the same spirit it was that the mother country lost America."

But that they were moved by simple patriotism was also not accurate. The company pursued a vast possession; the volunteers were each to get, under the Victoria Agreement, three thousand morgen (over six thousand acres) of farm land, twenty gold claims, and an equal share of Lobengula's cattle. Rhodes, it is true, did not value this farm land at more than forty pounds. ("And am I to be told that you left your occupation and employment and took the risk of being shot for the value of a farm worth forty pounds? The thing is ridiculous.") But the agreement valued the land at three pounds a morgen; eight hundred grants—about five million acres—were taken up; there were two hundred thousand cattle distributed, and

of the eighty thousand cattle left the company had forty-five
per cent. "It is your right," said Rhodes to the pioneers, "for
you have conquered the country."

No, one couldn't speak much of idealism.

Yet two things Rhodes said in this speech could not be questioned. It *was* impossible to deal with Mashonaland while
barbarism had the upper hand. They *had* created another state
in South Africa and ended savage rule south of the Zambesi.

The first private waggon that entered Bulawayo, like the
first private waggon that entered Salisbury, brought a load of
whisky and nothing else.

VII

Only one uncertainty—Rhodes would not, he said, call it a
disaster—marred their happiness this day. A party of men that
should have been with them were not. The leaders of the advance guard had failed to return.

They never, despite Rhodes' refusal to give up hope till the
worst was known, did return.

They had gone out—thirty-nine men under Major Allan
Wilson—to seize (no less) the person of Lobengula himself.
At various times six of them had been sent back to report. It
was not till February that the other thirty-four were found.
They were found on the Shangani River. Their skeletons were
found. They had been cut off by the suddenly rising river and
hemmed in by Matabele. They had fired their last round of
ammunition; the able had refused to abandon the wounded;
they had been killed, every one of them, in a space fifteen yards
in diameter.

Allan Wilson's patrol is today a saga in South Africa. A

story is told—a Matabele is said to have brought the news—of how, when only five or six of the thirty-four were left, they had taken off their hats and, standing, sung the National Anthem, and then fought on again until at last only one man was left, the tallest of them—Allan Wilson.

Their bones were discovered by that same Dawson, Lobengula's friend, who had written from his kraal saying that Lobengula would fight only in self-defence, and who had accompanied the *indunas* on their peace mission. In February, 1894, this man was sent out to find Lobengula and speak to him of surrender. He did not find Lobengula, but he came upon all that was left of these that had gone out to capture Lobengula, and he collected their bones and buried them beside a great tree, on whose trunk he cut a cross and the words, "To Brave Men." It is to Allan Wilson's Patrol the monument stands on the Matoppos near the grave of Rhodes. Their bones, too, were brought to surmount the View of the World.

But as Dawson's journey in search of Lobengula was fruitless, so had Allan Wilson's adventure been unnecessary. If Lobengula was not yet dead when Wilson's men went after him, he was soon to die.

On a tributary of the Zambesi Lobengula died of small-pox. It was not merely because they did not want to fight that the Bechuana under Goold Adams had talked of small-pox and clamoured to go home. Small-pox was over the land. The fugitive Matabele were full of small-pox.

In the heavy summer rains, beside the swollen rivers, they died of their starvation, their sickness and their wounds. The white men were against them, the nature of things, and the favour of the Lord.

It was a triumph for the Bishop of Mashonaland.

They say that a day before his death Lobengula called his *indunas* about him and told them to look to Rhodes for protection. "He will be your chief and your friend." To his soldiers he said: "You have done your best, my soldiers. You can help me no more. I thank you all. Go now to your kraals. Go in peace."

They wrapped his body in the hides of two newly-flayed oxen, and, when it was far decayed, they buried it there on the river bank. . . .

It was not until the Raid that Rhodes' world turned on him. But the Raid, unless one chooses to think it provoked the Boer War, is something that might have ruined Rhodes, not by its seriousness, but by its silliness—through laughter. There is no point in the breaking of Lobengula at which one can smile.

However, here is another aspect: It could also not have been very amusing for the Mashona to be assegaied by the Matabele, nor for the Barotse, nor for any of the other tribes in whose blood the Matabele had the habit of washing their spears. And this is what a missionary who was for many years in Matabeleland says: "Hundreds of innocent men, women, and children were murdered every year because they were supposed, in some way or other, to be traitors to the chief. . . . His own seven brothers were put to death, and his own sister also was murdered at his command. . . . The people were led by the nose, deceived, burnt to death, clubbed to death, driven out of the land, thrown to the crocodiles, murdered, and treated in all shameful ways by witch-doctors."

Other stories, too, are told, such as that Lobengula killed his wife for refusing to dance, and cut off the noses and ears of several young men for immorality.

228

There is probably truth in the reports that Lobengula was cruel. Savages are no doubt savages.

On the other hand, Europeans who had dealings with him say that (unlike, in Wellington's estimation, Napoleon) he was that thing morally so difficult to define—a gentleman. . . .

Legends have gathered round Lobengula. Many Matabele refused to believe, at first, that he was dead. To this day expeditions go northwards to look for the hidden gold and diamonds his subjects were supposed to have stolen for him on the Rand and in Kimberley. People talk in millions.

The idea is a plausible one, but its plausibility seems to be its foundation.

VIII

Well, and so it was not only a neat and swift little war; it was also—white people being what they are, and black people being what they are—an inevitable war.

It does not seem to have been a just war. But neither did the Matabele make just wars. And if injustice is not the moral reply to injustice, it is perhaps the natural reply—the distant justice of Nature, whose language to humanity is foreign.

There it stands in the dock, Humanity, like a Kaffir before a white judge, staring at him with intent wild eyes. And Nature delivers sentence; and an interpreter gabbles something; and a policeman taps Humanity on the shoulder. And Humanity starts and looks about in bewilderment. And the policeman gives a little push. And out of the dock Humanity stumbles and towards the cells. What for? What about? Who knows? . . .

Still—it was a very cheap little war, too. It cost the company only a hundred thousand pounds. Could the shareholders complain about that?

They did not complain. A fortnight after Jameson's men were piped into Bulawayo there was an Extraordinary General Meeting of the Chartered Company in London, and "I am sure," said the Duke of Abercorn, who presided—"I am sure you are of opinion that, as Mr. Gladstone stated in the House of Commons, it would have been a crime against justice and humanity if, on the refusal of Lobengula to put an end to his raiding and interference with the Mashonas, hostilities had not been commenced, and the cruel military system of the Matabele, so destructive to civilization, broken. [Applause.] It was clearly the duty of this company to take steps to fulfil the obligations imposed on it by the royal charter and afford to the white colonists, whom we had encouraged to settle in the country, and to the native Mashonas, protection of life and property."

It was a triumphant meeting. Only four people objected to its purpose, which was to increase the capital of the Chartered Company from one million to two million pounds by the creation of a million new shares. The meeting dispersed, says the report, amid cheers for Rhodes and the president.

CHAPTER ، 2 2

IDEAS NEED MONEY

I

I T WAS a Mr. Bennett, a solicitor, who led the dissentients against the Duke of Abercorn's resolution. He appeared, he said, in the interests of the Matabeleland Company. He said the shareholders were being asked to give a million shares for rights that did not exist. . . . Why a million shares? What rights?

He meant the Rudd Concession, which, at a propitious moment, the Chartered Company were to acquire for a million new Chartered shares.

This is the story of the Rudd Concession:

It belonged to the Rudd-Rhodes group. They amalgamated their interests with various rivals, and applied, jointly with them, for a charter. Before the charter was granted the petitioners formed themselves into a company called the Central Search Association, with a capital of one hundred and twenty-one thousand pounds.

When they heard the charter was to be granted, the principals of the Central Search Association agreed secretly that the forthcoming Chartered Company should have the Rudd Concession only in return for a fifty-per-cent interest. The board of the Central Search Association was, more or less, the board of the Chartered Company.

The capital of the Chartered Company, calling itself the British South Africa Company, was a million one-pound shares. These shares were not allotted to the public. They were allotted, most of them, to the promoters, and some were kept in reserve.

In July, 1890, as the pioneers were trekking northwards, the Central Search Association transformed themselves into the United Concessions Company, and their capital of a hundred and twenty-one thousand pounds into four million pounds. The difference of nearly three million pounds was the value they put on the Rudd Concession.

Next month it was agreed, for the first time in writing, that the Chartered Company should, as soon as possible, issue another million shares, of equal value to the first million, to pay for the Rudd Concession—"which shares shall be considered part of the original capital of the Chartered Company." Here, in short, was that fifty-per-cent interest.

The original million shares were thrown on the open market only when Salisbury was founded and there was talk of a new Rand in Mashonaland; and an excited public bought them for anything up to four pounds a share, thus justifying the value placed by the United Concessionaries on the million shares they were demanding for the Rudd Concession.

It was not until a year later the shareholders of the Chartered Company discovered that they did not own the fundamental Rudd Concession and would have to pay so enormously for it. Some of them threatened to go to law, and for the time being it was thought better not unduly to obtrude the Rudd Concession.

This reticence was broken in the atmosphere of triumph generated by the Matabele War. If ever the United Conces-

sionaries were to get their million Chartereds for the Rudd
Concession, now was the time.

And these were the million shares of Mr. Bennett's com-
plaint, and the rights which he said did not exist were the
rights of the United people to the Rudd Concession.

"We do not deny," said Mr. Bennett, "that the promoters
are entitled to remuneration for the manner in which they have
engineered this enterprise. The first issue of the capital was two
hundred thousand pounds. To whom was it allotted? It was
allotted to the promoters. I have seen the allotments and the
share register, and perhaps I am the only one of the public who
has seen them. Then there was a further allotment of five hundred thousand shares at the time when the shares were selling
in the market at four pounds. How were they allotted? They
were allotted to the promoters at par, and that alone was very
handsome remuneration for the trouble they had had. As if
that were not enough, the directors, without taking the shareholders into their confidence, gave away half their whole profits.
I say it is an outrageous agreement and should not be confirmed. By giving them today one million shares we are con-
firming that agreement. . . ."

Mr. Bennett had little support. The Duke of Abercorn,
K.G., put the resolution that the capital of the company be
increased to two million pounds by the creation of one million
new shares at a pound each. Mr. Albert Grey, he who had once
opposed the granting of the charter, seconded the resolution.

There were those four dissentients.

THE PRESIDENT: The resolution is agreed to almost unanimously. [Loud cheers.]

On December 19th, the day Rhodes stood on the ashes of
Lobengula's kraal and addressed the conquerors of Matabele-

233

land, the Chartered Company held its third ordinary general meeting, and the issue of the million new shares in payment for the Rudd Concession was ratified. For the first time the Chartered Company, that for three years had been spreading itself in Mashonaland and issuing land and mining claims, possessed at least the formal right to do so. It was to exercise that formal right for nearly another thirty years, to find then that no right at all had ever existed.

At this meeting seven hundred and fifty thousand pounds, at six per cent, was raised in debentures to pay for the war and other things, the interest to be funded and paid on January 1, 1896.

Later there were other debentures.

One may choose to connect these debts, this date, with the Jameson Raid.

II

At the next Chartered meeting Mr. Albert Grey, now Lord Grey, said: "Those who appeal to the Gospel of Humanity as their guide will rejoice that the first result of the Matabele War has been to enable the starved and wretched natives to descend from their rocky fastnesses and build their huts upon the plains, and for the first time in their lives to cultivate their rich fields in security and peace. . . ."

It was the Mashona Lord Grey meant who now became so happy. It is true the Mashona themselves, asked whom they preferred as lords, the Matabele or the Europeans, said: "The Matabele burn us and rob us and kill us and take our wives, but then they go away. The white people do not go away." And when the Matabele, three years later, rose against their

234

conquerors, the Mashona rose with them. But this merely shows their ingratitude. The white people make a war whose first result is their blossoming in security and peace, and they say they would rather be killed by the Matabele!

But was Lord Grey quite accurate? Was the bliss of the Mashona indeed the first result of the Matabele War? In actual fact, no one was thinking about the Mashona. Lobengula had not yet been traced, nor had his *indunas* come into Bulawayo to surrender, nor had Rhodes addressed his volunteers as conquerors, when Lord Ripon, the Colonial Secretary of the day, was telegraphing to the High Commissioner that, according to the newspapers, Lobengula's followers were dying of small-pox and starvation; the Matabele were not being allowed to sow until they had surrendered their arms; their cattle were being seized, and their land—even Lobengula's kraal— was being mapped out. These, despite Ripon's instructions that Jameson was "to moderate his proceedings and stop the looting of cattle," were the first results of the Matabele War. And it was partly to secure them, and partly to get fresh capital for railways and public works in the new country, that Rhodes, having congratulated his settlers, now hurried back to Cape Town.

III

In Cape Town Rhodes was entertained at a banquet by representatives of all political parties; the atmosphere was that of See the Conquering Hero. He was deeply moved, his audience was deeply moved; he made one of the great speeches of his life.

It was a speech delivered in a spirit of exaltation—one might say of almost divine ecstasy. With whatever motive settlers had gone into war and shareholders encouraged that war, Rhodes had undertaken it with one motive only, and this motive the religion of his life. He was spreading England, he was fulfilling his holy obligation, and that obligation was none the less holy because his desire and ambition were bound up with it. "I can assure you, gentlemen, that when you have to reply to your own fellow-citizens—when they have intimated to you that . . . you have deserved well of the state—I can assure you that it is exceedingly difficult to speak."

They say he did, in his emotion, find it difficult to speak.

But why were they thanking him? The question was rhetorical. He answered it. They were thanking him for his idea, that idea with which he had come to Parliament and for which he had thought it good and wise to work in season and out of season—the idea of obtaining the unknown interior—"your Hinterland."

He repeated to them now how Sir Hercules Robinson, the old High Commissioner, had asked him where he would stop, and he had spoken of the measure of his imagination. "I made the seizure of the interior a paramount thing in my politics, and everything else subordinate. . . . All I wanted was the painting of the map. . . . The future is clear—we shall be one."

But patience was the thing. Never hurry and hasten. He told them, to point his moral, a story he was often to repeat in the years to come: how in his impetuous youth he had met a very old man planting oak trees, and asked him why an old man should plant oak trees.

"You feel," said the old man, "that I shall never enjoy the shade?"

"Yes," said Rhodes.

"I have the imagination," said the old man. "I know what their shade will be. . . . I have laid my trees on certain lines. I know that I cannot expect to see them beyond a shrub, but with me rests the conception and the shade and the glory."

It sounds a little like the story of the retired admiral who planted acorns that England might always have oaken timbers for her ships—and then ships were built of iron. But Rhodes' old man seems to have been merely thinking of beauty. . . .

And so, said Rhodes, was he, too, working slowly and gradually for results beyond his own "temporary existence." And for what reward? "My motives have been assailed. I have many enemies, and they have insinuated many reasons for my actions. . . . They do not understand yet the full selfishness of my ideas. I will take you into my confidence and will say that I have a big idea that I wish to carry out, and I know full well the reward, a reward which is the highest reward a human being can attain, and that reward is the trust, the confidence, and the appreciation of my fellow-countrymen."

In England his partners in the United Concessions Company had just mulcted the Chartered shareholders of a million shares which were soon to rise to eight pounds, and by their action he would profit. In Matabeleland the land and herds of the Matabele were being distributed among their conquerors. Of their whole territory only two reserves were left them, and of their two hundred and eighty thousand cattle, their one possession, their title to life, they were allowed to keep forty-four thousand and to milk some of the others.

And in Cape Town Rhodes spoke of the trust, the confidence, the appreciation of his fellow-countrymen. That was the reward he wanted.

Was Rhodes a hypocrite? . . . Even his enemies do not

call him exactly a hypocrite. A rogue, a liar, a scoundrel, capital incarnate, an unscrupulous character, a curse to his country— these things they say of him, but that he exercised this subtle falsity which has been called the homage of vice to virtue, this they do not say. There was a sort of bluntness in Rhodes which even Labouchere and Harcourt felt bound to admit. His cynicism was open, not secret. He believed, with Robert Walpole, that every man has his price. "I object to the ballot *in toto*," he said, "because I like to know how a person votes." He threatened, when England's policy irritated him, to "hoist his own rag." He said such things aloud. But he himself sneered at what he called the British policy of "philanthropy—plus five per cent." He spoke with disgusted humour of having to meet, at the Raid enquiry, "the unctuous rectitude" of his fellow-countrymen. And he called the strictures on the raiders "a tribute to the upright rectitude of my countrymen who have jumped the whole world." Rhodes did not, in short, pretend to be a better man than he was.

How, then, is one to reconcile this ruthlessness against a dark humanity, this joy in acquisition, this combining of patriotism and profit, with an avowed idealism?

One might point out that it could also not have delighted the Turks and Saracens to be killed by Holy Crusaders; that holy crusading was the amusement of the age; that in the blood of Jerusalem the crusaders treaded the wine-press of the Lord; that the conquerors of Jerusalem died not merely of Western chivalry, but of Eastern luxury. As the younger sons of the nineteenth century emigrated to Rhodesia, so did the younger sons of the thirteenth century emigrate to the Holy Land. They too were colonists. They too were rulers and merchants. They too formed chartered companies. They too changed geography. Even idealism has earthly parents as well as a Heavenly Father.

Rhodes did sincerely feel that he deserved well of his country:—his hill in the Matoppos is specifically set aside as a burial-place for those who have deserved well of their country—so that in time he will not rest in loneliness, but merely under one of a number of memorial slabs. In spite of his sneer against "my countrymen who have jumped the whole world" he did think that the more the world was English the greater its chance of happiness. And who had spread England farther than he? Certainly he felt himself entitled to trust and appreciation.

Did the Matabele suffer? He was always a man who believed the lesser had to make way for the greater. Did he love money, power, and fame? So too did Alexander, Cæsar, Trajan, and Napoleon, the men whose lives he studied. Nor had he, like these, the thirst for military glory, which, says Gibbon, "as long as mankind shall continue to bestow more liberal applause on their destroyers than on their benefactors . . . will ever be the vice of the most exalted characters."

Rhodes despised professional soldiers, and his conquered were his children as well as his victims. While he lived the natives in his North had succour in time of need, they had just hearing and a friend. They said so, and they felt so. He used to bring young Matabele to Cape Town in batches to see his Groote Schuur and the oceans. They loved to serve him. They used to approach him crouching, as they had once approached Lobengula. They called him their father. They named their children after him. When he died they gave him, as they had never before given any white man, nor ever did again, the royal salute of *"Bayete!"*

239

He was even indignant with those men "that simply look on the Chartered Company as a means of making money through the sale of shares."

"You don't seem to care for money," a friend once said to him.

"For its own sake, no," he answered. "I never tried to make it for its own sake. It is a power, and I like power."

And stories are told of how he used to go around without money in his pocket; or pay a cabman with gold, or, on the other hand, forget to pay at all; or lend money or borrow money, and not think of it again.

But other rich men have had this indifference to physical money. Such money was not money to them, nor was it to Rhodes. When he said he did not love money for its own sake he was speaking primitively; he was thinking in terms of the ships and slaves and statues that were the cash of antiquity.

And when Spengler says: "The conquest and exploitation of Gaul—an undertaking motived by finance—made Cæsar the richest man in the world. It was for power that Cæsar amassed these milliards, like Cecil Rhodes, and not because he delighted in wealth"—even he does not appreciate the fundamental value of his millions to the millionaire.

A millionaire must delight in his wealth. He must love his millions because they are an extension of his own personality. They add to him as the tool adds a new limb to the craftsman.

They are, indeed, more a part of him than those with whom he is united by blood. They can more interpret him—his impulses, his feelings, his hopes, and his desires. They represent him to the world. They are his—while they are his—to command and use and enjoy as he likes it. His millions cannot refuse him, chide him, rival him, oppose him, deny him. "Men," says Machiavelli, "will rather hear of the death of a father than the loss of a patrimony." . . . "My daughter! O my ducats! O my daughter!" cries Shylock in an agonized confusion of wealth and paternity.

> "Nay, take my life and all: pardon not that:
> You take my house when you do take the prop
> That doth sustain my house; you take my life
> When you do take the means whereby I live."

Why does a millionaire—except when he wishes to avoid their diminution through death-duties—keep his millions until the last moment, millions that he cannot enjoy or take with him? He keeps them as he keeps his eyes, his hands, his thoughts: because those millions are his very self—like the art of the artist and the passion of the pilgrim—his soul.

It cannot, therefore, be said that Rhodes' money meant nothing to him but power—unless "power" is taken to be something much more comprehensive than Rhodes himself intended.

On the other hand, there is an aspect to a man's possession of money other than its spiritual relation to himself. And that is the physical way he uses it.

v

"There is no proletarian, not even a communist, movement," says Spengler, "that has not operated in the interest of money, in the directions indicated by money, and for the time permitted by money—and that without the idealist among its leaders having the slightest suspicion of the fact."

Granted that Rhodes was an idealist (and it ought to be granted), he disproves at least part of this assertion.

Rhodes was not unaware that his idealism—whether for the swifter pursuit of power or the outpacing of men—was mounted on money. Money was his Pegasus, and he knew it. "One is called a speculator," he told his Chartered audience when he faced them for the first time in England. "I do not deny the charge. . . . If one has ideas, one cannot carry them out without having wealth at one's back."

It was a thing he often said—and with a bluntness that was deliberate. To begin with, he knew it suited his type of an empire-builder to be a little bluff and rough. Should Rhodes of Rhodesia behave as if he had never gone beyond a drawing-room? He found (he said so) that he could do things in England "on the basis of a barbarian." It was expected. He traded on the savagery of Africa, although he knew this savagery to be a localized affair: "You must remember," he said, speaking of a land whose legal system is its pride—"you must remember that in South Africa, where my work has lain, the laws of right and equity are not so fixed and established as in this country."

But there was also another aspect than the cynical to this frank crudity of Rhodes. "I find in my life," he once wired to Beit, "it is far better to tell the town crier exactly what you are going to do and then you have no trouble." His enterprises involved very often secrecy and intrigue, but he was not a natural intriguer. To judge by his speeches, he seems really to have acted on his principle that "the idea of modern politics is to tell the people nothing, but I have an exactly opposite idea. The right thing is to tell them everything."

He was quite prepared to admit brazenly—not merely

brazenly, but boastfully—that he was doing things through his money. "I have tried to combine the commercial with the imaginative." He went farther. He believed that money could bring about the millennium. Again and again he explains to Stead that his lever for raising mankind is money.

The difference between Rhodes and his fellow-exploiters was this: that, whereas they looked upon the charter as a means of making money, he looked upon his money as a means of backing the charter.

In this very Cape Town speech he tells his worshiping audience how he himself had to raise the money to build the Mafeking railway; out of his own means had to provide for an extension of the Beira railway; and alone had found four-fifths of the money for six hundred miles of telegraph through Africa. He had also, of course, financed the administration of Mashonaland, subsidized individual settlers, and sold fifty thousand Chartered shares, when they were very low, for the conduct of the Matabele War. His money was poured out endlessly for his North.

It is true he died a very rich man—a multiple millionaire. He had so many assets. His money bred money. His de Beers bred. His Goldfields bred. His Chartered shares had the unique habit of rising whenever a South African war threatened—unique but not inexplicable, for a South African war inevitably and cynically (but often wrongly) suggested some benefit to the Chartered Company. Wherever Rhodes moved he seemed to be able to make money.

Nevertheless, there were days when Rhodes did not know where to turn for money. One of his secretaries mentions that at the time he was with Rhodes Rhodes' income was a quarter of a million, yet for nine months of the year he was overdrawn, and had to pay as much as five thousand pounds interest on his overdrafts; and he had even to pay interest on his charities. He was in funds only, says this secretary, during the two or three months immediately following the payment of his de Beers dividends. And his man of business writes that he refused to check his financial statements, did not know what he was worth until his balance-sheets were shown him, kept no books, had no idea what was owed him, registered his securities in the names of third parties, and left them lying about in odd pockets and odd corners.

One is apt to think of money as something acquired at the expense of other people. It is more often made through increasing the world's commodities. One may find a millionaire decent, and be right. Rhodes' money was not only, on the whole, put to creditable uses—the opening up of a closed continent, it was also (on the whole) fairly made. He robbed no one by possessing diamond mines, he robbed no one by possessing gold mines. There was no fake about the diamonds and gold: they were there. Investors were not offered paper. Nor did he grind the faces of the poor by making diamonds more expensive. The manipulations with the Rudd Concession may be questioned. But, on the other hand, Rhodes' North, so far from yielding him money, cost him money. He had, of course, his assets in the North. But they were a poor investment to him. No modern chartered company, except the Royal Niger, has been a financial success. And although it cannot be denied that with his money he bought men as well as civilization; and although it has been said that for money the Matabele War was begun, and even (it has been said) the Jameson Raid, and actually the Boer War itself; yet with the last, at any rate, Rhodes had no direct connection, and behind all Rhodes' deeds that were evil there was, as he himself pleaded, a high object. "There have been not a few men," he said at his old college three years before his death, "who have done good service to the state, but some of whose actions have partaken of the violence of their age, which are hard to justify in a more peaceful and law-abiding age. It is among those men that my own life and actions must be weighed and measured." He was thinking mainly of Raleigh, who also combined ruthlessness and the quest of money with a love of beauty and the desire to spread England, and who, no less, believed that the end justified the means. The money Rhodes wanted was money for his railways, his telegraphs, his Rhodesia, his North; money to meet his Chartered debentures of seven hundred and fifty thousand pounds and nine hundred thousand pounds; money to pacify his Chartered shareholders—and particularly when they were due to meet on January 1, 1896.

Rhodes has been decried for the way he spent his money in his lifetime, and lauded for the way he willed its disposal after his death, yet he gratified the same passion in each. Rhodes had no wife and children to whom to leave his money; and although he was passionately interested in his "young men" and wanted (as his Rhodes Scholarships prove) heirs to his tradition, he never found one he could adopt after the manner of the Roman emperors. As for his brothers and sisters—he dutifully did this or that for them, but there is no evidence that he much loved them. On the contrary. He often demonstrated his indifference to them. Not one of his many brothers and sisters participated in his larger enterprises or was nominated as trustee in his will. Only one was present at his death. And for all that he expresses in his will his "humble belief that one of the secrets of England's strength has been the existence of a class termed

'the country landlords' who devote their efforts to the maintenance of those on their property," and he therefore leaves a
country estate to a Rhodes heir, yet he makes it by no means
easy for this heir to enter upon his inheritance. "I object," he
says in his will, "to an expectant heir developing into a loafer."
And he specifies that the heir to his Dalton estate shall for ten
consecutive years be engaged in a profession or business—"such
profession or business" (here is the final expression of his dislike of professional soldiers) "not being that of the army."

Rhodes' attitude towards his family is interesting when one
remembers how eagerly he trusted those he loved, and in his
second will left, not only his great schemes, but also his growing possessions, to the care of the young Pickering.

He even mentions in his open letter to Stead that his secret
society for the regeneration of the world might be supported
"by the accumulated wealth of those whose aspiration is a
desire to do something, and a hideous annoyance created by
the difficult question daily placed before their minds as to which
of their incompetent relations they should leave their wealth
to."

A man does not, quite impersonally, write such words.

Rhodes' dispositions in his will are not, then, more remarkable for their generosity than the dispositions he made of his
money during his lifetime. Nor are they more altruistic. They
were devoted equally to the same cause. They aspired equally
to link his name with that cause. ("I find I am human and
should like to be living after my death.") They merely express
what he believed to be the justification of all his deeds: his
"high object." They also express in terms the principle on which
that object was founded. This principle is sometimes, in our
day, called the Nordic principle.

Rhodes thought of himself often as a Roman—a Trajan, a Hadrian. "Take care," he quoted Marcus Aurelius, "always to remember you are a Roman. . . . Have a care you are not too much a Cæsar." Marcus Aurelius was his companion, and Gibbon his mentor. He thought of himself also as a Greek— a Pericles. And as an Elizabethan.

Actually he was, by temperament, outlook, and fundamental predilection, a Teuton. "In our Germanic world," says Spengler, "the spirits of Alaric and Theodoric will come again. There is a first hint of them," he adds, "in Cecil Rhodes."

CHAPTER ᛫ 2 3

RHODES AND THE NATIVES

I

RHODES thought he deserved well of his fellows because he was spreading the rule of England and the blond men. At the same time, however, he had no racial animosities. "I have no feelings," he said, and it seems truthfully, "as to where a man was born; all I desire to know is whether he is a good man, and then I want him." . . . "In my social life," he said, again, "the majority of my friends—people on the Diamond Fields and in Cape Town—were men of a race other than English." In Kimberley these friends he speaks of were Jews—notably Beit. In Cape Town they were Dutch—notably Hofmeyr. Without going so far as to say that Rhodes did not prefer men of his own race—he thought an English gentleman the flower of humanity—it does seem that, like Alexander and Napoleon, he had no animosity towards Jews.

His companions at Oxford remarked on this idiosyncrasy. He appears to have liked the way Jews understood money, and their generosity. They admired his ability to beat them at their own game, and his idealism.

His feeling for the Dutch was also—Raid or no Raid—genuine. For if Rhodes was a natural financier and loved the money game he played among Jews, he was also a natural coun-

tryman and met the Dutch on a common passion for the soil.
He said, after the Matabele War, that his views were changed
and he had a new sympathy for the men who sold him things
across a counter, because among those who had helped him
destroy the Matabele power were butchers and bakers and
store-men. But he said that only in the emotion generated by his
triumph. As in his house he had wanted the "big and simple—
barbaric, if you like," so in his life he wanted the big schemers
and the primitive land-workers—not the bourgeois.

Rhodes did little for the South African manufacturer; he
believed, in fact, that he could not, and should not, compete
with the English manufacturer. But he helped the South
African farmer as no one else had ever helped him. He established a Ministry of Agriculture; became himself a practical
farmer; experimented with fruit and animals; brought out fruit
experts from California and Florida; studied the wines of
France; imported Arab stallions and Angora goats; discovered
a new cattle-grass; put through an irrigation scheme; established
cold storage; attempted to cure of their pests oranges and
vines and sheep. . . . He used to welcome parties of Dutch
farmers to Groote Schuur, give them his finest hospitality, give
them presents, and tell them that he too was a countryman,
descended from cow-keepers. He protested gravely in Parliament against the number of Sunday trains. They trusted him
to the extent of saying, concerning the charter (it was the
president of the Bond who said it), "If Mr. Rhodes and his
people are in charge, it is all right." It was they who, in the
Cape Parliament, defeated a motion that it was undesirable
for the official representative of the British South Africa Company to be also their Prime Minister. "We have never," said
Hofmeyr, "had a Premier who on most questions was more

249

of one heart and soul with our colonial Afrikanders than Mr. Rhodes." . . .

The Raid killed that amity and trust. Significantly, the original founder of the Bond, the anti-British Reverend du Toit, who was now the editor of *Di Patriot*, stayed with Rhodes after the Raid. Rather romantic. One might find a moral in such a story: the first enemy who remained the last friend. . . . And yet not so romantic, and the moral all wrong. . . . Rhodes came to control not only most of the English papers in South Africa; he controlled also *Di Patriot*. He said, very reasonably, that a man should be properly reported. . . .

The Bondsmen themselves, who had once unanimously followed Rhodes, after the Raid resolved "that every consideration of national self-respect, political honesty, and good faith compels the Afrikander Party no longer to give Mr. Rhodes an iota of political support either at political gatherings, in the press, at the polls, in Parliament, or anywhere else." At the next Parliamentary elections Rhodes said, "Whatever have been my mistakes, I still keep the strong support of a large section of the Dutch." He said: "You tell me I am against the Afrikanders. Surely my whole life's work proves the contrary." . . . Over and over again he speaks of the Dutch who are with him both in the Cape and in Rhodesia, and out then come the little moving stories of how he had given them a country as big as Europe and he would get only six feet of it, and of how de la Rey had roared, "Blood must flow," and so on.

In vain. Rhodes might plead, promise, prophesy. He might threaten. He might speak of his six by four of earth, and know, as he spoke, how soon he must claim that little space—as far as the Dutch were concerned, he troubled himself for nothing. The Dutch were gone from him. They would not come back.

They would not send him into Parliament to work for them, for their Hinterland, for his North, his dream of union, his dream of empire, his dream of world-domination by blond men —all those great things whose beginnings lay in the little Cape Parliament. . . .

And should he abandon them, his greater thoughts, as he called them? "I don't falter," he said. And again, "I am not going to be driven out of the country." And again, "I shall pursue the same course as I have done in the past." And again, "I have never altered my ideas, and I shall never alter them as long as I live." Whether the Dutch were with him or not—and so he told them—he was going on with his work.

But through what means? With what human material? It was his election agent who gave him the answer—the natives. . . .

In the year Rhodes founded his Goldfield Company, and was engaged in amalgamating the Diamond Fields, and was beginning to lay his trail northwards—in that year which inaugurated the period of his life when the gods, in their favour, seemed to make him their very equal—in 1887, Rhodes had said, in his arrogance, that if he could not keep his position on the European vote he would rather not be elected at all; he was not going to the native vote for support. "Equal rights for every white man south of the Zambesi," he had demanded. Every white man. It was only three years before his death that he proclaimed what is today in South Africa accepted as his guiding principle. On the margin of a scrap of newspaper he addressed his message to the coloured people of Kimberley thus:

My motto is, "Equal rights for every civilized man south of the Zambesi." What is a civilized man? A man, whether white or black, who has sufficient education to write his name, has some property or works, in fact is not a loafer. C. J. RHODES.

And in those words he wrote the abdication of his hope with the Dutch, and admitted that any man, black equally with white, was good enough to vote for Rhodes.

He lent himself also now to the Jingo South African League which hitherto he had scorned.

II

The first speech Rhodes ever made in Parliament concerned the natives—the disarming of the Basutoland natives. That was in 1881. His second speech, too, concerned the Basuto natives and their disarmament. Rhodes was against that disarmament, and he objected to the natives being subject to the whims of changing Ministries. He himself, he said, would prefer the natives outside the Cape border to be subject to Imperial rule. His wish was granted. In 1883 England took over the Basutos.

She had, however, hardly done so when Rhodes, excited suddenly by the thought of Bechuanaland and the great country beyond it, decided that there must be no Imperial interference in Bechuanaland, that the Imperial factor must be eliminated, and that the Cape, together with the Transvaal, must administer Basutoland. "I am perfectly consistent," he said, "in having voted for the transfer of Basutoland and in now holding these views. . . . What we want is to annex land, not natives."

He is not, politically speaking, so consistent. He is, in fact, with the entrance of Bechuanaland into his scheme of things, quite changed. Natives with land, land with natives—that is not the real question at all. He has just visited Bechuanaland and been struck with its situation. Bechuanaland (the thing has caught his heart and his head) is the key to the whole Interior. Can he afford to wait while England broods over what is best for the natives? He must, before anyone shuts it to him, make safe his path to the North.

Still, if not England, why the Transvaal?

The answer is Hofmeyr. Was Rhodes using Hofmeyr or Hofmeyr Rhodes? They both wanted a United South Africa and they used one another. Hofmeyr backed Rhodes. Rhodes backed Hofmeyr. Did Hofmeyr demand a northern ascent hand in hand with the Transvaal—was that his idea of union? Rhodes was with him. Did Rhodes then find that the Transvaal was going to be a nuisance and object to the establishment of Boer republics in his northern preserves? Hofmeyr was with Rhodes. Did Hofmeyr want Dutch as well as English taught in the schools? Rhodes supported him. Did Rhodes, putting his private above his public business, resent a tax on diamonds? Hofmeyr stood by Rhodes. As for missionaries, Hofmeyr's ancestors had been hindered by missionaries, and so was Rhodes always being hindered by missionaries. And Kaffirs? More than ever was Rhodes persuaded by his dislike of missionaries, and the feeling they created against him in England, to take the Dutch rather than the English view of Kaffirs.

In 1887 both Rhodes and Hofmeyr decided that the natives, while they were in a state of barbarism, should be treated as a subject people. "It is to me a matter of sorrow," said Rhodes, "that I am separated on this question from those gentlemen with whom I have usually acted, but I think they will give me the credit of fighting for my principles."

Were they his principles? Thinking of him as a Darwinian and an ancient Teuton, one might say they were.

But before he died Rhodes was demanding equal rights for the natives. And were *these* his principles? He was sick and desperate, and he was prepared to accept as his necessary allies any human beings who helped him to go on with his work.

A few years later Hofmeyr died. And he too ended a champion of the dark races. Because *his* ideas were changed? Hardly. He repudiates, indeed, his right to the "undying gratitude" they offer him. He cannot admit that he is without "prejudice of colour and race." It is merely, as he bleakly tells them, that he thinks the political and social security of white South Africa will be none the worse for their good will.

With him, as with Rhodes, the native franchise is a matter rather of expediency than of passion. His reasons, it is true, seem more disinterested. He is fighting a country's cause and not his own. Yet was not Rhodes, too—his end so near, and with no hope of averting that end—thinking of something beyond what he always called his "temporary existence"?

III

Even then Rhodes' change of native policy from 1887 to 1899 is not so sudden as the sharp turn in his battle-cry might suggest. There is a whole process of history, experience, and spiritual evolution between those two dates. There is his rise. There is his fall. There is his financial triumph. There is his political triumph. There is his human triumph. . . .

There is his taking of the North—his conquest of the Mashona and Matabele, the elation that brought him, the compunction, the responsibility.

There is his dream of world peace that had to be fed on things of the night—betrayals and shabby shifts.

There is his misdemeanour of the Raid—the humility it induced in him, the defiance, the despair.

There is his second—his human—conquest of the Matabele.

There is the young vision that he could grow a whole new world, and the final realization that he could but plant a limited garden for others to cultivate. . . .

The heart in his body was great not only with exultation, but with disease. His passionate blood was stemmed at its source. At thirty-four he was a man escaped from death, and at forty-five death's manacled prisoner.

IV

In practical terms, these were Rhodes' dealings among the natives:

He came to Parliament, a man whose concern with natives was that of master towards servant—good master, devoted servant; he had to consider natives by the hundred.

By 1887 he had consolidated his Goldfields, he was amalgamating all the diamond mines; he was considering natives by the thousand.

He went North, he took those hundreds of thousands of square miles and with them hundreds of thousands of natives. He became Prime Minister of the Cape, and laid it down that the Prime Minister should have charge also of the Ministry of Native Affairs. He added to the Cape the two Pondolands. He was, before 1899, to annex to the Cape still more territories. He could say, in moving the Glen Grey Act of 1894, that "by the instrumentality of Responsible Government and also by that of another position which I occupy, I feel that I am responsible for about two millions of human beings."

He called them human beings.

V

"Human" was a word Rhodes liked to use. "We human atoms," he always said, and he often spoke of the natives' human minds. "They have human minds." "Help them use their human minds."

Nevertheless, it may be questioned whether, for many years, Rhodes applied the term "human" to the natives in much more than a biological sense. He liked them, he could be very friendly with them, he could win their confidence and justify it, too, but that they were human as white-skinned people—mature white-skinned people are human—in their minds and passions, that, until doubt and pain entered his own heart, he could not feel.

He held the Colonial view. "These," he said in 1887, "are my politics on native affairs. And these are the politics of South Africa." He identified himself, in short, not with the missionaries and negrophilists ("I am no negrophilist," he point-blank said), but with the traditional, the Dutch, the standard South Africa.

There were various reasons for Rhodes' attitude.

To begin with, he was not much of a Christian. He was, whether he knew it or not, a Nietzschean, an ancient Teuton. He considered himself a Darwinian. "At some future period," says Darwin, "not very distant as measured by centuries, the civilized races of man will almost certainly exterminate and replace the savage races throughout the world. At the same

256

time the anthropomorphous apes . . . will no doubt be exterminated. The break between man and his nearest allies will then be wider, for it will intervene between man in a more civilized state, as we may hope, than the Caucasian and some ape as low as a baboon, instead of as now between the Negro or Australian and the gorilla."

So Rhodes might have found in Darwin that, not only would civilization exterminate barbarism, but that the black man was nearer the gorilla than the white man, and thus the white man's inferior.

He said, "I do not believe they are different from ourselves." But he said also, over and over again, "The natives are children." He considered them underdeveloped human beings.

And that Rhodes believed in the blond people is manifest through all his broodings. His wills, and particularly his last will, directly express it.

He was not, therefore, disposed to enroll himself among those he held to be the soft cranks who wanted to treat the black people as if they were white people. In this he was like the average European, who, whether he has ever heard of Darwin and Nietzsche or not, has hardly had his northern pink face tanned by the African sun before he has adopted the prevailing attitude towards the native.

Then Rhodes was anxious to link himself in the most obvious way with the Dutch. There might be some English against him, yet on the support of the English he could, generally speaking, depend. After all, he was an Englishman.

For the Dutch support, however, he had to work. There was hardly anything Rhodes did in Parliament which had not as its object the favour of the Dutch. He wanted union.

The leader of the Cape Dutch was Hofmeyr. For reasons

not only personal, but political, Rhodes attached himself to Hofmeyr. And that was for the same thing—union.

Then, again, because he wanted union, he had to make his native policy acceptable to the Boer republics. He could not have the natives as a stumbling-block to union.

Then there was his North; there was all Africa—Union.

Rhodes did to the natives what would please the Dutch, what would please Hofmeyr, what he thought would suit the Free State and Transvaal, what he thought would work in his North, what he hoped would carry him right up to Egypt. "This is a native bill," he said of his Glen Grey scheme, "for Africa."

Not the Cape; not South Africa; Africa.

VI

One of the first things Rhodes did as Prime Minister was to support what is known as the Strop Bill. He did it to please the Dutch farmers.

The thing the Dutch farmers were always complaining about was that they could not control the natives—their habits, their labours, their comings, and their goings. A native earned himself the money to buy a few cattle, and then he lay on his back in the sun, gazing up at high heaven. Nor, failing complete freedom, had he anything much against prison. Prison life was no worse than any other servitude; the housing was no worse, the eating was no worse. How was the farmer to punish the unsatisfactory native? By dismissal or imprisonment? Useless.

The Strop Bill was a bill empowering magistrates, in certain master and servant cases, to impose the lash (hence "strop").

Not only Rhodes, but Hofmeyr, supported the Bill. The Bill did not become law.

A year later there was what is called the Franchise and Ballot Act. This has been spoken of as a fair attempt, through political reward, to encourage industry and education among the black people.

That was not its intention. Its intention was to limit the native vote by raising, generally, the property qualification and adding an educational test. It was during this debate Rhodes objected to the secret ballot because he liked to know how a man voted. And Hofmeyr spoke of "a Teutonic population, surrounded or intermingled with a mass of barbarism." He said the only other country where, in similar circumstances, an equal franchise obtained was America; "and there the system has led to fraud, violence, bloodshed and a systematic falsification of the register." It was, he said finally, essential for the Cape to have a franchise that would induce the other South African states "to cast in their lot with us."

Rhodes supported him, crying Civilization and Union! The measure was effective. The European vote went up, the native vote went down. . . .

Just a year later there was set going the war in Matabeleland. When Rhodes came back from addressing the conquerors at Bulawayo he had new ideas on how to handle natives and annex native territories.

VII

It had happened, while Rhodes was in his North, that Sir Henry Loch, the High Commissioner, touring through Pondoland, a country over which Britain had a protectorate, was in-

259

sulted by Sigcau, the Paramount Chief of the Eastern Pondos. Loch had asked to see Sigcau, and Sigcau had kept him waiting three days.

There were troubles in Pondoland. The first and most serious trouble was that Pondoland lay between the Cape and Natal—the last of the independent native states in that region. It was in the way. One might call that a fatal trouble. As Rhodes said, the maintenance of a barbarian power between two civilized powers was almost an impossibility. For years it had been an understood thing that, at the right moment, Pondoland was to be annexed to the Cape. It was the only question the Cape had to consider, said Rhodes: the right moment.

Well, the position of Pondoland was the first trouble. The other troubles were like the saint's two-mile walk with his head in his hands: as Madame du Deffant felt—interesting but not, after the first step, significant. For instance, a white magistrate and his clerks had been murdered many years before. The murderer had never been delivered up to justice. Then the Pondos were, it cannot be disputed, savages. They had the customs of savages—witchcraft, rain-making, smelling-out and so forth. They quarrelled, they fought, they were a menace to the white people on their borders. Even while the Matabele were fighting in the North, Sigcau and a brother of his were having a sort of civil war over certain trading concessions held by two Germans; Germany had declined to interfere; the natives were arguing it out among themselves; and the half-brother was hiding in Natal.

There was not, in short, a happy atmosphere in Pondoland when the High Commissioner went to visit it.

Nothing was done about the insult to him or the other troubles until Rhodes returned from Matabeleland and decided that as "a native power in the North had been dealt with," the time had now come to deal also with the Pondo question.

But how? By force of arms? Not, according to Rhodes' tradition, if it could be avoided.

What actually occurred was that Rhodes travelled down to Pondoland in a coach and eight cream-coloured horse, some machine-guns and eight policemen, announced that he proposed to annex Pondoland, and sent for Sigcau.

Sigcau came. Rhodes kept him waiting for exactly the three days he had kept Loch waiting. He then offered to show Sigcau what would happen to him and his tribe if there was any further unpleasantness, took him to where the machine-guns were trained on a mealie-field, opened fire on the mealies, and brought down the mealie crop.

Sigcau noted the lesson, and ceded his country. The Chief of West Pondoland also ceded his country. Sigcau's half-brother was arrested and deported. Some mounted policemen were left in the country. The concessions to the two Germans were held by the Chief Justice "to create no legal obligation, because their execution depended solely on the will of the Paramount Chief, and there existed no possible means of enforcing them." As to this, the Government, said Rhodes in the House, might be right or it might be wrong. Accordingly "when you go into a native country you should obtain all the attributes of Government." He meant, speaking out of his own experience, the Government should itself possess the concessions. The annexation of the two Pondolands and their two hundred thousand inhabitants was achieved without the firing of a shot and at a cost to the Cape Government of under seven thousand pounds. "I do not ask for congratulations," said Rhodes.

It was not the end of Sigcau. Sigcau, unlike his brother, had been allowed to remain in Pondoland and given a pension of five hundred pounds a year. "Five hundred pounds a year," said Rhodes, "is enough for the maintenance of a native chief." Nor did Sigcau demand more. What he did demand was adequate recognition of his greatness. Like Lobengula, he persisted in thinking of himself as a ruler of men. His dignity: that was the fatal thing.

Next year Rhodes, as Secretary of Native Affairs, issued a proclamation charging Sigcau with "obstruction" and declaring his presence in Pondoland to be a public danger. Under this proclamation Sigcau was arrested and imprisoned. A commission held that, although he had maintained peace among his people, he had obstructed the magistrates by his insistence on his dignity. To Sigcau's question if that was enough cause for his imprisonment he received no answer. But he insisted on justice and he got it. He went to law with the Government. "The Governor," said the Chief Justice, "has arrested, condemned and sentenced an individual without the intervention of any tribunal, without alleging the necessity for such a proceeding, without first altering the general law to meet the case of that individual, and without giving him any opportunity of being heard in self-defence. . . . Sigcau, it is true, is a native, but he is a British subject, and there are many Englishmen and others resident in the territories who . . . if the respondents' contention be correct, would be deprived of their life and property as well as their liberty, otherwise than by the law of the land."

Rhodes, in short, was not always able to persuade South Africans that "in South Africa, where my work has lain, the laws of right and equity are not so fixed and established" as in an older country. But he could alter the law to give himself the power he wanted, and, after the Sigcau case, he did.

When, during the Great War, the matter of imprisoning British subjects without trial was being considered in England, General Smuts referred the commission to the precedent of Sigcau.

CHAPTER · 24

A BILL FOR AFRICA

I

IT WAS after the passing of the Glen Grey Act—Rhodes' charter to the natives—that he attempted thus to create his own law in Pondoland. The native had rights—the Glen Grey Act admitted it—but Rhodes could still not bring himself to believe that he had the rights of a white man. The Glen Grey Act, indeed, seeks specifically to distinguish those rights.

II

There is a river in South Africa called the Great Kei River. Where the coast line of South Africa begins to curve upwards to the east the Great Kei River flows into the Indian Ocean, and the country above it is called the Transkei and the country below it is called the Ciskei. In the Transkei are four regions taken at various times from the natives and Bastaards—Pondoland is one of them. In the Ciskei, at the foot of the Stormberg Mountains, lies the district of Glen Grey.

This land through which the Kei flows used to be known as Kaffraria—the land of the Kaffirs. Rhodes justly called it "the best portion of South Africa." It is no longer that. Many things have become different in Kaffraria since Rhodes' time. Only this

—since his time—has not changed: Kaffraria is still the land of the Kaffirs.

Two months after the annexation of Pondoland, in the month of the assignment by England of the whole of Lobengula's territories to the Chartered Company—in the ecstasy of this success—Rhodes moved the second reading of the Glen Grey Act.

The Glen Grey Act was Rhodes' scheme to solve what is called the Native Problem, which is a thousand problems of a hundred nations. It was his attempt to recreate, according to his design, that which he had helped to destroy. For two centuries the white men in South Africa had said that something must be done about the black men. Now, for the first time, it was done. Here was Rhodes' Bill for Africa.

This was the theory on which Rhodes worked: There were many of the natives' friends, he said, who "would hear of their minds being employed in no other pursuit than that of selecting members for Parliament." But he held that the natives were, in terms of civilization, children. They had human minds, but they were just emerging from barbarism.

At the same time, even if, socially, they were children, physically they were adults. They could work. "There is a general feeling," he said, in opening his speech, "that the natives are a distinct source of trouble and loss to the country. Now I take a different view. When I see the labour troubles that are occurring in the United States, and when I see the troubles that are going to occur with the English people in their own country on the labour question, I feel rather glad that the labour question here is connected with the native question. . . . If the whites maintain their position as the supreme race, the day may come when we shall all be thankful that we have escaped those difficulties which are going on amongst all the old races of the world."

In short, the natives, in their proper position, were an answer to the labour question.

What was their proper position? How were they to be accommodated in a civilized world? "The natives," said Rhodes, "are increasing at an enormous rate. The old diminutions by war and pestilence do not occur. . . . The natives devote their minds to a remarkable extent to the multiplication of children. . . . They had in the past an interesting employment for their minds in going to war and in consulting in their councils as to war. By our wise government we have taken away all that employment from them. We have given them no share in the government—and I think rightly, too—and no interest in the local development of their country. . . . There arises the question of the land, which cannot continue to provide enough for all of them. . . . In many parts of the country we have placed canteens. . . . We do not teach them the dignity of labour, and they simply loaf about in sloth and laziness. . . . These are my premises."

Here, then, considering the natives, not philosophically, but practically, was what Rhodes proposed to do: to find land for them, to give them employment, to remove liquor from them, to stimulate them to work, to train them to self-government, and to make this social experiment, first in the Glen Grey district, and then in the Transkei. If the experiment was a success it could be extended to other parts of the country. It could be extended to his North. It could be applied to the whole of Africa.

In Glen Grey was a surveyed piece of land of about six hundred acres. Rhodes proposed to divide this land into seventy allotments. These allotments would be forfeited if their owners did not cultivate them, but they might not be sold or ceded, and they might not be divided among numerous children in that manner which had created among South African Europeans the problem of the poor white. There was to be primogeniture—the English country landlord system which, in Rhodes' "humble belief" was one of the secrets of England's strength. The younger sons would have to go out and work. Natives who did not work would be taxed. They were South Africa's reservoir of labour.

The allotments would be controlled by village boards, the village boards by district councils, the district councils by a general native council.

It was to stimulate a man's ambition and effort that Rhodes advocated individual instead of, as heretofore, communal tenure. He had read about this system of separate holdings in a book on Russia by Sir D. Mackenzie Wallace. Rhodes was not to know that Russia would one day exchange it for the old Kaffir system he himself was discarding. . . .

And then, so settled, the natives would manage themselves, tax themselves, educate themselves, build their own roads and bridges, grow their own forests. Drink would not be allowed —Rhodes was prepared to suffer the wine-farmers' objections. Loafing would not be allowed—a special tax of ten shillings on loafing (and here, on the other hand, Rhodes was pleasing the farmers). Europeans were not to be allowed.

That was a very important part of the scheme. Except for a few officials, traders, and missionaries, no Europeans; no impossible mixture of races in different stages of development. . . .

There was an outcry over the ten shillings tax on loafing.

Negrophilists said it was nothing but a fine on those natives for whom there was no work at home, that it was a whip to lash them on to work on white farms and in the mines of Kimberley and Johannesburg.

And—partly—they were right. Nevertheless, Rhodes did have a sincere horror of loafing. He constantly expresses that horror. Even in his last will he states it. It was not entirely for sordid reasons Rhodes wanted this loafing tax, which, in practice, was never imposed.

One may take it that Rhodes meant to do the fair and decent thing in his Glen Grey Act, that he was moved by an impulse above the mere pleasing of his voters and shareholders. He had placed the limit of his life at forty-five years. He was now forty-one. Here was the most difficult problem in Africa, the crucial problem. It had to be settled before Africa could unite. ("All that—all one—that is my dream.") And who would settle it if he did not? Who else had the power, the wit, the will, the energy and the courage? Could he leave the world never having attempted its solution? Could he so betray his dream? . . . Not merely for the sake of voters and shareholders, but for the sake of a life-long ideal Rhodes had to make his native testament.

For the sake, too, of the natives. "The natives are children, and we ought to do something for the minds and the brains the Almighty has given them," he said. "We cannot stand by and do nothing," he said. "You are sitting," he told the Cape Parliament, "in judgment on Africa."

One has to consider Rhodes not merely as a monster, whether superman or devil, but as a man. How would a man, a big man, act who had a gigantic passion and knew he must soon die? Rhodes was an urgent man with too little time. That explains the whole of Rhodes. It softens his worst actions and enhances his best.

The Glen Grey Plan was Rhodes' retribution to the natives he had crushed that the white man might advance. It was a fair plan, tainted, some said, with self-interest. But the fairest human plans are tainted with self-interest, and, for all one knows, the plans of the gods.

III

Has the Glen Grey Plan proved a success? It has been largely applied; it is the only plan that has been largely applied; it has had enough success to justify its application; it has not been an entire success.

It has not been an entire success because the natives themselves have failed to make it an entire success.

It may be that, like the Teutons, who once, as Gibbon describes, lived a life not different from theirs—like the old Teutons, the South African natives will yet grow to what today we consider maturity. In the working out of Rhodes' plan they have proved themselves the children he always called them, children younger even than he calculated.

The South African natives have much Negro blood in them, and also blood Hamitic and Semitic. For, trailing down Africa, they mingled with those Hamites who include not only the Egyptians, Nubians, Abyssinians, and such others, but also the Hottentots; and they further met, in what is now Portuguese East Africa, in what was long years ago a great Arab state, the Eastern men who landed at the port of Sofala to trade in slaves and gold and ivory. These Hamites and Semites chiselled away the Negro thickness of the Kaffirs' faces. They gave the

Kaffirs their name: Kaffir, an Unbeliever. Vasco da Gama, the first man to round the Cape, speaks of these Kaffirs (or Caffres, as it used to be written, and as Rhodes once wrote it)—these Kaffirs of East Africa—darker or lighter according to the degree of their bastardization. . . .

And so the natives have in them the grasshopper merriment of the Negro, and his acquiescence in servitude. They have also—by blood or example—the mannerly indolence of the Arabs and Abyssinians, and their temper in war. The South African native, like the Negro, lives for the day, but he is prepared to work for a master as one whose ancestors were, over the centuries, sold so to work. He will uncomplainingly do work, when hunger drives him, that no white man will do in Africa, work that is called Kaffir work. If he cannot get it he will, as uncomplainingly, die of starvation. He would rather, like all his ancestors, have little than labour to possess much. One might say he labours in order to idle. . . .

It is nearly forty years since Rhodes initiated his Glen Grey Plan. In the year of 1932 a Government commission reported the following:

IV

The European, says the Report, has changed the environment of the native, but he has not taught him how to adjust himself to the new environment. The native plants as his forefathers planted, he practises the animal husbandry of his forefathers, he believes religiously in a plenitude of cattle, and it distresses him that "man begets, but land does not beget," that land does not increase with population.

Since the native believes in the agricultural methods of his ancestors, he suspects of witchcraft, and thus discourages, any exceptional native who successfully follows the methods of the Europeans.

Since cattle are his cult, and only cattle can bring him wives, his land is so overstocked with cattle, they have so ravished the earth, that a native area can be distinguished at sight by its bareness. There are deserts, there are dangerous weeds, where once were grasslands. From the mountain-sides of Glen Grey itself most of the plant life has gone, and with it the soil it once held together. The torrential rains have washed the loosened soil away. . . .

Since the native, as in Rhodes' time, "devotes his mind to a remarkable extent to the multiplication of children," since, in Rhodes' words, "the diminution by war and pestilence do not occur," since, further, European science now conserves life —not merely can the reserves no longer maintain the excess of cattle, but also not, so primitively developed, the excess of people. The adventurous and ambitious go to the towns. "A visit to Johannesburg frequently ranks with the circumcision school as a necessary preliminary towards the attainment of manhood." The standard left behind remains the standard of the lowest.

v

So then has the Glen Grey Plan proved a failure? Well, it is true that one may travel half a day in the Transkei and meet no tree under which to rest, that the natives have robbed their hills of green life and never replaced it. Yet still, when it rains, there is land in the Transkei greener than any other land in the country. The commission that speaks of "desert conditions" being created in the reserves, finds also that the reserves, duly improved, offer the only practicable method of natural segregation, and that, in the reserves, the native problem must be solved. And still the black man will try to govern himself, and still the white man hopes to teach him the art of it. Where Rhodes' experiment has failed, Europeans have their difficult material, their limited experience, and not their evil intentions to blame. The Glen Grey Act remains the basis of the solution of the Native Problem.

CHAPTER · 25

"IF ONLY ONE HAD A JOHANNESBURG!"

I

THEY say that, in these days, Rhodes was looking exhausted, he seemed shrunken, he was going rapidly grey, he was very neurotic. The year 1894 held for him not merely the official achievement of Matabeleland; his plans for Uganda; the annexation to the Cape of Pondoland; the passing of the Glen Grey Act—he fought also in this year a Parliamentary election; this was the year in which he decided that, as the native question was the fundamental question of South Africa, the Prime Minister must add to his work also the charge of native affairs; he sent de Villiers and Hofmeyr to the Ottawa Colonial Conference to speak of cable and steamship communications and Imperial reciprocity; he wrote, himself, to Washington about the unpleasant effect the new McKinley tariff would have on British trade.

Thirty-four United States Senators expressed their astonishment at what they clearly considered news from nowhere; and they replied to Rhodes' letter that, having been inspired by the nature of his business, they too had fresh ideas on taxation. "It is estimated that the United States now absorb from a third to a half of the annual product of the South African diamond mines, which are controlled by English investors, who have limited the output, created a trust, and practically control the price of diamonds in the world." Would not, the Senators pleasantly suggested, a thirty-per-cent tax on diamonds check consumption, beneficently operate on the excessive and artificial price, and "induce people of Cape Colony to believe that the present attitude of Great Britain in relation to silver is not only unfair and unjust, but is also injurious to the interests of that Colony"?

The only retaliation in Rhodes' power was to make it, as soon as he could, a part of the new Matabeleland Constitution that the duty on English goods—but not on imported goods generally—should not exceed the duty on Cape goods; to tell his Chartered shareholders that one day the United States might have to be dealt with as a naughty child and told, "If you will keep up this McKinley tariff, we, for a period, shall keep out your goods"; and to point out that the United States, with a hundred times the population of English South Africa, was importing only twice as much goods from England.

Insist on that preferential clause in the Matabeleland Constitution, he begged his shareholders. "It is the little things that change the world, not the big things."

II

Was it a little or a big thing that changed Rhodes' world? It was in action little to the point of childishness, and in thought monstrous. It was both in action and in thought so grotesque that through all the passion and sentimentality it engendered there were many who, from the beginning, could do nothing but laugh at it. It would probably not have happened but for an impatience born of a united arrogance and desperation. Rhodes had got to the point of feeling that his desire was his duty, and that if he did not soon fulfil his desire it would never be fulfilled. For his time was short; and no one else could do what had to be done. That terrible time was against him, the only unconquerable, as he said.

"Never hurry and hasten in anything," he had warned the Cape Town audience welcoming him back at the beginning of this same year of 1894 from his triumph in Matabeleland. "We can work slowly and gradually," he admonished them.

Now, suddenly, he felt that he could no longer work slowly and gradually, he had to hurry and hasten. He had spent fifteen years, twenty years (sometimes he said the one, and sometimes the other) in amalgamating the diamond mines, and so all things should be done, he maintained, step by step.

But today he could not give fifteen or twenty years to things, there were only a few years left him altogether. Ten years—if only he could have ten years more than the term of life destined to him, he always said (he did not demand the allotted span, he did not ask even to reach sixty) but if only he could have just one more decade for his work's sake!

He could not have it. What remained was to crush into months the work of years. The warning he had given to others he dared not apply to himself. He had to hurry and hasten. He could not progress step by step. He had to leap.

III

Nor had he to leap merely because time was short. In this year, through the very blare of triumphant trumpets, little faint instruments were playing thin minor notes—notes of warning

275

and menace. Obstacles were beginning to appear in Rhodes' path. Over these he had to leap.

For instance, his telegraph to the North. How glibly he had told his Chartered shareholders in 1892 that all he needed to ensure his telegraph to the Mediterranean was Uganda. If only England would keep Uganda for him he could go through to Wady Halfa. He could then square the Mahdi and reach Egypt.

So England had proclaimed a protectorate over Uganda. And as his own Chartered sphere extended to Tanganyika, and as he had got from Belgium cession of a strip of land along Lake Tanganyika which would connect Tanganyika with Uganda, nothing now hindered the northward path of his telegraph.

And what must suddenly happen? Belgium, inspired by Germany and France, must go and withdraw her cession of the strip of land . . . ruin for his telegraph! It was not until Rhodes met and charmed the Kaiser in 1899 that he got from him an alternative telegraph route through German East Africa. In the meantime, as far as he knew, his northward march was fatally interrupted.

Nor was that all. There was Lourenço Marquez lying between Rhodesia and the sea. Three years ago he had spoken to Kruger about taking Lourenço Marquez, and Kruger had icily told him that ill-gotten goods were accursed. Rhodes had then decided that the Cape must buy Lourenço Marquez. Lourenço Marquez had everything he needed—harbours, even a new railway—and times were bad in Portugal.

For years Rhodes had had this hope of buying Lourenço Marquez, and now Portugal (German interference again) said definitely she would not sell.

The second blow.

And then a third, if a lesser, blow. Swaziland had passed officially to the Transvaal.

But, finally, a blow at the very heart. In September, 1894, as if the year were not full enough already of work and trouble, Rhodes, together with Jameson and Hays Hammond, an American who was the consulting engineer to Rhodes Gold-fields Company, went to Matabeleland to look for the New Rand which they had not found in Mashonaland. It was in expectation of the New Rand that Chartered shares had risen to eight pounds. Rhodes had urgent need to tell his share-holders of a New Rand in Matabeleland.

And no New Rand! "Well," said a prominent shareholder, "if we have to depend on Hammond's geological report to raise money for this country, I don't think the outlook is very encouraging. If he cannot say anything stronger than that I have not much hope for the future of the Chartered Company." It was to this man Rhodes said, in his bitterness, that if he only wanted money he had better go and sell his Chartered shares.

But most shareholders, he knew in his heart, only wanted money. What was he to do now? With what words now comfort them? Was there, after all, only one Rand in South Africa, and that in the grip of Kruger? How gold shares were rising since the discovery that gold mines, like diamond mines, had treasure-laden depths! Was it not too maddening that Kruger, so bitterly anxious to keep apart, should have the Rand, and not he, who craved for union?

In Matabeleland, as they were travelling about, Hays Hammond had spoken of other things than a New Rand in Rhodesia. He had spoken of the old, the only, Rand in the Transvaal.

If there was much more trouble between Kruger and the Uitlanders (the Outlanders—the foreigners), he had told Rhodes, there would almost certainly be a rising in Johannesburg. And, after such talk, could one fail to think in one thought of Charterland and the Transvaal?

On his way home from Rhodesia Rhodes called in on Lourenço Marquez and asked could he help the Portuguese in their native troubles or do any other little thing for them? They said not. He went on then to Pretoria to talk to Kruger about his railway rates. But it was of a piece with the whole unsuccessful journey that he could do nothing with Kruger. He left Kruger, saying: "If you do not take care you will have the whole of South Africa against you. You are a very strong man, but there are things you may do which will bring the whole of the Cape Colony, and indeed the whole of South Africa, against you, and so strongly that you will not be able to stand against it."

Worst of all Rhodes' obstacles was the old tight-mouthed Kruger.

IV

Still, it was no wonder Rhodes had not found Kruger in a good mood. Did not Kruger know as well as anyone else the designs Rhodes had? Already in April of this year of 1894 a Johannesburg friend of Chief Justice de Villiers was agreeing with him that Rhodes' policy seemed to be "a threat and menace to the two republics. . . . I do not think that when Rhodes started his career he thought of getting rid of the republics in the manner he is now setting about it. I fancy his success has made him over-confident and I have become alarmed. . . .

Should Rhodes threaten the Republic he will be made short work of. Once he is removed from the scene there is no one to carry out his schemes."

And here was Rhodes threatening! Yet even that was not the immediate reason for Kruger's bad mood. The immediate reason was what had happened not long ago during Sir Henry Loch's visit to Pretoria. Kruger had gone to meet him, and jolly Englishmen had taken the horses from the official carriage in which they both sat, and dragged it to Loch's hotel, and for a whole mile waved the Union Jack over Kruger's head, singing "God Save the Queen" and "Rule Britannia" and, says Kruger, "the usual English satirical ditties." At one stage Kruger had been completely enveloped and muffled in the flag, and had struggled, accompanied by their music, to disentangle himself from it. At the hotel they had allowed Loch to descend, but had refused to pull the carriage farther and left Kruger absurdly sitting there until some burghers collected themselves to drag him to the Government Building.

It was considered by many people a very funny occurrence; but one may believe that to the President it must have been an outrage harder to bear than the Boer War itself, which, at least, had the consolatory grandeur of tragedy. He must have remembered, first, all the time, and then less often, and then, during his whole life to come, suddenly, sharply, irrelevantly, how Englishmen had made him look ridiculous in the presence of his burghers.

It is no wonder, really, that Kruger lacked inclination to parley with Rhodes.

But he never had cared to parley with Rhodes. Not from the beginning. Rhodes may have been the very man to deal with him—so many thought—and yet he was the signal failure among Rhodes' dealings. He had no sooner met Rhodes over the Bechuanaland business ten years before than he had spoken of trouble with "that young man"—and this, although Rhodes was nominally (he pretended to be, said Kruger) on his side in the business; at least he was against his own countrymen who represented those opposite callings he despised, the missionary Mackenzie, and the soldier Warren. Kruger had not been moved to goodwill even by Rhodes' offer to work in Bechuanaland jointly with the Transvaal. Why, so long ago, did Kruger already distrust him?

And then Kruger had tried to interfere in the Lobengula affair. He had gone clutching at Swaziland. He had snubbed Rhodes about Delagoa Bay. Burghers of his had aspired to make a republic in Mashonaland—they had actually, until England stopped them, done so in Zululand. He was even now linking himself for trade with the Portuguese of Lourenço Marquez rather than with the English of the Cape. He would not come into tariff or railway unions with the Cape. He would not come into any sort of union. He stood there immovably, like a rock in a flood, the great obstacle to Rhodes' whole scheme of union.

On top of it all, to him must happen the Rand. In his Republic must lie the wealth of Africa. "If only one had a Johannesburg," Rhodes spoke his brooding thoughts out to a Cape Town audience when the Boer War was already fomenting, "if one had a Johannesburg, one could unite the whole country tomorrow. . . . Then you would have a great commonwealth; then you would have a union of states; then, I think, apart from my mother country, there would be no place in the world that would compete with it. . . . There is no place to touch this; there is no place to touch it—for the beauty

280

of its climate and the variety of its products. And yet we stupid human mortals are quarrelling over the equality of rights instead of thinking of the great country that has been given us."

"There is no place to touch this; there is no place to touch it. . . ." It has the very rhythm of Solomon's passion for the Shulamite: "Behold thou art fair, my love. Behold thou art fair." Rhodes loved Africa beyond money. If only one had a Johannesburg!

If only one had a Johannesburg! What could one not do if one had a Johannesburg! But Kruger had it, the only, the miraculous Johannesburg. And he would not divide it with Rhodes. And, the great ultimate things apart, what was Rhodes to say to his shareholders, expectant of a New Rand in Matabeleland, when he met them in January, 1895?

v

If he could say to them that soon there would be a federation of all the states in South Africa, and Rhodesia would be in it, too! If he could tell them that no longer need they pay for the running of Rhodesia—a United South Africa would pay for everything! If his shareholders could participate in the boom on the Rand!

At the mere thought of it—when, next year, Kruger made a slip and there seemed a chance of war—what a gambling, what a rare gambling, there was on the Stock Exchange in Chartereds!

If one had a Johannesburg. . . . Jameson, too, had gone visiting Johannesburg, and was now lashing himself with that thought. They talked, he and Rhodes, about the troubles the Uitlanders were having in the Transvaal, and the opportunity

281

there might arise of assisting them, and the desirability, therefore, of having in permanent readiness a volunteer force.

To the world at large—as much of it as was interested—they explained that the company's extended territories needed fuller protection. The company's board, whether, as some say, in full knowledge, or whether in their deluded transports over the conquest of Matabeleland, authorized the expenditure on equipment. For a long time hardly anyone else wondered why the new Rhodesia Horse required so much equipment.

But Kruger wondered. And if Rhodes was beginning to equip his settlers, so, too, was Kruger beginning to equip his burghers.

VI

Nor had he need of warnings from Rhodesia. He knew as much as the engineer, Hays Hammond. He knew what the Uitlanders were saying and doing. That, at least, everyone knew.

"People have talked of a conspiracy," writes Bryce, who happened to be in the Transvaal shortly before the Raid, "but never was there, except on the stage, so open a conspiracy. Two-thirds of the action . . . went on before the public. The visitor had hardly installed himself in an hotel at Pretoria before people began to tell him that an insurrection was imminent, that arms were being imported, that Maxim guns were hidden, and would be shown to him if he cared to see them. . . . In Johannesburg little else was talked of, not in dark corners, but at the club where everyone lunches, and between the acts at the play. . . . All over South Africa one heard the same story; all over South Africa men waited for news from Johannesburg."

It is said that the plot that culminated in the Raid was set going when Jameson visited Johannesburg in 1894. Was it he or Rhodes who first saw in the agitation of the Uitlanders their Heaven-sent, urgent opportunity? Whichever it was, of one thing one could be sure: they were not going to let so lovely, so beneficent, an agitation die if effort of theirs could keep it alive.

CHAPTER ، 26

KRUGER AND THE UITLANDERS

I

THIS was, in summary, the trouble in Johannesburg, and the way it all began:

In 1852, by the Sand River Convention, the British Government "guaranteed to the emigrant farmers beyond the Vaal River the right to manage their own affairs, and govern themselves according to their own laws without any interference on the part of the British Government," and a Boer Independency, calling itself the South African Republic, arose.

Difficulties came upon the South African Republic—native wars and bankruptcy—and Sir Theophilus Shepstone was sent to find out if its unsettled state endangered British subjects in the Republic or on the Natal border; and also whether the will of the country favoured annexation by Great Britain. He found the Republic, under President Burgers, weak, harassed, and helpless, rode into Pretoria with eight civil servants and twenty-five policemen and annexed it. England confirmed the annexation as the will of the country.

But it was not the will of the country. Three years later the Boers reproclaimed their independence, attacked the British and defeated them at Majuba. By the Pretoria Convention that followed the independence of the Republic was again recognized, but it was limited by a British suzerainty and otherwise.

In 1884 Kruger did some bargaining which resulted in the Convention of London. This agreement dropped all talk of suzerainty, and the title of South African Republic was formally conceded. On the other hand, the Republic subjected to British approval its treaties with natives or countries other than the Orange Free State, and it was not allowed to discriminate by tariff or prohibition against British goods.

The—call it justice, or otherwise—of the Boer War rests on interpretation of these two agreements. The British said the preamble of the 1881 Convention, specifying the suzerainty, stood. The Boers said it did not.

The clause affecting British goods nearly, in 1895, brought about that war, the very hope of which caused Chartereds and Rhodes' other shares so to rise.

A year after the London Convention—one ironical year too late—the gold reef was struck on the Witwatersrand, and the Transvaal became the life-source of South Africa.

In 1886 Johannesburg was founded.

II

Now, as adventurers had come to Kimberley, they came also to Johannesburg. When Lord Bryce visited Johannesburg in 1895 he found nothing in it to remind him that he was in a Dutch country except the names of some of the streets. The mixed population was English-speaking and its social character was English. In the Transvaal generally, there were, at this time, Kruger says, eighty thousand foreigners—adult males— and they outnumbered the burghers by four to one.

What was more, they could not forget that from 1877 to 1881 England had owned the state. They still felt it to be, somehow, an English state.

One might well imagine that a man who had actually been in the Great Trek which had fought and suffered a thousand miles to be free of interference, whose idyllic dream it was to live like a patriarch among his own, must have been maddened by this roaring, pursuing, overwhelming flood of foreigners. In 1888, at the septennial commemoration of the Declaration of Independence, even while Moffat, at Rhodes' instigation, was at Lobengula's kraal persuading Lobengula to reject any dealings with the Transvaal and to make a treaty of amity with England against all other powers, Kruger addressed his world as follows: "People of the Lord, you old people of the country, you foreigners, you newcomers, yea, even you thieves and murderers!" And by this, he said, when the Uitlanders complained of outrage, he meant only that "everybody, even thieves and murderers, if there were any such at the meeting, should humble themselves before God and acknowledge the wonders of God's dealing with the people of the Republic."

The Uitlanders, however, did not believe him. No, they said, Kruger meant they were thieves and murderers.

It does seem the more likely interpretation. One has to recall Kruger's state of mind. There was, at this very moment, the Lobengula business. If Rhodes wanted to expand, so did Kruger. Had he been in Rhodes' way? But how Rhodes had been in his way! Kruger had wanted to expand in the days when he hadn't, as Rhodes said, a sixpence in his treasury. Now where was he to expand? He could not expand south: Britain had ruined his hopes in Zululand. He could not, but

286

for his bit of power over Swaziland, expand east: Britain had a treaty of preëmption over Portuguese territory. He could not expand west: Rhodes had hindered him in Bechuanaland. He could not expand north: Rhodes had turned from him the ear of Lobengula.

As if that were not enough, as if it were not sufficiently galling that he could nowhere stretch himself, could nowhere even find an outlet to the sea, he was now being fenced inside his own domain as Job by his bones and sinews. Rhodes himself had just consolidated his Goldfields. Other men who had begun in Kimberley were today in Johannesburg buying up claims, farms, building-sites. Foreigners owned the gold. Foreigners ran the shops, the clubs, the racecourses. Foreigners were making the money, having the excitement, the pleasure, the power, the pride. Foreigners considered themselves the best society. Bryce conjectured "the English and colonial elements to compose seven-tenths of the white population, the American and German about one-tenth, while Frenchmen and other European nations made up the residue." The Boers? Hardly any except Government officials. The Boers came to Johannesburg to sell their farm produce to the rich Uitlanders, and then humbly slipped off home again.

Was it not enough to madden a man? Although Johannesburg was the very meaning of the Transvaal, although it was only thirty-five miles from the capital, although the law prescribed that the President should visit each town and district of the Republic at least once a year—in nine years Kruger could not bring himself to go to it more than three times. This town, his town, bearing his name, the town that should have been his triumph and his hope—he felt about it like an old Puritan father whose daughter has become a flaunting courtesan, or like the father of a Juliet who has given herself to the son of his hereditary enemy. He wanted none of it.

How much more likely that Kruger meant, not what he said he meant, but what the Uitlanders said he meant. Actually from the standpoint of literature and oratory and Kruger's essential Bible, should not the word "even" convey emphasis rather than differentiation? Is he not addressing two separate groups of people: "People of the Lord, you old people of the country! . . . You foreigners, you newcomers, yea, you thieves and murderers!"

It was not by accident Kruger spoke simple-seeming words that on reflection had so curious a flavour. He once opened a synagogue "in the name of Jesus Christ."

III

Who understood Kruger's bitterness so well as Rhodes himself? "I pity the man!" he burst out in Parliament a few months after the Moffat Treaty. "When I see him sitting in Pretoria with Bechuanaland gone, and other lands around him gone from his grasp . . . with his whole idea of a republic vanishing . . . likely to have to deal with a hundred thousand diggers who must be entirely out of sympathy and touch with him . . . I pity the man. . . . When I see a man starting and continuing with one object, and utterly failing in that object, I cannot help pitying him."

One might imagine that if there were still something needed to make Kruger completely boil over, this triumphant pity of Rhodes must have supplied it. . . .

The first time Kruger came to Johannesburg was in the days before Rhodes had pushed through the Moffat Treaty, before he was in the position to gloat over him. Rhodes was then in Johannesburg, consolidating his Goldfields, and he proposed Kruger's health at a banquet and called himself prettily one of Kruger's young burghers.

After Rhodes had his concession he appeared, one Saturday morning, to see the President in Pretoria. The President said Rhodes could wait till Monday; his burghers were in town to celebrate Nachtmaal—the Holy Communion—and he always reserved the Saturday of Nachtmaal week for his burghers. As for Sunday, he did not do business on a Sunday. Rhodes could wait or he could go. "The old devil!" said Rhodes to his companion. "I meant to work with him, but I'm not going on my knees to him. I've got my concession, however, and he can do nothing."

The second time Kruger visited Johannesburg it was to reassure the citizens during a collapse of the stock market and also to talk about railways. Perhaps he liked the citizens of Johannesburg better in their troubles than in their triumphs. But a rabble crowded round his house and upon it, broke its railings and pillars, pulled down the Transvaal flag and trampled upon it, and had to be driven back by police.

Kruger vowed then never to come to Johannesburg again. Nor did he, until five years later, when he was persuaded, both by his officials and by his farmer's heart, to forget his vow and open the first agricultural show. This time—the third time—nothing unpleasant happened. And at the end of the year there was the Raid.

IV

Of course, Kruger hated the Uitlanders and did what he could to hinder them. His officials were either Boers or Hollanders. He tried to keep the Uitlanders' unpleasing voices out of his Government. The Constitution of the country laid it down that "the territory is open for every foreigner who obeys the laws of the Republic." A law was then passed making an Uitlander's vote contingent on either ownership of landed property in the Republic, or otherwise a year's residence. In 1882 there was, on one hand, a great acceleration of gold-rushing, and, on the other, renewed independence and an enlarged patriotism. And when it was seen how many foreigners the gold of the Transvaal was bringing in, five years' residence became the stipulation.

More gold appeared, and still more foreigners; the Witwatersrand itself appeared, and tens of thousands of foreigners. They outnumbered the burghers, as has been said, by four to one.

To combat this preponderance, Kruger thought out a new plan. He would set up a second Volksraad—a second parliament, a special inferior parliament for the foreigners, the Uitlanders. This Raad, over which the First Raad had the right of veto, could deal with the things that peculiarly concerned the Uitlanders, it could deal with business matters and gold laws. Two years' residence entitled a stranger to vote for the Second Raad. Another two years (provided he was a Protestant, thirty years of age, and had landed property in the Republic) gave him the right of election to his particular Raad. A further ten years brought him the full rights of burghership: he was now promoted to vote for the first Raad; he had the privileges that a true-born Boer acquired at the age of sixteen.

By such measures—by giving the franchise to a Boer at the age of sixteen and to an Uitlander not before forty—Kruger hoped to make good the difference in their numbers.

He hoped to do more. How many Uitlanders, by the year 1890, had lived in the Republic for fourteen years? Most of them had not come until 1886. There were going to be few indeed foreign voters tampering with Kruger's Republic before the twentieth century. . . . And the deep levels had not yet been discovered. And who knew how long the gold would last, and how long, therefore, one would stay in the Republic. The twentieth century! What was the use of a vote in the twentieth century? In effect, by the law of 1890, the Uitlanders were disfranchised.

That was not, was it? very pleasant for a proud population. But stay! A proud population. Did the Uitlanders *want* to become burghers? That is to say, did they want to be merely burghers, to give up their English or French or German or American nationality and link themselves, for what it was worth, not only here and now, but in the world and for ever, with this little primitive nation on the veld? . . . In fact, what the Uitlanders really wanted was what they called the dual nationality. They wanted to remain English, French, German, or American. But, for immediate, practical, temporary purposes they wanted also to be Transvaal burghers.

Another thing they wanted was that their children should be taught in the English medium at the Government schools. They provided, they said, all the money, so why could not the state (whatever might be the practice in other parts of the world) arrange that the children should be taught in their mother tongue even if it were not the language of the country?

Then there were the monopolies Kruger gave away—he believed, he said, in monopolies: they stimulated industry. He gave, therefore, the railway monopoly to a German-Hollander group; and the dynamite monopoly to that same Lippert of the

Lobengula land-concession. It was said the country lost hundreds of thousands a year through these monopolies. There was also a liquor monopoly. That, again, debauched the natives.

Then there were the tariffs and taxes. True, the Chartered Company taxed the gold of their own settlers fifty per cent where Kruger taxed the gold of his foreigners ten per cent; but Kruger did see to it, against the Convention to which he had agreed, that English goods should be expensive.

Then there were, the Uitlanders complained, the unjust awards of the courts and the general corruption.

And there were the police, the Zarps—their name, like those of Russian organizations, made out of initials: the Zuid Afrikaanse Republikeinse Polisie. They suffered, cried the Uitlanders, at the hands of the brutal Zarps.

J. A. Hobson, a Boer partisan, denies that the police were such an evil. "The country Boer drafted into the police force was certainly," he says, "ignorant, possibly rude in manner and more than possibly corrupt, but to suggest that out of such matters intolerable grievances could be constituted is a bold defiance of common sense."

It is not, however, so apparent as he seems to think that the combination of power with ignorance, rudeness, and corruption is easily bearable. It is, of all things, the least bearable. The only point is, to what extent did the general population encounter the police? Hobson says not at all; these troubles merely skirted the lives of the quiet tradesmen, business men, or professional men. "Many of them hated the Boer and believed him corrupt and incompetent; some of them exhibited a certain fervour on the franchise issue, but none of them had undergone any serious personal trouble with police or other officers of state. . . . As for general liberty and even licence of conduct, it existed nowhere if not in Johannesburg. Every luxury of life, every extravagance of behaviour, every form of private vice, flourished unchecked; every man and woman said and did what seemed good in his or her eyes. The helot" (there was talk of the Uitlanders being in the position of helots) "bore his golden chains with insolent composure. . . . The entire wealth of the country, drawn from the bowels of the earth by Kaffir labour, passed easily into his hands, with the exception of a toll taken by the Government. . . . In a land of simple-mannered, plain-living farmers he alone had material luxury and the leisure to use it."

And, indeed, if one asks a moderate sort of Uitlander today if he suffered much under Kruger, he smiles as the pageant of his youth passes before his eyes, and he says: "Well, it wasn't so bad. The franchise and all that: what did we really care about the franchise? There'll never be such days again as the old Johannesburg days."

Certainly over thirty-five thousand Uitlanders once presented a petition to the Volksraad praying for relief of their grievances. But then almost anybody will sign almost anything. If one has the necessary education it is easy, and somehow adventurous, to sign one's name.

v

Nevertheless, that the Uitlanders had just grievances one may infer from what—as against Hobson—Bryce says. Those early Republicans, he says, were "brave, good-natured, hospitable, faithful to one another, generally pure in their domestic life, seldom touched by avarice or ambition. But the corruption of their legislature shows that it is rather to the absence of temptation than to any superior strength of moral principle that these merits have been due. . . . The old Boer virtues were giving way under new temptations. The Volksraad (as is believed all over South Africa) became corrupt, though of course there have always been pure and upright men among its members. The civil service was not above suspicion. Rich men and powerful corporations surrounded those who had concessions to give or the means of influencing legislation, whether directly or indirectly. The very inexperience of the Boer ranchman who came up as a member of the Volksraad made him an easy prey."

The Uitlanders used to speak sneeringly of a Third Raad. They used to call the go-betweens, the representatives of the bribers, the Third Raad. It may be remembered that there was now also beginning to be a certain amount of corruption in the Cape Parliament. . . .

And it was in these circumstances that a number of Uitlanders, resenting the rule of people they thought their inferiors, and feeling themselves important and impotent, both together, persuaded a number of Uitlanders who wanted some excitement, and a further number of Uitlanders who were prepared to do whatever anybody suggested to them, that one ought to form a National Union.

The object of the National Union was "to obtain, by all constitutional means, equal rights for all citizens of the Republic and the redress of its grievances."

A Mr. Charles Leonard, a solicitor, was the chairman.

The National Union had not at first been joined by the most important of the Uitlanders—the mine-owners. These were busy taking the gold out of the mines: they did not intend staying in the Republic after the gold was gone and could exist quite comfortably without the vote; many of their principals lived in Europe and certainly could live without the Transvaal vote; agitation might do their enterprises more harm than good. What the mine-owners, for their part, did was to raise a fund "to get a better Volksraad"—"whether," comments Bryce, "by influencing members or by supplying funds for election expenses has never been made clear."

The Volksraad was pelted not only with petitions, but also, it would seem, with money. And neither helped. Kruger became President for the third time, a new Volksraad was elected, and it acted no differently from the old Volksraad.

On top of everything, clinching everything, deep-level mining had come into profitable existence: inexhaustible gold, no speedy departure now from the Rand. It grew worth the while of the mine-owners to consider their grievances more seriously: the dynamite monopoly; the heavy railway rates for coal; the tariff on mining machinery and on the food of their labourers; the sale of liquor to the mine natives.

In 1894 Rhodes and Jameson visited Johannesburg and found that things were as Hammond had told them. It was in these days the Rhodesia Horse came into being, and Rhodes grew more urgent, and the mine-owners, through him, more demonstrative.

Rhodes made dissatisfaction fashionable. He inspired them. To begin with, he was himself a mine-owner. But he was also much more than a mine-owner. He was the deity of de Beers, Charterland, and the Cape House. He had the ear of England. He was Rhodes the empire-maker, who had merely to decide he must have Matabeleland or Pondoland or any other piece of Africa and it was his. Could one resist the feeling that Rhodes' desire and the Lord's accomplishment were indissolubly mated?

In Rhodes' heart were other things than the Uitlanders' sorrows: Africa; union; the need for Rhodesia to come into that union; his whole plan of life that the one obstinate old man was blocking; his knowledge that this life must soon be over; his terrible compulsion, therefore, to hurry.

As for Jameson, Jameson was actually the man with the practical experience of how to bring troubles to a head. He was the instinctive surgeon: he could operate, with a few swift cuts, not only on people, but on history. He had discovered that, without any training, he could run wars, countries, and men. He had walked, alone and full of fever, into native territories to take their lands from native kings. He had, single-handed, turned away a trek of Boers designing to establish a republic in Mashonaland. Everyone was praising him for the way he had just conquered the Matabele. Had he given up his practice and his cronies in Kimberley merely to sit, for the rest of his life, with his feet on a desk in Salisbury? He wanted renewed excitement, renewed applause. He saw Rhodes' brooding eye. He loved Rhodes. He wanted anything Rhodes wanted. Jameson, too, inspired the mine-owners.

Towards the end of 1894 Rhodes and Jameson were in England, receiving the worship of the nation. On January 1, 1895, Rhodes was gazetted a Privy Councillor, and this was a preliminary to the official proclamation of Rhodesia as the name of the territories Rhodes had added to the Empire. In the circumstances he could no doubt bear it that he was also, in the month of January (perhaps through the instrumentality of such men as Wilfrid Blunt), blackballed at the Travellers' Club. Later in the same month he met his shareholders and found them some comforting things in Hays Hammond's report, yet warned them more than once not to "discount possibilities as if they were proved results." He also told them that he needed no more money from them, and that Rhodesia's relations with Kruger continued to be friendly. At a banquet given to Jameson, with the Prince of Wales in the chair, Jameson prophesied the imminence of a South African economic federation, soon to be followed by a political federation.

Jameson was not the only speaker at banquets. Towards the end of the month Kruger too made a speech at a banquet. At a German club he proposed the health of the Kaiser; suggested that the Transvaal was no longer an infant nation; complained that "when we asked Her Majesty's Government for bigger clothes they said, 'Eh, Eh? What is this?' and could not see that we were growing up"; and ended with the confident expectation that Germany would help provide the Republic with an adult's wardrobe.

Nor was Jameson's Rhodesia Horse the only new military organization in South Africa. Kruger was using the Uitlanders' own money to complete the fort at Pretoria and to build the new fort at Johannesburg. He had imported big guns from Krupp's, and Maxim's. "We are even told," said the great Manifesto the leaders of the Uitlanders presented to Kruger three days before Jameson started out to save them, "that German officers are coming in to drill the burghers."

Rhodes declared afterwards it was this Germany-minded speech of Kruger's that finally impelled him to action. And this is quite likely. He had said, not ten years before, in the Cape House: "Do you think that if the Transvaal had Bechuanaland it would be allowed to keep it? Would not Bismarck have some quarrel with the Transvaal? . . . There would be some excuse to pick a quarrel—some question of brandy or guns or something—and then Germany would stretch from Angra Pequena to Delagoa Bay." . . .

On top of everything else, then, Rhodes did fear the incursion of Germany into Africa, and further hindrance of his schemes. Kruger's speech may very well have stimulated his decision that if there were to be a quarrel picked—"some question of brandy or guns or something"—and a stretching across Africa, not Germany, but he, Rhodes, should do that quarrelling and stretching.

Beit had been anxious to protect Rhodes, and had asked the mine-owners not to embroil him in their Uitlander difficulties. It was, nevertheless, left to Rhodes and Beit to decide "whether it was necessary, from the capitalist point of view, to resort to extreme measures."

Early in 1895 Rhodes returned from England, went up to Johannesburg, and told his mining friends that it was necessary. And urgently necessary. There had been talk enough. The business of a movement was to move. He was prepared to back this movement. He would do for it what he had done for the Matabele War—sit in Cape Town and provide the arms, the men, and the means. Only not openly—not, as in the other case, with a brazen insistence to England that the thing must be done—and let no one stop him. Rhodes was to say, a few months before the Boer War: "When I am told the President of the Transvaal is causing trouble, I cannot really think about it; it is too ridiculous. If you were to tell me that the native chief in Samoa was going to cause trouble to Her Majesty's Government, then I would discuss the proposition that the Transvaal was a danger to the British Empire." And it is true Rhodes was then nearing his end, he was sick and frustrated and reckless and could not, they say, control the enormous angers that he afterwards repented. It is possible that these words are the words of wild passion. Nevertheless, there was one thing that had, from the beginning, infuriated Rhodes against Kruger, and it infuriated him until he died—the fact that he had been hindered, throughout his career, not by the representative of a great power, but by the unlettered leader of a struggling nation. He did mean, passion or no, that Kruger wasn't a fit opponent for him.

And yet he might think, feel, say, mean what he liked: there were things he knew: Kruger was not, after all, a Samoan, nor, indeed, a Matabele chief; the Prime Minister of one country could not foment, subsidize, assist a revolution against another and nominally friendly government. It was not for him to pick the quarrel about "brandy or guns or something." He could not, this time, come riding in to join his triumphant cohorts as he had done in Matabeleland, nor stand in Church Square, Pretoria, as he had stood in Lobengula's burnt-down kraal at Bulawayo, saying: "Dr. Jameson, officers and men of the various columns, I have to thank you for all the excellent work you have done." Dr. Jameson, in truth, would be there in Church Square (one hoped), and also the officers and men of the various columns, and, come to think of it, he himself. But not at all in the usual capacity. Far from it. He would arrive, Rhodes, not as participator, but as mediator. He would say—surprised—in Kruger's words to the German Club: "Eh, Eh? What is this?" There would not really be bloodshed as with the Matabele—if there was a thing Rhodes hated, it was bloodshed. There would not even be a demonstrative shooting down of mealie fields as with the Pondos. It would be rather a recapitulation of the Shepstone affair. Rhodes would be in Pretoria merely to ask if it was the will of the Transvaal people to enter the Union of South Africa. And "Yes!" would cry the great voice of the Uitlanders. As for the still, small voice of the Boers, let it whisper "No!" if it dared.

CHAPTER · 27

THE IMPATIENCE OF JAMESON

I

DURING the year 1895 plans went forward. Frankie Rhodes, Johannesburg manager, since Rhodes' recent visit to England, of the Consolidated Goldfields, was now in the plot. Jameson came often to Johannesburg, and it was he, the infallible, who made the arrangements.

In September, writes Sir Percy Fitzpatrick, Jameson "visited Johannesburg, and it was then agreed that he should raise a force of fifteen hundred men, fully equipped, a number of Maxims and some field artillery; that he was, in addition to this, to have with him fifteen hundred spare rifles and a quantity of spare ammunition; and that about five thousand rifles, three Maxim guns, and a million rounds of ammunition were to be smuggled into Johannesburg. It was calculated that in the town itself there would be, perhaps, a thousand rifles, privately owned. Thus, in the event of a junction of forces being effected, Johannesburg would be able to command about nine thousand armed men, with a fair equipment of machine-guns and cannon."

This junction of forces would naturally not be effected until the appropriate moment. First the Reformers would send an ultimatum to Kruger. This would, of course, be treated with contempt, because all their communications to Kruger were treated with contempt. The Reformers would then rise, take possession of Johannesburg, declare a provisional government, march that same night on Pretoria, seize the fort and its munitions, seize the railway and carry off these munitions. The fort was undergoing those alterations they complained of, it was completely vulnerable—it could be taken, they reckoned, without the firing of a shot. . . .

But now, it followed, the Boers would gather themselves together and trouble would begin. The Reformers would here cry out that they were in danger, and Jameson, handily but lawfully doing something with a large force at a convenient spot, would rush in and save them.

Then Rhodes, as Prime Minister of the Cape, would solemnly appear to mediate between the combatants. Then the High Commissioner, as the representative of England, would come to assist him.

Then the Boers would give in, and Rhodes would say, as Jameson to Lobengula, that he was their former, and he hoped their present, friend; peace would follow, bliss for the Uitlanders, the Rhodesians, the Chartered shareholders, the Greater Englanders—bliss for everybody: the Union of South Africa.

II

That was the September plan—a very good plan, but for one difficulty. Johannesburg and Pretoria are somewhere about the twenty-sixth parallel. Rhodes' territories adjoin the Transvaal somewhere about that twenty-second parallel he was always talking about in the early days. Was Jameson to be hovering around the Limpopo River when the faint distant wail of

Kruger's victims reached him—to travel, by horse and Scotch cart, across hundreds of miles of open country to their help?

Impossible, of course. Most clearly other arrangements had to be made, very subtle arrangements. Those arrangements had been begun, indeed, months ago. They were, unfortunately, not yet completed.

It will be remembered that, after all the trouble with Mackenzie and Warren and the Dutch and the Bechuanas, Britain had declared the southern part of Bechuanaland a crown colony which was called British Bechuanaland. The Charter had trading concessions over Northern Bechuanaland, which was called Bechuanaland Protectorate. It had not, however, administrative rights there. And what Rhodes had been demanding for a long time were these two things—that, in the interests of homogeneous management, eventual union and his own various schemes, Britain should hand over British Bechuanaland to the Cape; and that, for the same reasons, in inverse order, the Chartered Company should be granted administrative rights over Bechuanaland Protectorate.

Now, just a month ago, the first demand had been granted. Only that was not, at the moment, the crucial demand. It did not help Jameson. The really important thing was to have a legitimate foothold in Bechuanaland Protectorate within easy reach of Pretoria and Johannesburg. And all this year Rhodes had been struggling with the Colonial Office over the question of the Protectorate. Fruitlessly.

The Uitlanders were, at the moment, blowing hot. He and Beit were ready with the money. The difficult High Commissioner Loch had been exchanged, against the Queen's will, for the easier, the older, Hercules Robinson. Jameson was so popular in Rhodesia through the Matabele business, his men asked for nothing better than to assist his further ventures. Rhodesia, for all that, was sucking the company dry. Despite his assurances earlier in the year, Rhodes had, after all, found it necessary to ask his shareholders to authorize a new issue of five hundred thousand Chartereds at three pounds ten. There were his predictions, and Jameson's, of a speedy South African federation with Rhodesia in it. It was urgent that the revolution should be brought to a head. Yet, despite all sorts of understandings and promises, first Ripon, and now Chamberlain, sat there in the Colonial Office and made difficulties about giving Rhodes the Protectorate.

In his necessity, in his perplexity, Rhodes thought of a new scheme. Did he really need the whole of the Protectorate? Would not a mere passage to that striking-spot they were after be enough?

He was busy in the Cape. Jameson was busy in Rhodesia. Rhodes sent Dr. Rutherfoord Harris, the South African secretary of the Chartered Company, to England to tell Chamberlain that the company required a strip of land along the Protectorate border for reasons of railway construction.

Harris was joined in his campaign by several English Chartered representatives.

Rhodes' old friend Shippard was still Commissioner of British Bechuanaland. While Harris was seeing Chamberlain, Shippard and Frankie Rhodes were seeing the Bechuanas about a site for Jameson's camp.

III

All the company wanted, Harris explained to Chamberlain, was a strip just six miles wide, and, in return, they would make reserves for the natives, they would forego the annual railway subsidy promised them by Ripon, and they would save Britain much expense in connection with her Bechuanaland police by themselves maintaining a police force to guard their railway construction parties.

It was in August Harris saw Chamberlain, and he then, as he afterwards testified at the Raid Enquiry, "referred to the unrest at Johannesburg, and added a guarded allusion to the desirability of a police force being near the border." . . .

Chamberlain, at the Enquiry, here intervened, saying he did not deny Harris' statements, but neither had he understood his confidences, nor had he allowed him to continue them.

To this Harris countered that he had also explained everything to Chamberlain's confidential assistant, who had soon after died. So, for that matter, compelled by her suspicious questioning, had he explained everything to Miss Flora Shaw, a journalist on *The Times* and the first person to scent a connection between the trouble on the Rand and the six-mile railway strip in the Protectorate.

This lady, afterwards Lady Lugard, the wife of the Administrator of British Nigeria, was Rhodes' friend, and the article on Rhodes in the *Encyclopædia Britannica* is by her. She now, on Harris' invitation, became the link between the conspirators and the Colonial Office. Various people in England began to hear this or that about the six-mile strip. *The Times* correspondents were given warnings.

It was while Harris was waiting to know about the strip that there occurred something which made Chartereds rise, which made de Beers and other shares in Rhodes' companies also rise, which pushed into the background the Uitlanders' grievances, Jameson's preparations, the six-mile strip, the very revolution itself. During the months of September and October there was a prospect of war between England and the Transvaal.

IV

It was not without justice the Uitlanders were always complaining about the heavy railway rates. Kruger was doing whatever he could to shut out British goods.

There were two routes from the coast to Johannesburg: one from the Cape through the Orange Free State, and one from Delagoa Bay. Where each line met the Transvaal border, the Netherlands Railway Company, to whom Kruger had given the railway monopoly, continued it. A distance of fifty miles separated Johannesburg from the Free State terminus on the Vaal River border. And now what Kruger had done was, first, to make the rates on the Transvaal section of the Cape line so prohibitive that it could not compete against the Delagoa line, and, later, when, in desperation, the Cape merchants sent their goods by waggon from the Free State terminus to Johannesburg, to close the drifts by which the waggons crossed the Vaal River, and so shut them out altogether.

And by doing this Kruger, it was contended, broke that clause of the London Convention according to which he might not discriminate against goods coming from any part of the British dominions.

Chamberlain sent ultimatums to Kruger. Rhodes arranged with Chamberlain that the Cape would share with England the expense of a war. Troopships on their way to India were told to call at the Cape. It was now shares rose so spectacularly. . . . Kruger climbed down.

306

He climbed down. He opened the drifts. War was averted. Shares fell. Back again Rhodes was compelled to the revolution business.

He had one comfort. On October 18th, in the midst of all the war talk, the company had been given formal authority over a six-mile railway strip along the Transvaal border. At a place called Pitsani, about a hundred and eighty miles from Johannesburg, Jameson, drifts or no drifts, was mobilizing his men. Whichever happened, war or revolution, he intended to be ready.

v

While Jameson was collecting his forces, the Reformers at Johannesburg were no less busy. They were holding meetings, delivering speeches, passing resolutions, forming committees, selecting leaders, making decisions, inspiring the newspapers, and penning a truly magnificent declaration of their rights.

It took the form of a manifesto that was to be delivered by Charles Leonard, the chairman. It was several newspaper columns long, and it began:

"If I am deeply sensible of the honour conferred upon me by being elected chairman of the National Union, I am profoundly impressed with the responsibilities attached to the position. The issues to be faced in this country are so momentous in character—" and so on.

It is perhaps not surprising that the contemporaries of Mr. Leonard did not think much of Rhodes as a speaker.

With the Manifesto, Leonard and a companion now travelled down to Cape Town to see Rhodes. They read it to him. Rhodes leaned against the mantelpiece, smoking a cigarette—

one might suggest, several cigarettes. He said nothing until they were four lines from the end, when he suddenly turned round at the words "Free trade in South African products." "That is what I want," he said. "That is all I ask of you."

Over what had Rhodes been brooding while they read him the long story of their disappointed hopes, their tragic plight, and their just demands?

He added: "If you people get your rights, the Customs Union, Railway Convention and other things will come in time."

They asked him then, the emissaries, how he hoped to recoup himself for the money he was spending that they should have those rights. He gravely replied that he had large interests in the country and "would be amply repaid if living conditions were improved."

That was all Rhodes wanted.

VI

Yet even the Manifesto was not the most striking piece of literature produced by the Reformers. When, towards the end of November, Jameson came down from Pitsani to make final preparations at Johannesburg, true inspiration fell on the Reformers—from what source is not clear. In one blow the world should hear of their terrible situation and the Chartered directors be made to realize Jameson's knightly compulsion.

What they proposed to do—what they did do—was to write Jameson a Letter of Invitation, a letter begging him to come to their assistance. It was a letter without a date, but the date was to be filled in when the time arrived for Jameson to join them in Johannesburg. It was to be the reason for his joining them. But he was not to use it, he was not to come, the Reformers finally arranged, until they sent for him.

As the rising, they now decided, was to take place either on December 28th, or on January 4th, the letter, written in November, was provisionally dated December 20th. According to the Reformers, it "was to be used only privately and in case of necessity." It has, however, no suggestion at all of a personal appeal. This is the way it goes:

DEAR SIR,
The position of matters in this state has become so critical that we are assured that at no distant period there will be a conflict between the Government and the Uitlander population. It is scarcely necessary for us to recapitulate what is now a matter of history; suffice it to say that the position of thousands of Englishmen and others is rapidly becoming intolerable. . . .

This private letter, in short, is twin brother to the great Declaration of Rights. It is in the celebrated Manifesto style. It is even more impassioned, and, naturally, it is appropriate to the occasion.

The Government [it goes on] has called into existence all the elements necessary for armed conflict. . . . What will be the condition of things here in the event of a conflict? Thousands of unarmed men, women, and children of our race will be in the greatest peril. We cannot contemplate the future without the gravest apprehensions. All feel that we are justified in taking steps to prevent the shedding of blood and to insure the protection of our rights.
It is under these circumstances that we feel constrained to call upon you to come to our aid should a disturbance arise here. The circumstances are so extreme that we cannot but believe that you will not fail to come to the rescue of people who will be so situated. . . .

Several copies were made.

It was with this comforting, protecting letter Jameson returned to continue his preparations.

The people at Johannesburg lacked an equal sense of comfort and protection. While they had been producing literature, what had Jameson been doing? He had promised them fifteen hundred men. It was not till this November meeting they heard that he did not hope to start with more than eight hundred or a thousand. They had expected so many rifles, cartridges, and Maxims to be smuggled in by de Beers, like Ali Baba's forty thieves, in oil-drums. The slowness with which these munitions came dribbling in to Johannesburg, to be hidden there in one of Rhodes' mines, was bitterly disheartening. Jameson had suavely told them that as long as there were men and arms enough to take the fort at Pretoria, what more did they need? And what more, it is true, did they need?

They couldn't say. They merely knew they were unhappy. This whittling down seemed to be a bad sign. They did not like it. They did not like Jameson, either—not at the moment. He was taking too much on himself. After all, whose revolution was it, theirs or his? Was he assisting the Reformers, or they him? One might think, from his manner, that the Reformers existed merely to help the Chartered Company.

Nor did they like his brisk habits. For years now they had gone their way, alternating their protests and petitions with gamblings on the Stock Exchange or race meetings. It was, one might say, that final touch to bliss: this anger to which they could stir themselves by remembering their grievances. They had learnt the benefit of ill, "That better is by evil still made better," and

Sick of welfare found a kind of meetness
To be diseased ere that there was true needing.

They had spoken of risings and revolutions before Jameson
and Rhodes had come in 1894 to Johannesburg. Where was
the hurry? The market was booming. Why this impetuosity?
Like a tornado Jameson and Rhodes had blown in and whirled
them through the air.

And to what were they now committed? Who could tell its
result? What would even a successful revolution do for them?
Who could say the decorum of a good Government would
make for their greater happiness? Did they, in their hearts,
want a good Government? What, in fact, was a good Government? They had licence. Did they need liberty? And the market
so active!

In bewildered excitement they found themselves being rushed
towards finality. The doings of the month of December were
terrific. More committees were formed. More meetings were
held. More petitions indited. More deputations sent to Kruger.
More emissaries sent to Rhodes. An intelligence department
was created. A code was arranged. The busiest of all affairs
was naturally the Intelligence Department. Everywhere strong
men, not so silent as they might have been, were rushing by
train, horse, or bicycle. Along all the wires telegrams in code
were buzzing.

The code fascinated them. If there was one thing they really
enjoyed, it was the code. Jameson's Intelligence and Commissariat Department, whose head was a Kimberley friend, Dr.
Wolff, became in the code the Rand Produce and Trading
Company, and Dr. Wolff was the partner. Jameson himself
was, sometimes, the Veterinary Surgeon, in which case his men

311

were horses; or else he was the Contractor, in which case his men were "boys," and his business, railway construction.

Or, again, the revolution was a polo tournament, and then the revolutionaries were horses or betting sums. Most frequently, however, the revolution was a directors' meeting or a shareholders' meeting or a flotation; whereupon the Reformers naturally became our foreign supporters, and the rank and file on either side, shares or subscribers or shareholders, and the High Commissioner, the chairman. Even the Boers were most appropriately the opposition Boer shareholders. The Transvaal Boer opposition shareholders, Rutherfoord Harris once wired, were holding a meeting on the Limpopo River and at Pitsani—for the benefit, no doubt, of the locusts. . . .

There were, however, occasions—and particularly in December, after Rutherfoord Harris returned from England and put a really imaginative mind to the code, when messages were sent that nobody understood—not even the Boers. He sent, for instance, one urgent telegram about the veterinary and his horses, signed Godolphin, which only the events it foreshadowed duly interpreted. Who was Godolphin? It wasn't in the code. Did anyone remember that Godolphin was Shippard's second Christian name? Still, it wasn't Shippard sent the telegram. It was Harris. Harris, quite recently Ichabod, had suddenly become Godolphin. . . .

But there was one really troublesome affair—the question of a flag. Under which flag should the revolution take place? The English demanded the Union Jack—and particularly because of Majuba. The Colonials were against the Union Jack, for they were afraid this might afterwards mean direct British rule. The Americans and Continentals certainly did not want the Union Jack.

In fact, what the Reformers really wanted was—well, what should they want but the good old Transvaal flag? Were they not Reformers? Wasn't their object—not change but reform? Far indeed was it from their minds "to deprive the Boer of his independence or the state of its authority." Far indeed. They craved merely what they had always craved—the things they had, only more of them.

So now Rhodes having thoroughly understood, from their Manifesto, why exactly he was making a revolution, more emissaries were sent down to Cape Town to consult him about a flag. They returned to Johannesburg with the reassuring news that Rhodes considered the matter of a flag a relatively unimportant one.

But did he? Rhodes had answered Harris, while Harris was in England: "I, of course, would not risk everything as I am doing except for the British flag." On whose behalf was Harris enquiring? It has not been declared. It would be interesting to know. . . . As for Jameson, the Reformers might, said Jameson, be indifferent, but he unequivocally demanded the Union Jack.

That meant another journey to Cape Town.

The new envoy—he was the correspondent of *The Times*—found Rhodes at Groote Schuur, entertaining, as was now his custom, a number of guests. Rhodes dragged him away to see his hydrangeas. "Quick! What is it?" The envoy said it was that the revolutionaries would just as soon not rise at all as rise under the British flag. "All right," said Rhodes. "If they won't go into it, they won't. I'll wire to Jameson to keep quiet."

And then whom should *The Times* correspondent meet on the train back to Johannesburg but Dr. Harris, with the information that Rhodes would not hear of a rising except under the

British flag: he had merely said it didn't matter about the flag in order to pacify the objectors.

What were the Reformers to make of such news? Was the revolution on or was it off? There were many who felt that, what with munitions, flags, and Jameson's impatience, their dearest desire was to scrap the whole Chartered coöperation scheme, start over again from the beginning, and manage everything in the good old way they understood. To ward off a climax just a little longer they told the Charterlanders there was one thing on which they absolutely insisted—the intervention, on their behalf, of the High Commissioner. No High Commissioner, no revolution. He and Rhodes were to leave Cape Town for Johannesburg on the day of the rising. They wanted this assurance.

Beit answered them. "Chairman starts immediately flotation takes place," he wired, ready to promise Robinson would do anything Rhodes asked him.

But the Reformers were still not happy. They sent two more emissaries to Rhodes to tell him so—to explain how wrong they felt everything to be. In the meantime, as it was already Christmas Day, the provisional date of December 28th was definitely abandoned, and the date for the rising and the seizure of the Pretoria fort now remained January 4th. And, in order to throw the Boers off the scent, a meeting was announced for January 6th.

VII

There was another reason why the revolution could not take place on December 28th. The Christmas-New Year week was race week. Would not a revolution absolutely ruin race week?

314

Frankie Rhodes sent an urgent telegram: "Tell Dr. Jameson the polo tournament here is postponed for one week, as it would clash with race week." . . . "Surely," wired Jameson back, so exasperated that he could no longer trouble himself to be secretive—"surely in your estimation do you consider races is of the utmost importance compared to immense risks of discovery daily expected, by which under the circumstances it will be necessary to act prematurely?" . . .

Prematurely! For Heaven's sake, not prematurely!

The latest emissaries had hardly left for Cape Town to see Rhodes when the Reformers decided once for all that they were not going on with the Rhodes-Jameson program, that the meeting announced for January 6th should take place on January 6th as a final demonstration to Kruger (no blind), and that two messengers should at once post across country by horse and special train to stop Jameson.

The three days before Christmas were spent by Jameson and the Reformers in sending telegrams: He was coming! He must not come! He was coming! Oh, let him not come!

And now from every quarter echoes were reaching Jameson: He must not come! Let him not come!

Sunday arrived, the 29th, the day after the first provisional date of the rising, and it brought Johannesburg two telegrams—a reassuring one from the Cape Town emissaries, "In view of changed condition, Jameson has been advised accordingly." And one from Jameson, "I shall start without fail tomorrow night."

Both telegrams had been sent on Saturday. So this Sunday night, if he were not stopped, Jameson would set out.

But, of course, he would be stopped. Any time after the dispatch of his telegram he would get the warnings of Rhodes, of Harris, of the Reformers, of the cross-country messengers. And certainly, then, he would not start.

The last few days of December were occupied by the Reformers, not only in telegraphing, but in holding meetings and sending deputations to Kruger. People began to leave Johannesburg. The Manifesto was published in Johannesburg and in Rhodes' other newspapers. Rhodes now controlled wholly, or in part, all the important newspapers in South Africa. Nothing hindered the public utterances of the Reformers on platform or paper. They libelled President, Executive, and Judiciary and were not apprehended. They called on the armies of England to come to their aid: Pretoria suffered it.

Would days so glorious, a Government so divinely apathetic, return after the revolution?

If only Jameson would not rescue them!

CHAPTER ' 2 8

THE RAID

I

SOMEWHERE about this time Rhodes must have awakened, cold and weak, but once more clear in his mind, from his long delirium. The Reformers, the revolution, the Manifesto, the Letter of Invitation, the Intelligence Department, the flag, race week, the oil-drums, the six-mile strip, Charles Leonard, Frankie, Dr. Jameson, Dr. Harris, Dr. Wolff —was it on these—was it, after twenty years among the exultant gods, on such as these his schemes, his dreams, his name, the very meaning of his life depended?

Until the 28th he had tried to convince, not only himself, but others, that this world of delusion was the solid earth. "My judgment is it is a certainty," he had cabled to Harris just before Harris' departure from England—in answer again to whose enquiry? From Flora Shaw he had received heartening news: "Chamberlain sound in case of interference European Powers, but have special reasons to believe wishes you must do it immediately." . . . Though, also, news not so heartening: "Delay dangerous. Sympathy now complete, but will depend very much upon action before European Powers given time to enter a protest, which, as European situation considered serious,

317

might paralyze Government. General feeling on Stock Market very suspicious."

Delay dangerous. Still, sympathy now complete. Surely one could go on with that reassurance. On December 27th Rhodes wired to Jameson not to be "alarmed at our having six hundred men at Pitsani . . . we have a right to have them. . . . If people are so foolish as to think we are threatening the Transvaal, we can't help that." Even on the 28th he was still begging Frankie to "keep the market firm"—to stiffen the wavering Reformers, and promising Jameson that everything would be all right if he would only wait.

But that was the end. Too many things were happening on the 28th. The Reformers' deputies were telling him they were not prepared to go on, and, simultaneously, Jameson was telegraphing that he was leaving. On the one hand, the Chartered people were expecting a rising on January 4th to save the market. And, on the other hand, Chamberlain, on whose support he had relied, was cabling to the High Commissioner that, concerning this "endeavour . . . to force matters to a head by some one in the service of the Company advancing from Bechuanaland Protectorate with police . . . intimate to Rhodes that, in your opinion, he would not have my support and point out consequences which would follow."

To this Rhodes cabled Flora Shaw: "Inform Chamberlain that I shall get through all right if he supports me, but he must not send cables like he sent to the High Commissioner in South Africa. Today the crux is I shall win and South Africa will belong to England." And, again, presumably after seeing the Reformers' delegates and hearing once more their difficulties about the flag, race week, and the High Commissioner's intervention: "Unless you can make Chamberlain instruct the High

318

Commissioner to proceed at once to Johannesburg, the whole position is lost. High Commissioner would receive splendid reception and still turn position to England's advantage, but must be instructed by cable immediately. The instructions must be specific, as he is weak and will take no responsibility."

But that was the last effort. Then reality struggled through fancy. The Reformers were failing him. Chamberlain was failing him. Only Jameson was still with him, and that, in truth, was the greatest failure of all. It was the solitary clinging of the too passionate adherent when fortune and the jolly company it has brought are together gone—it was the very emphasis of failure. To Jameson's message of that day: "Unless I hear definitely to the contrary, shall leave tomorrow evening . . ." Rhodes answered, "You must do nothing till all is clear." "Shall leave tonight for the Transvaal," was Jameson's simple retort next day. But Rhodes did not at once get that telegram. And when he replied, saying: "Things in Johannesburg I yet hope to see amicably settled, and a little patience and common sense are only necessary. On no account whatever must you move. I most strongly object to such a course," it was too late. Two things had happened to complete Rhodes' ruin: In the Johannesburg office of the Intelligence Department Dr. Wolff had taken a holiday, and, simultaneously, in the Cape Town office of the Intelligence Department Dr. Harris had also taken a holiday, so no one duly received Jameson's final message. That was the first thing. And the second thing was that Jameson did not get Rhodes' emphatic prohibition, for by the time it was sent the telegraph wires to Cape Town had been cut. The only wires that had not, in the interests of secrecy, been cut were the wires to Pretoria. For, naturally, before Jameson left there was much drinking to the success of the campaign (the talk is that waggon-loads of whisky and thirty-six cases of champagne had been distributed among the men with leave to get drunk for three days), and the trooper deputed to cut the wires to Pretoria went forth and methodically cut and buried the barbed wires of a farmer's fence.

Accordingly, the only person who knew all about Jameson's movements was President Kruger in Pretoria.

II

Rhodes walked up and down his bedroom that Sunday, caged in fear, hoping Jameson had got his wire, hoping he would not move, afraid he had moved, and seeing before him the ruin not only of Rhodes the man, but of Rhodes the empire-builder. Schreiner, his Attorney-General, came to warn him not to see too much of the Reformers. "People will be saying you are mixed up in the affair."

Should he tell him? Had Jameson left or had he not?

"Oh, that's all right," said Rhodes.

Next morning telegrams came to Schreiner over the restored Mafeking wire, and he went again to Groote Schuur to see Rhodes. Rhodes was not to be found. It is generally said he was wandering about the mountain. But it is also said, without precise description, that he was having a heart-attack. In the evening a message came for Schreiner, and a guide with a lantern to conduct him through the dark woods to Groote Schuur.

He found Rhodes in his study—a man he had never seen before, a man utterly different. He had not opened his mouth, Schreiner afterwards told the Cape Committee of Enquiry, he had not spoken, when Rhodes said: "Yes, yes, it is true. Old Jameson has upset my apple-cart. It is all true."

"I said," Schreiner went on to tell the committee, "I had some telegrams."

"He said: 'Never mind. It is all true. Old Jameson has upset my apple-cart.'

"I was staggered. I said, 'What do you mean?' . . .

"He said: 'Yes, it is true, he has ridden in. Go and write out your resignation. Go. I know you will.'

"I asked, 'Why did you not say anything to me yesterday when I was here?'

" 'I thought I had stopped him. I sent messages to stop him and did not want to say anything about it if I stopped him.'

" 'Why do you not still stop him? Although he has ridden in, you can still stop him.'

" '. . . Poor old Jameson. Twenty years we have been friends, and now he goes in and ruins me. I cannot hinder him. I cannot go in and destroy him.'

"He was really broken down," said Schreiner. "He was broken down. He was not the man who could be playing that part. He was broken down. . . . He was absolutely broken down in spirit, ruined. . . ."

III

Jameson himself was having his troubles that Monday night, but he little understood even then what was before him.

He had set out on his ride for the simple reason that he could no longer wait. He was wild with impatience. His position was becoming not merely untenable, but ridiculous: drilling his troops there at Pitsani, with the Boers knowing why, with the uncertain, sun-parched men themselves gradually drifting away. He was maddened by the irresolution of the Reformers: their delays, as he wired Rhodes, meant only one thing—fear. He was angry even with Rhodes: "Rhodes," he told one of the cross-country messengers, "has cold feet along with his Johannesburg friends." So had Chamberlain, it seemed, cold feet. Seventeen telegrams (including, says Wilfrid Blunt, one from Queen Victoria) came to Jameson from various people who had cold feet.

Jameson himself had no fear; he hadn't cold feet. There is one thing no one has ever said against Jameson—that he had fear. As for cold feet, so far was he from having cold feet, he was dancing on coals, he was burning to get away.

Nor did he think he could fail. Three weeks before the Raid he told a friend that "anyone could take the Transvaal with half a dozen revolvers." And he was sure, as he afterwards said, that with success would come forgiveness.

He rode forth. He had not the fifteen hundred men originally promised to the Reformers; nor the eight hundred or a thousand men he had spoken of in November; nor yet the seven hundred he later, on his way, announced by telegram: "The Contractor has started on the earthworks with seven hundred boys, hopes to reach the terminus on Wednesday"; nor even the six hundred men concerning whom Rhodes had wired him. In the end a number of men had refused to fight otherwise than under the Queen's orders, and so Jameson, seeing himself soon left with no men at all, had ridden out from Pitsani with under five hundred followers.

But how full of righteousness, courage, and good whisky were those five hundred. For days they had toasted success to one another. Sir John Willoughby, Jameson's assistant against the Matabele and in command here, had congratulated them

322

on their smart appearance and hoped they would give a good account of themselves. Jameson had stirringly addressed them and read them a part of the Letter of Invitation: "Thousands of unarmed men, women, and children of our own race will be at the mercy of well-armed Boers. . . . We cannot but believe that you and the men under you will not fail to come to the rescue of people who will be so situated." . . . Great melting hearts. Thunderous applause. God save the Queen. Pitsani in the middle of summer, the hot sand, no hills, no trees—Bechuanaland.

They were still cheering when they rode through the streets of Mafeking, followed by their eight Maxims, their three machine-guns, their six Scotch carts, and their Cape cart, and so announced the news that next morning was telegraphed to Schreiner. They did not cheer again.

IV

There was hardly a thing that failed to go wrong. They had provisions for one day. After that they had to depend on Dr. Wolff's commissariat. And the food for men and horses did duly meet them; it kept on meeting them; it met them every twenty miles or so, but as they were allowed only half an hour's pause each time for resting and eating, they merely, as often as not, threw themselves down in their sweating weariness and tried to get a few minutes' sleep, and made no attempt to eat. The horses, too, never of the best, were exhausted. The remounts were unsuitable, and some were not used. They thought they had cut the wires. How was it they were always hearing about Boers—bands of them, hundreds of them, now ahead, now behind, along their path?

On Monday night, just about the time Rhodes was saying

to Schreiner, "Old Jameson has upset my apple-cart. . . . It is all true. Old Jameson has upset my apple-cart," just about then two Boer messengers were asking Jameson, on behalf of their commandant, why he was breaking the law. On Monday, too, the High Commissioner, advised by Hofmeyr, was instructing the Resident Commissioner at Mafeking to tell the raiders "that this violation of a friendly state is repudiated by Her Majesty's Government, and that they are rendering themselves liable to severe penalties."

On Monday night, again, Kruger was issuing a proclamation calling upon "every peaceful inhabitant of Johannesburg, of whatsoever nationality he may be," to support him, and upon persons, evil-intentioned or not, to remain within the pale of the law; he was offering to protect life and property in Johannesburg, and still . . . "to take into consideration all grievances . . . and to submit the same to the people of the land without delay for treatment."

On Monday Shippard (yes, he was here, too) was saying to the Reformers: "Whatever may be your other aspirations, you have a great duty to that man and his gallant companions, and under the circumstances it is your duty to lay down your arms as men of honour." By "that man and his gallant companions" he meant Jameson and the raiders.

v

And the Reformers themselves? What were the Reformers doing this busy Monday night?

What should they be doing? They were arranging a committee, of course—the very committee of committees, the absolute queen ant of committees: the Reform Committee itself—

324

sixty-four strong, and all of them, in due course, to be lodged in gaol.

And then, besides, they were also forming subcommittees.

VI

And was Dr. Harris idle on Monday? By no means. Instructed by Rhodes, hardly, at this moment, sane, he was cabling to Flora Shaw the Letter of Invitation, that it might be published in *The Times*. On his own initiative, however, he was altering the provisional date of December 20th to December 28th—a date which made it impossible for Jameson to have received by post or messenger this letter that, on Sunday, he read to his troops. Another letter, dated December 29th, was found by the Boers and brought forward as evidence against its signatories.

Next day Harris cabled to Flora Shaw, "You can publish Letter."

The Letter appeared in *The Times* on New Year's day of 1896. It had the effect for which Rhodes had hoped. The heart of England burst out in flares of anger, sympathy, and admiration—anger against the cruel Boers; sympathy for their helpless victims; admiration for their noble rescuers.

This was Wednesday, the day on which the Contractor, having started on his earthworks, was to have reached the terminus.

VII

Jameson did not reach his terminus on Wednesday, despite his anxiety "to come to the rescue of my fellow men in their

325

extremity" (so ran his answer to the High Commissioner's warning proclamation); despite a letter from those unfortunates themselves, saying he was a fine fellow and they would send out to meet him and duly drink a glass with him. . . . An entrancing picture: the victorious rescuer. The accompanying cavalcade. The welcome. The toasts. God Save the Queen in Johannesburg. . . . But Jameson was not there that Wednesday, because he had other engagements to fulfil. At a village twenty miles from Johannesburg, appropriately named Krugersdorp, Jameson fought the Boers and was compelled to retreat. Next day he found himself manœuvred into a trap by a force two or three times as large as his own, and had to hoist the white flag. His hungry and exhausted men stacked their arms and dropped to sleep where they had fought—on the open veld in the hot morning sun.

Jameson's surrender asked for safe conduct for his forces. The Boer commandant accepted his surrender on those terms.

The Boer losses were nine killed and wounded, Jameson's fifty-eight.

The prisoners could barely sit their stumbling horses as they were escorted into Krugersdorp by the Boers—farmers in the clothes of farmers. They had not eaten for twenty-four hours. They "devoured with ravenous hunger" the food their captors gave them. Jameson was hooted.

VIII

In Johannesburg the Reformers had seen the old year out by closing the mines, shutting the bars, distributing three thousand rifles among twenty thousand volunteers, placing women and children in safety, and collecting money to support a campaign. They were hurriedly rising. The matter of the flag had not yet been settled, but they had been suddenly inspired to rise under the Transvaal Flag—flown upside down to express their ideal of reform.

They heard with derision Kruger's offer to remit taxes on food, but agreed to a twenty-four-hour armistice for further negotiation. Had they even wanted to, they were thus prevented from going, at the crucial time, to Jameson's assistance, and Frankie Rhodes was against the armistice. "My view," he wrote in a postscript to the letter that comforted Jameson with the assurance that he was a fine fellow—"my view is that they are in a funk at Pretoria." Yet—so much for Frankie's view—on that very day the German Consul-General at Pretoria, presenting the Kaiser's compliments, had asked if he might bring up some German marines from Delagoa Bay to defend his consulate, and Kruger, laughing, had offered him the protection of fifty of his burghers.

And why was Kruger laughing? How could he be so lavish with his burghers? Was he not concerned about his unprotected fort, his arsenal? "Nothing in the world," writes Sir Percy Fitzpatrick, "could have saved it [the fort]—except what did." While the Reformers were delaying their revolution on account of race week, Boers from all over the country had congregated in Pretoria to celebrate Nachtmaal. Kruger had all the defence he could possibly need. The moral is beautiful.

The Letter of Invitation was in *The Times*, wringing the heart of England, Jameson was on his way to defeat at Krugersdorp, when a Reform deputation opened the new year in Pretoria by (quite seriously this time) putting the Uitlanders' grievances before a Government Commission that had offered the Reformers an olive branch. And for whom, asked the Commissioners, did the deputation speak? What was its authority? It spoke, said the deputation, proudly, for every member of the Reform Committee: here were the names. The Commissioners expressed their thanks. It was the evidence they needed, the only evidence they were ever to have, concerning the exact composition of the Reform Committee. And it was while the deputation was thus engaged in giving itself away that news came of the High Commissioner's proclamation which Jameson had turned aside, saying he must rescue his fellow men, the proclamation which had called on him, under pain of penalty, to retire, and on all British subjects in the South African Republic to discountenance his violation of the territory of a friendly state.

The Reformers honorably guaranteed "with their persons, if necessary," that, provided the Government allowed Jameson to come in unmolested, "he would leave again peacefully with as little delay as possible." Jameson was, just then, engaged in rescuing them.

Dr. Harris was still cabling cheerful information to England, operations on the Johannesburg Stock Exchange were in full swing, when next morning the news came of Jameson's surrender. But the first man to receive the news held it back a little for the necessary purpose of first disposing of some shares.

CHAPTER ˈ 29

THE FALL OF RHODES

I

WHAT had happened—was happening—was going to
happen? No one knew. There were men on the very
Reform Committee itself who did not know, never had known,
and to this day do not. "And what took place then? No, I
really can't say. I don't suppose I was at that meeting." . . .
"The flag? Was there trouble about a flag? I don't remember." . . . "Why did I join? Well, I was young. I wanted
the fun." The present-day recollections of many Uitlanders
quite bear out the discovery Arnold Bennett made when he
wrote *The Old Wives' Tale*. People remember the little personal incidents, not the great historical facts. . . .

Now suddenly the air was charged with repudiations. The
rank and file of the Uitlanders repudiated the Reformers, crying: The gallant Jameson, their rescuer, why had not the Reformers gone to rescue their rescuer? The Reformers repudiated
Jameson: "The position taken up and maintained by them to
the end was that they were not responsible for Dr. Jameson's
incursion and were simply prepared to defend the town against
attack." Jameson repudiated the Reformers: he impugned their
courage. The Reformers repudiated one another: Where was
their leader, Charles Leonard? Why had Charles Leonard not

329

come back after his last mission to Rhodes? . . . He never did come back.

The High Commissioner, he who, at Rhodes' orders, was to have intervened after the revolution, repudiated Jameson and the Reformers, both together. The man who urged him to that repudiation was Hofmeyr, and Hofmeyr wired to Kruger repudiating "Jameson's filibusters."

"Filibustering," too, was the word Chamberlain used in warning the Chartered Company of England's repudiation of their charter, should it be found they had assisted Jameson. The Little Englanders repudiated not merely the Chartered Company, but the Rhodesians themselves. "If ever men died with their blood on their heads," wrote Labouchere, "they are the men who fell in this Raid, and if ever prisoners of war deserved scant mercy, Jameson and his comrades are those prisoners. They may thank their stars that they have fallen into the hands of men who are not likely to treat them as they themselves treated the Matabele wounded and prisoners."

And then the Kaiser leapt forward and, in congratulating Kruger on his stand against the "armed bands" and on "maintaining his independence," repudiated England. Whereupon everybody, from *The Times* in London to Hofmeyr in Cape Town, turned round and repudiated the Kaiser.

And once more the bowels of England were moved towards Jameson, and Alfred Austin, the new Poet Laureate, expressed its mood:

> "I suppose we were wrong, were madmen,
>   Still I think at the Judgment Day,
> When God sifts the good from the bad men,
>   There'll be something more to say.
> We were wrong, but we aren't half sorry,
>   And, as one of the baffled band,

I would rather have had that foray
      Than the crushings of all the Rand."

He meant he would rather have had the experiences here recorded than three thousand million gold pounds.

And Rhodes, reading the Kaiser's telegram, said to himself, and he said it, in effect, at the Raid Enquiry, and he said it, laughing, in due time, to the Kaiser himself, "This justifies me!"

But it never justified him with those who had always opposed him in England. It never justified him with those he had striven, for fifteen years, to make his brothers—the Boers of South Africa. It did not justify him with the friends and followers he had deceived. The people in South Africa whose affection and support he most craved repudiated Rhodes. Men who had not repudiated him after the Matabele War, nor in the days when he was corrupting their Parliament, repudiated him now. "Mr. Rhodes is unworthy of the trust of the country," said Merriman. Men who had always repudiated him, repudiated him the more. "Put money in thy purse, and then call it expansion of empire and the progress of civilization," said Harcourt.

The Bond members who had stood by him even against their own blood repudiated him.

Hofmeyr repudiated him. "If Rhodes is behind it, then he is no more a friend of mine."

II

They met the day after Rhodes' confession to Schreiner, and his instruction to him: "Go and write out your resignation.

331

Go." He had himself, the very next morning, tendered his resignation.

But that was not enough, Hofmeyr now told him. He must dismiss Jameson from his Administratorship, set the law against him, and altogether repudiate him.

It was the only repudiation that did not occur. "Jameson has been such an old friend. I cannot do it."

"I quite understand," said Hofmeyr. "You need say no more."

Rhodes *could* not do it. He was not in a position to do it.

A few days later a cousin of Hofmeyr's, whose intervention Rhodes had sought, wrote to Hofmeyr to "take pity. He does not defend himself. He admits he was wrong." Whereupon Hofmeyr drove out to Groote Schuur.

Rhodes' secretary has described how Rhodes spent the days immediately after the Raid—a disintegrated man, unable to collect himself or confront the life about him. He could not rest. He could do nothing but walk with his thoughts—staring vaguely at people who addressed him, looking unseeingly at the telegrams that came, one on another—walking continually.

He did not undress for forty-eight hours. He barely slept for five nights. At all hours of the night, there he was still walking. They heard him walking up and down his locked bedroom. But sometimes he broke into an endless monologue. A guest reports that one midnight Rhodes came into his room and for four hours did not cease speaking of Jameson. . . .

It was just after this period Hofmeyr went to see Rhodes, and found him—as one might imagine.

"What am I to do? Live it down? How can I? Am I to get rid of myself?"

He must have wanted to be told that he was not so bad, that all great men stumbled, that Hofmeyr, for one, still believed in him, that he was not to suffer so deeply: it would all blow over—such things as those.

But Hofmeyr, far from comforting, sombrely considered how, indeed, Rhodes could live down the Raid. He thought he might perhaps work out some sort of salvation by resigning from Parliament and exiling himself in Rhodesia for a term of years. After this probation he would have a chance to win back the Bond favour that he had now forfeited. Hofmeyr was to make this advice public in years to come. It *was* a sort of getting-rid-of-himself he recommended to Rhodes.

Even a smaller man, a man less maddened and sick, might have rejected, at such a moment, such advice. Rhodes had met Hofmeyr in humility. He seems to have sent him away with the impression that he had presumed to dictate to "a young king, the equal of the Almighty." The words are Hofmeyr's.

They did not meet again. Hofmeyr said he felt "as a man feels who suddenly finds that his wife has been deceiving him." And Rhodes, after hearing this too many times from too many people, interrupted one informant derisively: "Oh yes, I know —about the wife and so on."

Schreiner, indeed, wrote to him: "Whatever you suffer and whatever you seem to have lost or be losing, don't let them induce you to do anything small. You must go on living your life on big lines." But he refused, henceforth, to differentiate between all these too-virtuous people. In later years he went about telling election audiences how Schreiner and Merriman and Sauer were being "used" by Hofmeyr; they were no more

333

than his servants. They had to do as he told them. So had all that party: they had to vote, not according to their feelings, but according to Hofmeyr's orders. . . . And would his audience like to know the name Merriman himself had found for Hofmeyr? The Mole—that was what Merriman called him. "There is a little heap of ground thrown up which tells you he is somewhere near, but you never see him." And thus, said Rhodes, from underground, in back passages, Hofmeyr worked.

Rhodes went from platform to platform in the year 1898, deriding his old colleagues, "the men with whom he had once," as he said, "been friends together." These had ceased to be, after the Raid, his friends and colleagues, nor was Hofmeyr's little heap of ground ever again thrown up in his direction. He was also never again to address his audience as Prime Minister, or as an Independent who had the Bond and Hofmeyr behind him. "Dead flies cause the ointment of the apothecary to send forth a stinking savour; so doth a little folly him that is in reputation for wisdom and honour." Rhodes was rank in the nostrils of the men who had once worshipped him, they turned from him with compressed noses. In his need he found himself a new set of colleagues, he joined a new party called the Progressive Party, and the Bond was the party against which he worked. He was the god now of those he had once scorned— the Jingoes. And he found himself other friends. They say that a self-respecting man could not, in the days after the Raid, feel easy at Groote Schuur—the place was so full of panderers to his sore spirit, and Rhodes so contemptuously, even while he threw at them what they were seeking, emptied over them too the gall that filled and refilled him.

It seems as if Hofmeyr's advice to Rhodes to "Get thee to a nunnery, go. . . . To a nunnery go, and quickly, too," was the thing Rhodes needed to kick him into life again. He did, indeed, now set out for Rhodesia, but by no means in the spirit of repentance suggested by Hofmeyr. On the contrary. He was full of bravado. *The New York World* cabled to ask if he had declared South Africa independent, and what were his views? And he gave them a version of the situation which extremely annoyed Hofmeyr, and also told *The World* that the Uitlander population was "largely composed of Americans." And when, on his way north, he stopped at Kimberley and found that here he was still adored, he made what has been called his great "fighting speech," in which he rejected his friends' advice to retire and said his political life was only just begun. He did not, however, go on to Rhodesia, for while he was in Kimberley he received a cable from the Board of the Chartered Company calling him to London, and a week after seeing Hofmeyr for the last time he was on his way overseas. . . .

In September, 1895, during the talk of war over the Drifts crisis, Chartereds had stood at nine pounds. By December 28th, the first provisional date of the rising, they were down to five and a quarter pounds. On the same day notice was given that the five hundred thousand new shares at three and a half pounds, authorized the previous July, would be issued on January 8, 1896, and it was urgently hoped that the rising promised for January 4th would actually take place then, and a victorious result once more send up Chartered shares.

But since, so far from a rising taking place on January 4th,

Blunt was writing in his diaries: "Those blackguards of the Chartered Company in South Africa, under Dr. Jameson, have made a filibustering raid on the Transvaal and have been annihilated by the Boers, Jameson a prisoner. I hope devoutly he may be hanged"—since such was the news, Chartereds, on January 4th stood at three and five-eighths pounds. And Rhodes had not left for England in the middle of January when they were selling at three and one-eighth pounds, so that the people who had hoped last year to make a fortune by taking up the five hundred thousand Chartereds at three and a half pounds were in the position of losing now on the deal.

It was not a Rhodes with flags flying who this time went to meet his fellow directors. Whatever he might say to the workmen of de Beers, proud words would not restore his shareholders their money. And the very charter itself was being threatened by Hofmeyr and Chamberlain. Hofmeyr had vehemently demanded of Chamberlain "a radical change in the government of the territories under the rule of the B. S. A. Company, now that such a rule has proved to be a source of danger to the public peace of South Africa," and had asked for enquiry into "the conception and development of the conspiracy." And Chamberlain had meekly agreed to do anything—everything— "to prevent further embitterment of relations between British and Dutch"; his tone was very different from that strident voice in which he had addressed Kruger during the Drifts crisis. Over the Atlantic, like mournful doves, flew his messages, cooing conciliation. When Rhodes saw him now in England he reassured him about Rhodesia; that would not be taken out of his charge. But as to an enquiry—an enquiry could not be evaded.

And so the Chartered directors too requested Her Majesty's

Government "to institute a full enquiry into the circumstances attending the incursion of Dr. Jameson." Such a request looked well, and since the situation was not in their hands, it could do no harm.

In the meantime, the issue of the five hundred thousand new Chartereds brought them in the money to pay for their various liabilities, and they were also left with some cash in hand.

IV

Jameson had soon followed Rhodes to England. From Krugersdorp, after his capture, he had been sent, with his staff officers, to the Pretoria gaol. Despite the conditions of their surrender, they were to be shot, the rumours went. Hofmeyr wired to Kruger and the Chief Justice of the Transvaal for authorization to contradict these rumours, so "harmful to the Transvaal cause." "Rhodes retires as Premier and Chartered Company will be punished by England," he wired. "For God's sake," he wired to a violent Free Stater, ". . . drop all talk of shooting." Kruger says the burghers wanted to shoot down the rebels and he prevented them.

It was by Hofmeyr's arrangement with Kruger that the High Commissioner now journeyed to Pretoria to intervene— in circumstances, alas, how different from the Reformers' expectations of only a week ago. The result of the High Commissioner's mediation was that the Reformers surrendered on condition that Jameson and his men were turned over to the Imperial Government for punishment.

An amnesty was proclaimed for all but the ringleaders of the rebellion. The Reform Committee were put in gaol. Jameson and his officers were sent out of the country. The relieved

Chamberlain, having cabled to thank Kruger for his magnanimity, now began to instruct the High Commissioner to use firm language about the President's "neglect to meet the admitted grievances of the Uitlanders."

The Reformers were duly committed for trial and pleaded guilty. The result of the trial was that four out of the five signatories of the Letter of Invitation (Charles Leonard having left the country, never to return) were sentenced to death, but their sentences were the same afternoon commuted to sentences of fifteen years' imprisonment. The other members of the Committee were sentenced to two years' imprisonment, a fine of two thousand pounds each, failing which another year's imprisonment, and three years' banishment from the state.

There followed appeals for clemency by the sentenced and their friends—among others Barnato, who threatened to withdraw from the Transvaal, not only himself, but his expenditure of two hundred thousand pounds. Some rather unorthodox bargaining took place between Government and prisoners. All the prisoners, except one who had died, and one who became ill, and two who had refused to petition, were released on payment of fines and a promise not to "meddle" for a term of years in politics. The four leaders (Frankie Rhodes and Hays Hammond among them) were fined twenty-five thousand pounds each, and Rhodes paid their fines; but Frankie Rhodes would not undertake to give up meddling in politics (having now reason to believe himself a gifted statesman), and so he was banished. The others merely paid their original fines. The man who was ill duly pleaded not guilty, and was let off. The two who would not sign the petition were released, on Hofmeyr's advice, as a present to the Queen on her Diamond Jubilee.

Two months later Jameson and his principal officers were

338

committed for trial at Bow Street, London. They were then tried before a three-judge court presided over by Lord Russell of Killowen, who pinned a wavering jury down to a verdict of guilty. They were sentenced to various terms of imprisonment without hard labour, ranging from fifteen months to five months. They were sent, first, as ordinary convicts, to Wormwood Scrubs, but soon after, as first-class misdemeanants, to Holloway.

Jameson had ceased to be Administrator of Rhodesia in February. He lived to become Prime Minister of the Cape; a member of the National Convention that framed the Constitution of the Union of South Africa; leader of the Opposition in the Union Parliament; a baronet and a Privy Councillor. He lost not a friend through the Raid. And why the Boers, having triumphed all the way against him, did not laugh at the Raid must be sought for in reasons that concerned not only the Raid itself.

Earl Grey succeeded him in Rhodesia.

CHAPTER ، 30

THE MATABELE RISING AND HIS
REDEMPTION

I

BEHOLD, the hand of the Lord is upon thy cattle which
is in the field . . . there shall be a very grievous mur-
rain." However Jehovah might trouble his chosen, he remained
with them. Rhodes was not long to languish in shame. In the
grand old way there fell, for a sign, a wonder, and his redemption, a plague on Africa. It was such a plague, such a foul,
infectious, deathly cattle-pest, as the Egyptians had known in
the time of Moses. All Asia had known it since. Europe had
known it. They had known it again, a generation ago, in Egypt.
It was in Abyssinia in the year Rhodes' pioneers went to Mashonaland. Now, even while he was on his way back to Rhodesia
(still his Rhodesia) after one week's sojourn in England, it
appeared in Matabeleland. Within the year, of the hundred
thousand cattle in Matabeleland, five hundred were left. . . .

The year 1896 is remembered in South Africa as the year
of the rinderpest. The rinderpest was treated as veld fires are
treated when the grass is burnt down and a cordon of desolation
made to save the fire from reaching the grass. Infected cattle were
segregated; and not merely infected cattle, but infected herds.
Whole herds among which the rinderpest had been discovered,
and even herds among which it was merely feared, were taken

away, and sometimes all were killed, and, if they were not, the sick sickened the healthy, and they died just the same, except for a meagre few who recovered and were then considered to be "salted": they were safe, that is to say, against further infection. Nature had immunized them as, in that very year, man attempted to do, by following Nature and giving them mildly the disease itself.

But man had not learnt to do this before the land was desolated. The rinderpest which came to South Africa in 1896 is one of the godparents of the poor white. It marks the final calamity of the Kaffirs. Thousands of people, black and white, had nothing left of their beasts but the skins. In March the High Commissioner gave permission for the segregating and slaughtering of herds affected with rinderpest, and such few cattle as the Matabele had left to them after the war of 1893 were so segregated and slaughtered.

II

When Bryce visited Bulawayo in 1895, not two years after its occupation by Rhodes' settlers, he found that "everybody was cheerful because everybody" (and with good reason, he thought) "was hopeful." Bulawayo, standing, not exactly as Rhodes had romantically planned it, on the site of Lobengula's old kraal, for the gold reef was supposed to be under that, but two miles away—Bulawayo was prospering. Streets had been made wide enough (so Rhodes had decreed) for the turning around of an ox-waggon with its team of oxen. Quick-growing trees, by Rhodes' command, had been planted; they were already twelve or fifteen feet high. He had called for "Homes, more homes," in the country of his name, and brick houses

341

were appearing among the corrugated iron. A cricket-ground and a racecourse had been laid out. There was talk of an opera-house. Building sites had gone up to prices "which nothing," as Bryce says, "but a career of swift and brilliant prosperity could justify." For the Rhodesians were remembering the fortunes made out of property during the Kimberley boom. They had their eyes on Johannesburg. They dreamt of a new Rand going past Bulawayo, through the very heart of what had once been Lobengula's kraal.

And certainly gold was being found: not so much, perhaps, as in the days, four hundred years ago, when Vasco da Gama reported it to be the principal traffic in Mozambique, still, enough to keep them hopeful. The diggers were coming in daily with samples of ore. The farmers were coming in. The bars and shops were busy. The white man was a superman in this land of black men, a bearer of romance and a pilgrim of civilization. He was not merely an adventurer, a rough seeker after gold like the diggers of Klondyke and Ballarat. He had something of Rhodes' own spirit. He was a builder of empire, and conscious of it. He had actually a sort of breadth, an air, a quality.

He did not think of the native except as a tool. It was only two years since the Matabele had been despoiled of their land and cattle, and it never entered the mind of any Rhodesian that they might be other than satisfied with their lot. He had no fear of their resentment. And, certainly, if he had no fear of the proud and warlike Matabele, he had no fear of the meek Mashona. No one remembered that if there is a thing which outrages a native it is—not punishment or the natural results of defeat—but what he considers an injustice. The talk was that the Matabele themselves were happy to be free from the tyranny of Lobengula. The tradition was comfortably accepted, without any regard to circumstances, that a native tribe once conquered remained conquered.

It did not matter that there was conscription—often brutal —of able-bodied male labour at ten shillings a month; that the company took the natives' cattle—still as war payment—whenever they chose; and that, in the very year the white man settled in Mashonaland, locusts appeared for the first time, and now came regularly to eat up the young mealies, for which also the white man, as the Matabele believed, must be responsible.

Settlers lived on lonely farms or reefs and were not afraid. So unafraid were they, that Jameson hardly thought twice of taking all but forty-eight of the company's white police away with him to raid the Transvaal (the force had been increased again after the Matabele War).

But it was Jameson's departure with his policemen; his raid and the rising in Johannesburg; his ignominious defeat; the locusts; the conscription of men and cattle; the harsh administration; the memory of old days—it was finally the rinderpest; the consequent removing and killing of the few beasts left them; their famine—that maddened the natives to action. They could not understand—no one explained to them—this taking away, this wanton slaughter, except as another example of the white man's devilishness. Their prophet, who lived in a cave, their M'limo, told them to rise against the white people, and on March 20th, the day Rhodes landed at Beira, they rose. The Mashona (so much for Grey's pronouncement to the Chartered shareholders of their new-found happiness) joined their old enemies in attacking their saviours. On March 23rd the first white settler was killed. The savages spread themselves over the country, butchering in lonely places—unrecog-

343

nizably mutilating—white men and women and children. They did to death two hundred people.

III

Rhodes had come, as usual, with gifts for his Rhodesia. Past his private perturbations, he had thought to go by Egypt and there arrange, among other things, that Egyptian donkeys should be sent in substitution for the horses that another of Africa's plagues, the tse-tse fly, had wiped out in Rhodesia. Whatever he had lost, at least Rhodesia was left him: "My North" (he actually spoke these words)—"My North. They can't take that away. They can't change the name. Did you ever hear of a country's name being changed?"

And now Rhodesia—sinking already on account of the Raid and the loss of confidence in the company, was in further trouble, the worst trouble yet—blood trouble.

With malaria still on him, Rhodes joined a column marching to the rescue of his settlers. He little saw in this blood trouble the Lord's assistance.

There is a letter that, just about this time, he wrote to Harcourt. With it he enclosed a cable he had received concerning Harcourt's indictment of the raiders in the House of Commons. "The most brilliant women in society," writes A. G. Gardiner in his *Life of Harcourt*, "stood *en queue* to take their places in the ladies' gallery, and crowds of Stock Exchange men stood humbly below, waiting for a chance to get into the crowded galleries. Two great issues were at stake—the honour of the nation and the price of Chartereds, and there could be little doubt which issue was of most moment to the brilliant throng inside and outside the House."

344

Here is Rhodes' letter, and it reads strangely like the final letters of young men who have gone wrong and found the world too much for them. Such letters are written before suicide or battle. The writers say they have not been bad, but merely unfortunate or misunderstood. They ask for forgiveness and give it. If they have ruined their own lives, they offer advice to everybody else. If they have been bad, they tell other people to be good. They feel in these moments, with the painful blood bursting their hearts and heads, good themselves—Christlike, and as if they now understand everything. . . .

GWELO, MATABELELAND, May 13th, 1896.

The enclosed explains my letter. It has come just as we start to try and make a junction with Bulawayo. We are two hundred and fifty men and the Bulawayo column is five hundred. There are about six thousand natives between us and Bulawayo, and we may make a mess of it.

I would be sorry to think that you thought I was "capable but not honest". I have tried to unite South Africa, and no sordid motive has influenced me.

You might say why do I write, certainly not to mitigate your censure, but in case we come to grief I wish you to know that I feel that, whatever you have said you have said from a sense of public duty, and that I hope you will understand in the future that I understand the reasons of your censure, though bitter, and I am still pleased to think that you had an affection for me. But remove from your mind the idea of a sordid motive.

This letter is only written because I do not know what will happen during the week.   C. J. RHODES.

May 14th. We start in an hour. I am minded to tear this up, but the outlook is gloomy, and I would not like you to misunderstand me. If I get through, well, tear this up; if I do not, I think when you are sitting in that smoking-room at Rothschild's, you will be pleased to think that I understood your reasons, but I could not go out from here to an uncertainty without saying, blame me as much as you like, but do not do the cruel thing of attributing my conduct to sordid motives. Good-bye.

Had Harcourt received this letter by June 21st? If so, he was not moved by Rhodes' reiterated comprehension of his patriotic motives. For on that date he wrote to Chamberlain: "As long as Rhodes remains as managing director there can be no peace in South Africa. He is in his own person the red flag—perhaps I should say the black flag."

Nor, although Rhodes got through well enough, did Harcourt obey Rhodes' request to tear up his letter, so much more revealing than Rhodes himself appreciated, the most revealing letter—in its romanticism, its youthfulness—of all Rhodes' letters. The deliberate openness of his Open Letter to Stead does not so clearly exhibit him—just as the conscious autobiographies of writers show their inmost hearts less than the works in which they do not know that they are giving themselves away. . . .

Fighting took place and Rhodes was in it. Despite the Cape tradition that denies Rhodes' physical courage, his Rhodesians found him to be in these encounters cool (so they say) to the point of recklessness.

One may be romantic, yet truly express a state of mind. People who speak in terms of melodrama have quite often the sensations they so turgidly describe. It is necessary to look for truth beyond even taste. Rhodes felt innocent, noble and self-sacrificing; he appreciated his romantic situation; he was determined to justify himself; and he was now courageous because the drama of his life demanded heroism and, for all he knew, death. Down in his heart he may not have believed the words he wrote to Harcourt: "We may make a mess of it . . . In

346

case we come to grief . . . The outlook is gloomy . . . I
do not know what will happen during the week . . . If I get
through . . . If I do not"—but he thought he believed them,
and it was as a martyr-hero he went against the Matabele.

v

The starving, slaughtering Matabele hid among the hills of
the Matoppos, and from these desolate fastnesses, from secret
caves, came out to fight and kill. By July the terrified Rhodesians had prevailed against them not at all, and Imperial
troops were helping them. Within a fortnight the new force
had lost twenty per cent of its thousand men, and there was
talk of sending for five thousand more.

It meant ruin for the company. They had only just, through
their issue of the half million new shares at three pounds ten,
paid off, among other things, their liabilities on the Matabele
War of 1893, already what had been left over was gone, and
here they were faced with a fresh campaign that was costing
the company four thousand pounds a day, and that might, in
the end (so they feared), cost them anything up to five millions. It was not merely that they had the ordinary expenses
of a campaign: Providence, as Rhodes said, had sent them the
rinderpest, and the outcome of this, he said, would be the
swifter replacement of the trek-ox by the railway. In the meantime the nearest railway was six hundred miles away. Supplies
had to be brought by mule-waggon. Not only was food scarce,
but because the oxen were dead, the rate for bringing food by
mule-waggon was terrific. What was to be done? "Your list
of killed and wounded," Rhodes told the people of Bulawayo,
"is severe in the extreme. . . . Now we shall have to hunt the

347

Matabele in the bush and in the stones and in the kopjes, in a country nearly half the size of Europe. . . ." "I am here," he told them later, "and you have done me the favour of giving this country my name. My return for that will be to make this country as great as I can." . . .

He felt, to the point of passion, the responsibility he owed his settlers whom he had brought into this wilderness merely, it seemed, to be ruined and killed. There was his honour, his pride, so tragically reduced by the Raid, to make whole again. But five million pounds? Where was he to find five million pounds? His shareholders had lost on the January issue of new shares. He had borrowed one million two hundred and fifty thousand at five per cent. He would be compelled to issue new shares. Where was it all to end? How long would his shareholders, already shaken in their faith by the Raid, suffer this watering down of their possessions? They were even now complaining of the *way* these shares were being issued—so many set aside for secret underwriters who were selling behind their backs. Was ever a man in so suicidal a position?

Suicidal? We have seen Rhodes' romantic mood. It was the enlightening word. Let it be suicide or let it be redemption. Out of Rhodes' predicament was born a plan.

He would do with the Matabele what he had done with Groot Adrian de la Rey: "Blood must flow." . . . "Give me my breakfast, and then we can talk about blood."

VI

This was what Rhodes proposed to do: He proposed to go alone, and unarmed, among the Matabele, where they lay in the Matoppos, and talk to them. He had always held that

348

dealing was better than fighting. It was here not only better—it was the only course possible. However impractical it might seem, nothing was more practical, nothing else was practical at all. Soldiers could merely lose themselves in this wilderness of monotony. Machine-guns would not find the limit of its caves and fastnesses. Starvation might move the Matabele from their Matoppos, but Kaffirs can starve a long time before dying. The settlers would yield to final despair, and the Chartered Company go bankrupt before there arrived an end to this trouble.

He sent a young and devoted native, a Tembu who had fought against the Matabele and knew their ways, to find out what chance there was of dealing with the Matabele. It was Rhodes' hope that the starving men might want to deal, that they were fighting because they had no idea what else to do, because they were afraid even to surrender.

The Tembu, with field-glasses, a blanket, and a few days' food, set out. Two friends accompanied him. They walked among the hills by night.

VII

Rhodes remained waiting for them at the camp.

They returned on the sixth day with good news. Not all the chiefs were there, but such as were would meet Rhodes if he went to them with no more than three companions, and unarmed.

This was what had happened to the Tembu and his friends: Lying hidden, they had heard two Matabele women, on their way to fetch water, talking of their hunger and the troubles of the Matabele. The men had come out of their hiding-place and offered the women food, and told them of their mission, and asked them to report it to their chiefs. The Tembu had given the women a piece of his shirt for a flag, and, if they had a favourable answer from the chiefs, they were to raise this flag at a place agreed upon, and then the Tembu and his companions would go to meet the chiefs there. They would stay four days for an answer. No fighting would take place during those four days. If, at the end of this time, the flag did not appear, they would return to Rhodes and fighting would begin again.

They saw the flag on the fourth day, but no human being came forward, no chief to parley. Next morning, however, an old woman, a most ancient crone, one of Moselikatze's wives and Lobengula's stepmother, appeared through the bush. She was here to answer for the coming of the chiefs. They would come, she said, at noon.

This is the old woman with the bunched-together face and the rheumy slits of eyes and the arms like sapless branches and the hands like dead twigs and the empty sacks of breasts, whose portrait hangs in Rhodes' bedroom—the only portrait of a woman in Rhodes' house today, the only one he ever did have except a painting by Reynolds he had coveted as a youth and bought out of his wealth.

The chiefs came and told the Tembu they would meet Rhodes. . . .

There were men who thought that Rhodes should not go. They remembered what Dingaan had done to the Voortrekkers —the luring and the killing.

Rhodes said he had no such fears. He could not tell what their M'limo might induce them to do, but he was prepared to trust the Matebele.

With the three white men permitted him he set out on horse-back for the meeting-place. One of Rhodes' companions was that Colenbrander who had gone with Lobengula's *indunas* to England to protest against the Charter, and afterwards remained at Lobengula's kraal as the company's agent. He had since fallen out with the company, but Rhodes he could not resist, and he was the interpreter. Another of Rhodes' companions was Vere Stent, a journalist, who recorded the proceedings. The Tembu, on foot, guided them.

They entered the hills and passed through a cutting whose path lay between high-crested rocks on one side and, on the other, a wooded valley. Among the rocks they saw watching natives.

Their path led to a small open space surrounded by kopjes, and empty but for a few tree stumps and an ant-heap. There they stopped, undecided whether to remain on horseback or to dismount. "Dismount," said Rhodes. "Dismount, of course. It will give them confidence. They are nervous, too. How do they know we have not an ambush ready for them behind the hill?"

They dismounted, and sat down on the ant-heap to wait. Then a white flag appeared among the bush. Black men appeared. Men and flag came towards Rhodes. He turned with exultation towards his companions. "This is one of the moments in life that make it worth living."

There were twenty Matabele, chiefs and their attendants, and they planted the flag in the soft ground, and sat around Rhodes in a semicircle.

"Mehle 'mhlope," said Colenbrander for Rhodes—"The eyes are white," not flushed, that is to say, with passion, not, as the phrase goes, seeing red.

351

"Mehle 'mhlope, 'Nkosi, 'Nyamazane"—"Chief, Great Hunter."

RHODES: Is it peace?

SOMABULANE: It is peace, my father.

RHODES: Speak, Somabulane.

Somabulane spoke. Time is nothing to a native, and Somabulane gave Rhodes the saga, from its beginnings, of the Matabele. He himself, he said, had been one of Moselikatze's young men in those days when Moselikatze had fled from Chaka's wrath along a path of blood to a new home in the north. On that path they had fought black men and they had fought white men, and at Gebulawayo, the Place of Killing, they had finally rested. . . .

Lobengula had succeeded Moselikatze. Peace had come, happiness had come, but then the white men had come, too, and that was the end of peace and happiness.

For the white men had seen the gold in Lobengula's land, and whatever Lobengula could do for them it was not enough. When they approached him on their knees, begging him for his gold, he might treat them as a brother, and shelter them, and kill his oxen for them, and send them his young women, and offer them half his kingdom—it was not enough. They wanted everything. For only three years they had sat in the half of his kingdom he had given them. And then they had come between the Matabele and their justly punished vassals, the Mashona; they had brought their guns "that spit bullets as the heavens spit hail"; who were the naked Matabele to stand against these guns? . . . The white men had won the land from the Matabele as the Matabele had won it from the Maholi and the Mashona. Their king had been driven into exile. And the presents he had sent for peace offerings had been taken, but the peace had been refused him.

The white men were silent before Somabulane's truths. Rhodes told him to continue.

He spoke then of their present troubles, the tyranny of the native commissioners and the magistrates. How were they treating the Matabele? Like Mashona and Maholi, like dogs—the Amandabile, the sons of Kumalo, the Izulu—Children of the Stars—as dogs.

"You came. You conquered. The strongest takes the land. We understood. We lived under you.

"And you treated us as dogs. Should we not choose to die? Is it not better to be wiped out" (he passed his hand over his mouth and away, as they express annihilation) "than to live as dogs?"

"Ask them," said Rhodes to Colenbrander, "by whom and how they were made dogs."

By the native police (answered Somabulane), who raped their daughters, insulted their men, disdained their chiefs, offended their old women, collected taxes at the point of the assegai, and trod them into the earth. . . . By the native commissioners themselves. By the men above these.

"Once I myself visited Bulawayo. I came to pay my respects to the Chief Magistrate. I brought my *indunas* with me, and my servants. I am a chief. I am expected to travel with attendants and advisers. I came to Bulawayo early in the morning, before the sun had dried the dew, and I sat down before the courthouse, sending messages to the Chief Magistrate that I wanted to pay my respects to him. And so I sat until the evening shadows were long.

"And then, my father, I again sent to the Chief Magistrate

353

and told him that I did not wish to hurry him in any unman-
nerly way: I would wait his pleasure. But my people were
hungry. And when the white men visited me it was my custom
to kill that they might eat.

"The answer from the Chief Magistrate, my father, was
that the town was full of stray dogs—dog to dog: we might
kill those and eat them if we could catch them.

"So I left Bulawayo that night, my father; and when next
I came to visit the Chief Magistrate it was with my *impis*
behind me; no soft words in their mouths, but the assegai in
their hands. Who blames me?"

Not Rhodes. He could not discuss his white officials with
black men, but he knew the truth of what Somabulane said.
He knew, too, the native police—the scum of tribes once conquered by the Matabele, avenging themselves now, under the
white men's protection, against their black superiors.

"Tell them," said Rhodes to Colenbrander, "that the native
police shall go. I can promise them that. There will be no more
native police." . . . "Tell them," he interrupted Somabulane's
further recital of their grievances against the white officials—
"tell them I have listened to all that; that is past and done with.
Such things will not happen again. Now I want to know, is it
peace? Are the eyes white?"

Somabulane threw down a reed he was carrying, in token of
submission.

"There is my assegai. There is my rifle."

"Tell the chief I accept his word. He will send in his
arms. . . . I will stay among them to see that right is done."

The sun was going down. Somabulane stood up. His men
stood with him.

"It is peace?" said Rhodes.

354

They agreed. *"Ea vumbu."*

"How do we know it?"

"You have the word of Somabulane—of Babiaan—of Dhliso, chiefs of the House of Kumalo."

"It is good, my children. Go in peace."

"Hamba gahle, Baba."

"Hamba gahle, Aminduna."

"Mehle 'mhlope, Baba."

"Mehle 'mhlope, Aminduna."

Go in peace, father. Go in peace, chieftains. The eyes are white, father. The eyes are white.

It was the prelude to those *indabas* in the Matoppos that were to save Rhodesia and renew Rhodes. But there were people in Bulawayo who could not bear to see Rhodes parleying with the murderous savages. They wanted, they said, to see the Matabele killed off until the last few came crawling on their hands and knees for mercy.

VIII

A week later Rhodes, with him four other white men—two bringing their women—set out on horseback to meet the Matabele chiefs. The place of meeting was a mile and a half from the soldiers' camp. Contrary to their agreement, there stepped forth several hundreds of armed and hostile-seeming natives, nor had all the chiefs come; many, it appeared, were still seeing blood, their eyes were not yet white.

There were some moments of tension while Rhodes rebuked the chiefs present for the misdemeanour of the armed warriors. "Tell them," he said, "to lay down their arms at once."

He dismounted then, and sat down on a boulder, waiting

355

for obedience as one who is aware that he must be obeyed. Nor had he to wait long. The old men harangued the young men; the young men threw down their assegais, sticks, and rifles; called Rhodes their chief and their father; gave him now the name by which he was henceforth known among them: Lamula 'Mkunzi, Separator of the Fighting Bulls; they recited their grievances again; Rhodes told them they were his children; they asked him for salt, tobacco, and food. The end of the affair was that Rhodes returned to his camp accompanied by a cavalcade of prancing and singing natives.

Next day he travelled to the kraals of those whose eyes were red, and there pitched his tent. As Lobengula had done in the days of his power, so Rhodes did now. His house was open, and his hospitality endless. His patience, too, was endless. First one chief came, then more came, then they all came. Whenever they wished to unburden their hearts of their troubles or even merely of their oratory, there they were. Daily, weekly, Rhodes waited for their coming and their talking, and answered them according to their needs and understanding. "I used to be fat before the fighting. Now I am only bones. I look to you, U'Rhodes, to help me get round in body again." Rhodes accepted the obligation.

He would repeat the simplest sentences over and over. What was time to the Matabele? What could they do with time? What did they know of Rhodes' thousand urgencies? A native will describe the tolling of a bell by saying ata-ting, ata-ting, as often as the bell said it. Three days, four days, seven days to talk over this or that—they were in no hurry at all. They would put their points to Rhodes, hear what he said, go home to make explanations to their people, return for further talk.

They maddened Rhodes' companions. The sight of the chiefs coming again and again, day after day, week after week, irritated them to their limits. Rhodes himself, the impatient, the arrogant—more than ever, since the Raid, impatient and arrogant—Rhodes went on repeating himself to the naked savages:

"Tell them they are all fools. Ask them do they want peace, ask Babiaan does he want peace, and also Dhliso, does he want peace, do they all want peace? . . . Tell them they are fools, they are children. If they do not want peace, why do they not come down here in the night and murder me and all of us? The thing would be very simple; they need only send down a few of their young bloods one night—twenty-five would be enough—and the business would be over. They would have me. They would have him" (he indicated his companions) "and him, and him, and him. If they were not fools they would do this. . . . Tell them, if they want peace, then why do they not all come and shake hands with me, and then they could go back to their wives and children and be happy."

The conversations continued. The chiefs spent the day. They stayed overnight. They brought their wives. The Matabele were hungry; they had not planted; their cattle were dead; they were living on roots, berries, wild hares, in caves and forests. At Rhodes' camp there was food, there was tobacco and the comfort of talk.

Earlier in the year Rhodes had gone to London to discuss with Chamberlain and his directors the future of Rhodesia that had been made so lamentably different by the Raid, and those *indabas* had taken a week.

Here, in the Matoppos, August made way for September,

357

September passed—his companions protested, officials protested, the waiting soldiers protested, and it was not till the middle of October that the last chief had admitted that his eyes were white, that Rhodes was his father, and there was now forever peace between black and white in Rhodesia.

Rhodes kept his promises to the Matabele. He gave them food—a million bags of mealies, to be paid for, if necessary (but it was not necessary—the company was agreeable), out of his own pocket. He gave the chiefs the authority they prayed for. He compensated the settlers. The peace he made has been kept.

IX

One writes the words chiefs, warriors, royal houses, Children of the Stars—the words of the Matabele themselves—and romanticism invades the mind. A memory comes then of a photograph of Matabele chiefs taken after this trouble of 1896, and good-bye to the pretty words. The chiefs are not shining-naked and battle-plumed. That one spoke truly who said he had been round and was now but bones, and could Rhodes make him round again? The haggard chiefs wear old military hats and caps, bits of second-hand uniform, second-hand—fifth-hand—coats, overcoats, waistcoats. Some of them have trousers, some, below an upper garment, an apron of leopard-skin, monkey-skin, or leather thongs. They are barefooted. They look no better than the drab and dusty natives who crowd round the pass-offices in towns, waiting to be examined for their diseases, compelled to return to their hungry kraals if they cannot get work.

358

The old chiefs on the photograph crouch on the ground. The faces of the chiefs, like their clothes, wear a discarded look. Their minds, like their clothes, are half-savage and half-civilized. The past is gone and there is no future. The Matabele may well keep the peace. They have little else to keep.

CHAPTER ' 3 1

RHODES FINDS HIS BURIAL PLACE

I

IT WAS during these *indabas* on the Matoppos that there
came to Rhodes one day an indignant band of chiefs, crying a desecration! a desecration! Soldiers, belonging to the
camp Rhodes had left behind him, had found—sitting on a
natural chair of rock in a great circular tomb of granite—the
skeleton of a man. Around the skeleton was an accumulation
of old waggons, carriages, furniture, glass, savage battle loot.
The soldiers had robbed the cave and disturbed the skeleton;
and the skeleton was the skeleton of Moselikatze.

Rhodes accompanied the infuriated chiefs to the tomb to see
for himself what had happened. He found there hundreds of
excited, shouting natives. The bones of Moselikatze, the tomb
of Moselikatze, the spirit of Moselikatze had been affronted.
See what the white man had done!

Rhodes entered the tomb. Its entrances were broken down;
the ground within dug up for treasure; its contents rifled. The
head of the skeleton rested on its thigh-bones. Rhodes' indignation satisfied even the indignant chiefs. He offered to make
reparation.

It was decided finally that black men should be allowed,
unhindered by white men, to repair the tomb, and that they

should be paid while they were working. To purify the tomb and appease Moselikatze's spirit, ten black oxen were to be sacrificed, and the vandals punished.

They were punished, the tomb restored, the oxen sacrificed, their bones arranged round the tomb for its future protection, ten more oxen given by Rhodes for a feast.

The memory of Moselikatze sitting on his chair of rock, looking in death over his kingdom, remained with Rhodes. Death was in his mind in these days, and so, he thought, a monarch should rest at last, erect and overtopping his world.

II

It was during these *indabas*, too, that Rhodes, riding out one day with Earl Grey, the new Administrator, found his tomb. He came upon the hill of granite on whose black floor giants had played at marbles. Beneath it lay this rocky waste, this endless desolate waste, this stony figure of a world, unsmoothed, unsoftened, neglected even by that terrible Time. Rhodes stood there muttering of its peace, its chaotic grandeur, and the littleness of man. "I shall be buried here," he said.

III

The things that Rhodes did in these days were beginning to shape themselves in his mind as memorials. He knew he had little longer to live, but he was not yet so ill that he could not bear the thought of death. After what had seemed the breaking for ever of his life, he had found, in the Matoppos, his greatest moments. He had done here a good work—the best, indeed, of his accomplishment—and he knew it. He had made a hundred thousand enemies in the south, but in his North he was loved. "My Rhodesians have never bitten me."

How pleasant to brood among the Matoppos on the panorama of his life, his legacies to the future, and his dominance in death.

It was with pain he drew himself from these romantic thoughts of annihilation to go and answer for the things he had done in a bygone life which hardly now seemed to be his.

In December Rhodes left Bulawayo for Cape Town—thence to face in England an Enquiry into the Raid. He was hardly perturbed—so distant was the old life—when he was told, just before leaving, that Groote Schuur with all its contents had been burnt to the ground. "Is that all? . . . I thought you were going to say Jameson was dead." . . . "What with Jameson's Raid," he agreeably informed a friend, "the Raid, rebellion, famine, rinderpest, and now my house burnt, I feel like Job, all but the boils."

The Cape Enquiry into the Raid was past; he had not attended it, and it had perhaps gone the more lightly for him because of his work in the Matoppos. The Committee found that he had not directed or approved Jameson's final act, yet could not be absolved of all responsibility, since he had assisted at the whole scheme's inception.

Things he had not expected—a greater welcoming than he had dreamt of—met him on his way from Beira to Cape Town. True, this approbation came almost entirely from one class of colonist—the Jingoes he had once derided. He was aware of that. Yet he was moved. At Port Elizabeth forty old Rhodesians took the horses from his carriage and drew him through the streets to the Town Hall where he was to speak. It was in this speech he said he was going to meet the "unctuous rectitude" of his countrymen. "Anxious rectitude?" a solicitous journalist suggested. "No, unctuous rectitude," Rhodes insisted with relish.

At every station between Port Elizabeth and Cape Town vociferous crowds met him. In Cape Town people ran after him, shouting their welcomes, touching him, clutching him.

The year had been too full—he was too exhausted—he could not bear the emotion all about him and within himself—the tears streamed down his face. He said something about its being moving to see the kindness of one's fellow men. "Such appreciation," he told the crowd, following the thought that was always with him now—"such appreciation as this generally comes after a man is dead." At a private dinner he offered to do his best to make atonement for his error "by untiring devotion to the best interests of South Africa." He was prepared, he wrote, to say as much in public. He began, a few days later, to do so, and acclamatory crowds interrupted—finally—the declaration.

He met a Parliamentary Committee of Enquiry in England on February 16, 1897. The ghosts of Raleigh, Clive, and Warren Hastings stood behind him.

CHAPTER ˒ 3 2

THE SHAREHOLDERS TURN AT LAST

I

WHEN Harcourt indicted the Raiders, his audience were more perturbed about the price of Chartereds than about the nation's honour. So his biographer suggests. And certainly Chartereds, irony or no, gave cause for perturbation.

Rhodes was still in Matabeleland when, in November, 1896, there took place an extraordinary general meeting of the Chartered Company. The shareholders had been called to make arrangements for meeting the expenses of the war and rinderpest. The various moneys raised during the year were gone. It was proposed to issue now still another million one-pound shares. The capital of the company would thus be: The original million one-pound shares. The second million of equal value raised to pay for the Rudd Concession. The half-million issued in July of this year, and the latest million—three million five hundred thousand pounds in all.

Of the million new shares, five hundred thousand were now to be issued to the shareholders *pro rata* at a price slightly less than the current market value—namely, two pounds. Three hundred thousand of these shares were to be underwritten.

The second five hundred thousand shares were not yet to be

issued except for a hundred and fifty thousand at two pounds fifteen, on which the underwriters of the other three hundred thousand had an option.

A Mr. de Pass, a shareholder, objected to this. He said they did not need underwriters. "The same people who have under-written these shares have been the sellers of Chartereds. It is altogether a monstrous business. We are asked to give the call of a hundred and fifty thousand shares at two pounds fifteen each, and yet we are told the prospects of Rhodesia are most favourable, and most likely they are. It is only fourteen months since these shares were worth nine pounds ten each, and yet this option is to be given at two pounds fifteen. If the directors carry out this underwriting business it will be a detriment to the interests of the shareholders, and it ought not to be done." ("Hear, hear," and uproar.)

The president, the Duke of Abercorn, repeated his resolution, previously seconded by the Duke of Fife, to increase the capital to three million five hundred thousand pounds, and the resolution was carried.

The motion concerning the underwriting was now seconded to cries of, "No, no."

Mr. de Pass: I oppose the granting of this underwriting. The price of the shares has been knocked down to about two pounds.

A Shareholder: We can see through it.

Mr. de Pass: I move an amendment that the shares be offered to the shareholders without any underwriting.

A Shareholder: What are the names of the underwriters?

The secretary of the company suggested the withdrawal of these arrangements if the sense of the meeting was against any underwriting.

The president thought the resolution had better be put.

A Shareholder: May we know who the underwriters are?

The President: No, I do not think that is necessary. I will now put the resolution.

A Shareholder: Who are the underwriters?

The President: Order, order, if you please. . . . I will now put the resolution. [Interruption.] Order, order. The resolution is, "That the underwriting arrangements referred to in the circular accompanying the notice convening this meeting be and the same are hereby approved." Those who are in favour of that resolution will please hold up their hands.

A Shareholder: Put the amendment first.

The President: Those who are against the resolution will please hold up their hands. [Voices: "Against, against."]

A Shareholder: It is not understood.

The President: I will put it again. Those who are in favour of the resolution will be good enough to hold up their hands. On the contrary, those who are against the resolution will also hold up their hands. [Great uproar.] If the meeting will be good enough to keep quiet— [Interruption.]

A Shareholder: Is any portion of the money now proposed to be raised to be devoted to Mr. Kruger's indemnity? [Laughter.]

The President: No, sir. Now, one moment, gentlemen, please, while I put the resolution.

A Shareholder: Let us have the names of the underwriters first.

The President: I must ask you to keep order for one moment.

A Shareholder: Is it true that Mr. Rhodes and Mr. Beit are going to pay up?

THE PRESIDENT: I have been asked to read the resolution once more, and if you will kindly listen, I will do so. . . .

A SHAREHOLDER: Put the amendment first.

THE PRESIDENT: There is no amendment; it is a direct negative. Those who are in favour of the resolution will hold up their hands. ["No, no."] Those who are against the resolution will hold up their hands. The resolution is lost, gentlemen. [Loud cheers.] Now, gentlemen, I have only to say this, that I rely upon you to take up the shares which are asked for at this meeting, and show your confidence in the company.

A SHAREHOLDER: Half a million?

THE PRESIDENT: Half a million, yes.

THE SECRETARY: Half a million shares at two pounds each.

II

It will be seen that things were no longer so sweet at Chartered meetings as once they had been—when eager crowds were ready to do anything Rhodes demanded of them. The resolution about the underwriters was lost almost unanimously, but the underwriters, it was declared, were not directors of the Chartered Company. Were Rhodes and Beit the underwriters? It does not emerge. Certainly they had resigned their seats on the board of the Chartered Company in the previous June, and so had Dr. Harris. The resignation of Rhodes had involved the resignation also of his English representative on the board. In February there were further resignations—one by the Prince of Wales' son-in-law, the Duke of Fife. In Rhodesia practically the whole administration resigned in the years 1896 and 1897.

No wonder the House of Commons had been thronged with

anxious shareholders during Harcourt's indictment, and Rhodes had gone out to do or die among the Matoppos.

But if there were two great issues at stake when the Chartered shareholders (among them the fashionable women who had bought just a few shares that they might see and hear Rhodes at shareholders' meetings), when these notable people so crowded the galleries to hear Harcourt, there were two questions that all the world wanted clearly answered at the Raid Enquiry: What was the true purpose of the Raid? Had Joseph Chamberlain any complicity in it? And as much as the issues concerning the nation's honour and the price of Chartereds were ever resolved, so were the world's questions about the purpose of the Raid and Chamberlain's complicity ever answered.

As in the last act of a revue or comic opera, all the actors lately on the South African scene appeared now in a body on the English scene, and with them a few others who had made the fun merely in England. Rhodes came, of course, and Jameson; the Reform leaders came—Charles Leonard, and the truthful Frankie Rhodes, and the other three; the doctors of the Intelligence Department came, and Flora Shaw, the head, one might say, of the English Intelligence Department of the Raid. Everyone made speeches, and Rhodes made many, but Dr. Rutherfoord Harris and Flora Shaw, too delicately placed as the links between Rhodes and Chamberlain, threw up the thickest smoke-screen of all.

The Select Committee used time even more extravagantly than the Matabele in the Matoppos; its *indaba* lasted a year;

368

and what, at the end, emerged quite clearly was that Jameson had indeed ridden into the Transvaal.

IV

For the rest, certain documents were allowed to be withheld for reasons so vaguely stated that it was rumoured they inculpated the Prince of Wales and contradicted the Queen's personal statement to the Kaiser that her Ministers were not involved. Certain Imperial officials, who had known things and not told them, were deprived of their positions, and duly given others. Certain officers were dismissed the service and then reinstated. Neither the Secretary of State for the Colonies (it was held) nor any of the officials of the Colonial Office "received any information which made or should have made them or any of them aware of the plot during its development." Rhodes was censured for being simultaneously a Prime Minister in one country, a Chartered ruler in a second, and a conspirator in a third, and Chamberlain followed up this censure in committee by saying in the House that Rhodes had done nothing in any respect inconsistent with the character of an honourable man. . . . Whereupon the talk was that if Chamberlain had not, in the words of Swift MacNeill, M.P., who was present in the House, "fulfilled the conditions required by Rhodes—at a signal from a confidential friend who was sitting under the clock, Mr. Thomas" (Q.C., a Liberal Member) "was to disclose correspondence which would make Mr. Chamberlain's complicity in the Jameson Raid incontrovertible."

Yet why more evidence was needed to involve Chamberlain than had already appeared is not, humanly speaking, clear. The giving of the railway strip. Flora Shaw's cables to Rhodes:

369

"Chamberlain sound," etc. "Sympathy now complete," etc. Rhodes' cables to Flora Shaw: "Inform Chamberlain that I shall get through all right if he supports me." . . . "Unless you can make Chamberlain instruct the High Commissioner to proceed at once to Johannesburg, the whole position is lost." Chamberlain's own last-minute cable to the High Commissioner to stop Jameson. Rutherfoord Harris's statement at the Enquiry that Chamberlain's confidential assistant knew everything; that he had presumed Chamberlain understood his guarded allusions, upon which presumption the conspirators had acted. More than anything, Chamberlain's very intervention at this point that he had stopped Harris's confidences: an action implying so obviously that he knew what must not be spoken—all these and more make, one may suggest, a good *prima facie* case against Chamberlain, which is the most that can be said of any man never brought to trial.

However, one who was at the heart of the conspiracy has written down the truth. His document, sealed, is deposited at a certain institution in South Africa. It is to be opened on January 1, 1946. And on that date knowledge will take the place of speculation.

Yet to Chamberlain, of all people, Harcourt wrote: "I have always believed that Rhodes since the Raid has been, and still is, the evil genius of South Africa."

CHAPTER · 33

THE RHODES SCHOLARSHIPS

I

IN FACT Rhodes, after the Raid, had little influence in South Africa. He certainly became the leader of the South African Jingoes and the bogeyman of the Boers. Yet the Jingoes of South Africa could not have made the Boer War, nor did the Boers wish it. Over Milner, who was now sent out as High Commissioner, Rhodes had little power. Milner's own letters—the declarations, on the whole, of a lonely, suspicious foreigner—attest this. "Rhodes," he writes, "is just the same man as he always was, undaunted and unbroken by his former failure, but also untaught by it." And, in an access of that knowingness which is the mental gambling of the lonely and suspicious, he adds some recommendations about keeping a hold on Rhodes by interminably dangling before his desirous vision the otherwise valueless Bechuanaland Protectorate. "The North," says Milner, "is perhaps going to be of more immediate urgency than the Transvaal."

Milner was wrong, not only in this last idea, but in many of his thoughts about Rhodes. Rhodes was bitterly taught by his former failure. He said himself, concerning the Transvaal: "I made a mistake there and that's enough for me. . . . I keep aloof from the whole Transvaal crisis, so that no one will be

able to say, if things go wrong, 'Rhodes is in it again.' . . ."
"I must say to you," he said, "that one has had great troubles
during the last two years—most probably, as one might say,
owing to my faults; but with a high object. The methods have
been worthy of condemnation, but, gentlemen, remember this,
you all have your trials, you all have your troubles, and then
you are better men." . . . "I honestly believe that my years of
trouble have made me a better man."

He had thought himself, as Hofmeyr said, the equal of the
Almighty. He had imagined, like Napoleon, that the human
laws of morality and decorum did not apply to him, and that
he was invulnerable and invincible. Now, after the Raid, he
not only many times echoed Napoleon's sentiments, "When I
was happy I thought I knew men, but it was fated that I
should know them in misfortune only," he went further, saying: "If I may put to you a thought . . . a man does not
know himself, his own mind or character. It is a good thing to
have a period of adversity." . . . And though these are not
profound discoveries—they are any old woman's platitudes—
yet such words do suggest a certain new humility in Rhodes
which Milner could not realize; they do mean Milner was
wrong in his conviction that Rhodes remained untaught by
the Raid.

Rhodes himself always dated everything from the Raid. He
told an election audience this in one of those asides which are
intended to cause amusement. But he meant it. And even if
he still wanted the Union he had always wanted, and was often
angry and unpleasant and violent about it, nor ever ceased
demanding the eventual inclusion of Rhodesia and the Transvaal in that Union, there is little in his conduct after the Raid
to suggest that through him occurred the Boer War. "It is not

372

Rhodes," he said himself, "that is causing unrest in South Africa. It is the Transvaal position that is causing unrest in South Africa. And if I were dead tomorrow the same thing would go on." The Boer War was not, as many think, the outcome of the Raid—except in that the Raid vivified Kruger, an old man losing grip. It was the outcome of those things which, as a most significant incident, also produced the Raid: the century-long hostility between Boers and English that had never, for a generation, abated; the warring of different ideals of life; the annoyance caused the English by the fact that the wealthiest part of South Africa had fallen, under their very noses, into the accidental hands of a primitive people; the ex-emplification of that primitiveness in Kruger himself; the ambition of Chamberlain; the passion of Milner. The actors in the scene that closed the nineteenth century in South Africa were not Rhodes and Kruger, but Chamberlain and Kruger. It was Chamberlain who broke Kruger because Kruger would not elude him by bending, while Rhodes stood on one side, thrust out by his own deed, sighing: "If you were to ask for a prac-tical solution, I should say the best solution possible would be for myself and President Kruger to meet. . . . I am afraid that such a solution is an impossible one, because we are not broad enough." Yet Rhodes himself was broad enough.

Spengler speaks of men who become History's commanding officers. But even such men must work with the materials left by others, when they die their accomplishment falls into fresh hands, and behind all is an unknown design. Chamberlain him-self entered upon a scene set long before his time, and the scene that was to follow had been conceived in a mood of mockery.

People said, after the Raid, after what they called Rhodes'

betrayal, that he had destroyed faith itself: he had been so trusted, who could again be trusted? But this very fact threw Rhodes clear of the whole business, and, in one blow, both relieved him of responsibility and punished him.

II

In the end, the only person punished for the Raid was Rhodes. The Reform leaders became wealthy men, the conspirators who had been deprived of their ranks and honours received them back again, Jameson in particular triumphed over the past—Rhodes lost what he most truly cared for: the mould of his work was broken. "The fool foldeth his hands together and eateth his own flesh." Rhodes was not the man to sit in idle grief. "If I have ever so many faults . . . the best atonement I can make is to work for this high object" (union). . . . "They have devised all sorts of retreats for me . . . a hermit's cell on the Zambesi. . . . I am going to continue to take a share in public affairs." . . . "My public life is only beginning. It is not over. It cannot be over. I must go on. . . . My time must be spent in the service of this country." . . . Such were the things he said. And "work," he insisted, "survives the worker." And, "Does it matter," he urged, "what people say about us so long as our work goes on?"

But work needs a shape, and if the mould is smashed, and there is little time to make a new one, and the hurried fingers are clumsy and the eyes strained and the heart exhausted, what then?

Goethe suggested to Eckermann that there was perhaps a divine reason in what seemed like the untimely cutting-off of great men: that every extraordinary man had a certain mis-

374

sion to fulfil, and when this mission was fulfilled there was no
further need for him, so he was scrapped and the next great
man had his place. Sad that this Divine economy should not
be exercised on other than great men, and proof of the theory
be so humanly inaccessible. South Africa has not recovered
from the ruin of Rhodes' work.

In this year in which Milner writes that Rhodes is just the
same man he always was, and that, regarding Bechuanaland,
"Let him wait for it and deserve it," in 1897 Rhodes, so far
from settling down to wait for his deserts, has another heart
attack; and at about the time Milner is writing his letter
Rhodes is discussing with his man of business the terms of the
will which was finally drawn up in 1899. That will becomes
now the dearest companion of his life. His thoughts are henceforth on death, his plans are testaments and his labours
memorials.

He rebuilds his house, Groote Schuur, and it is to be the
abode of the Prime Ministers of a United South Africa. He
builds a home in his garden where artists may come and dream.
He sets aside grounds for a university. He buys farms in
Rhodesia to leave to Rhodesia's people. He makes a dam to
hold fifty million gallons of water, beside it an agricultural
college. He settles four thousand natives on his estate—notably
the rebellious chiefs and their witch-doctors, both for their
comfort and for the convenience of having them all assembled
under his eye. He plans a sanatorium for disabled workmen,
and a three-mile avenue to Government House in Bulawayo.
"You say I shall not live to see those trees grow? I tell you
that in imagination I already see people passing and repassing
under their shade." . . . "Get that avenue through," he says

375

on his death-bed. "See it through. We have got to fulfil our promise to give shade to the nurse-maids in the afternoons."

He plans a railway from Bulawayo to the Matoppos, "so that the people of Bulawayo may enjoy the glory of these hills from Saturday to Monday." He asks one of his engineers if the spray from the Victoria Falls will splash the train that is to cross the Zambesi bridge on his Cape to Cairo line. "That would depend on the way the wind was blowing." "But if it blew the right way, would it?" "It might, and probably would."

Rhodes will never see this spray, but the thought enchants him. If Mark Twain's "When he stood upon the Cape Peninsula, his shadow fell on the Zambesi," carries a sinister tinge, there is no equivocation in Bryce's less spectacular "From Cape Town to the Zambesi it is all Rhodes. When I ask who built that, who made this industry, who created that, who is responsible for this, I get one reply—Rhodes." Rhodes' monuments, Rhodes' legacies, are memorials to himself.

But what of his larger thoughts, as he called them, what of his dreams beyond South Africa? Are they gone? "It is ridiculous," he said, "to lose one's ideas by death."

They are not gone, but the will Rhodes begins to plan in this year of 1897 declares that he has come down to earth. He has folded up youth's manuscript—five manuscripts, indeed—all the other wills. His first will speaks of "extending British rule throughout the world," of "the restoration of the Anglo-Saxon unity destroyed by the schism of the eighteenth century," and "the foundation of so great a power as to hereafter render wars impossible." The next four wills are merely variations of the first will; not more, really, than manifestos, with no declaration as to how these grand ideas are to be effected or even, practically speaking, initiated. The sixth will is the will of a mortal man. This man has certain assets that shall be applied in a certain manner towards a certain purpose. The sixth will has its own glamour, but it is not the glamour of moonshine. In this will Rhodes makes various arrangements for his relations, for the people of South Africa, and for his old college, Oriel; but the essence of the will, as the world knows, is the Scholarship Foundation. In the end all that Rhodes can do towards extending British rule throughout the world and restoring Anglo-Saxon unity and founding a guardian power for the whole of humanity is to arrange for a number of young men from the United States, the British colonies, and Germany to go to Oxford.

The proportions of that number are not, today, as Rhodes planned them. When Rhodes assigned his scholarships—so many for each state and colony and a complimentary few for Germany, he believed there were still only the original thirteen states in the Union of America. Nor did his man of business in South Africa, nor the solicitor of the Chartered Company, who drew up his will, know better. There are, accordingly, rather more Rhodes Scholars from America than from all the British Dominions put together.

The germ of his scholarship idea had come to Rhodes in the year 1891. In that year, as he told a Bond Congress, he "saw at Bloemfontein the immense feeling of friendship that all the members had for the Grey College where they had been educated and from which they had gone out to the world. . . . I said to myself: If we could get a teaching university founded in the Cape Colony, taking the people from Bloemfontein, Pretoria, and Natal . . . the young men who will attend it will make the Union of South Africa in the future. Nothing will overcome the associations and the aspirations they will form under the shadow of Table Mountain."

Since then his plan had grown. It had grown until it seemed to him the only practical plan—all he, personally, could do towards Teutonizing the world and thus regenerating mankind. If the Union of South Africa could be made under the shadow of Table Mountain, why not an Anglo-Saxon Union under the spires of Oxford? After thirty years there would be, in the words of Stead, "between two and three thousand men in the prime of life scattered all over the world, each one of whom would have had impressed upon his mind in the most susceptible period of his life the dream of the Founder"—each one of whom, moreover, would have been specially—mathematically—selected towards the Founder's purpose—thus:

Thirty per cent for "literary and scholastic attainments."

Twenty per cent for "fondness of and success in manly outdoor sports such as cricket, football and the like."

Thirty per cent for "qualities of manhood, truth, courage, devotion to duty, sympathy for and protection of the weak, kindliness, unselfishness and fellowship."

Twenty per cent for "exhibition during schooldays of moral force of character and of instincts to lead and to take an interest in his schoolmates." . . .

In speaking of these attributes to Stead Rhodes defined them, with that defensive cynicism of the romantic, as smugness, brutality, unctuous rectitude, and tact.

He added the Germans after meeting the Kaiser.

Before his death his plan was tested on a South African school.

It is thirty years, the period mentioned by Stead, since the first Rhodes Scholar went to Oxford. About eighteen hundred Rhodes Scholars have been selected for Oxford, fostered by Oxford, sent out from Oxford. What has been the effect on the world?

Well, eighteen hundred young men have been given a time of happiness, and chances in life they might not otherwise have had. Most of them have married and begotten families that will participate in the enhanced opportunities of their fathers. Five thousand beings are probably the happier for Rhodes' dreams. And more men will be selected, fostered, sent out, more generations get something in life they might not have had, but for Rhodes. One speaks in terms of the likely and obvious, not in terms of O Life! O Fate! and of what seems good fortune, yet may not be. Rhodes Scholarships have brought things to a number of people, which, accumulated, may have some meaning. And that, in itself, is a satisfactory result.

Whether the Scholars have done their share towards fulfilling Rhodes' plans, whether many of them have gone out from Oxford with the sense of a particular responsibility, is another matter. One would suggest that, on the whole, the Rhodes Scholars have taken, but not given. But was it in them to give?

The Rhodes Scholars have been selected for being—one might say shortly—decent fellows. Decent fellows are the best fellows for composing the world. The Rhodes Scholars must be better than average men. They are today creditably following their professions, they are good citizens. But that, as Rhodes expected, they have had any influence on the world at large is not apparent. Few of them, proportionately speaking, have even gone into public life—hardly more than would have done so, Rhodes Scholarships or not.

It may be said that thirty years is only one generation, and what can be proved in a generation? The response of a certain type of individual in given circumstances can be proved in a generation. The final test, indeed, is the individual. The sum of the world's suffering or happiness is only one man's suffering or happiness, for no man can feel more than it is possible for a man to feel, and that, therefore, is the limit of feeling. In our linked and opened world the accomplishment of any nation, young or old, great or small, is not a national accomplishment, but merely the work of its individuals, for the past is a general inheritance and the present an equal spectacle.

Similarly, decent fellowship is merely one decent fellow, and its quality and influence a constant thing. Eighteen hundred decent fellows are always eighteen hundred decent fellows, and one may test all the generations of decent fellows by one generation of decent fellows.

The greater number of Rhodes Scholars today must be between thirty and fifty years of age. If a man is going to do anything he will, between thirty and fifty, at least begin to give some indication of his likelihood to do it. The impression the mature Rhodes Scholars have made on the world is the impression an equal number of them will probably make in the future. And since, as some come and others go, the number of Rhodes Scholars between thirty and fifty will be fairly constant, their influence in the world may be considered as permanently what it is today. One may allow for those killed in the war. But the accidental must always be part of a regular calculation. And, on the other hand, some men might have received Rhodes Scholarships who would have gone to Oxford without them. It may occur that a Rhodes Scholar will do something significant. One must assume, however, that such a man will achieve distinction, not because he is a Rhodes Scholar, but because he is this particular individual. The material for judgment exists. . . .

Rhodes' idea was twofold. There was this going forth into the world of young men with certain associations and aspirations, and the world's benefit from young men so ennobled. This he indicated in his speech concerning a university at Cape Town. And then, according to Jameson, he wanted another Rhodes; he wanted, as the Roman emperors adopted their heirs, to design his successor.

It seems not to have entered his mind that he himself could never have won a Rhodes Scholarship: he was nothing of a scholar, he was nothing of a sportsman, he lacked most of those qualities he lumped under "unctuous rectitude," and there is no evidence that he ever led or took an interest in his schoolmates. Even Kipling, who dreamt as Rhodes dreamt, and came to do that dreaming in the cottage Rhodes built, and wrote "The Light That Failed" as Rhodes was taking up his North and the white man's burden—even Kipling, a man more sentimental than Rhodes, knew better than to make his heroes fit subjects for a Rhodes Scholarship.

IV

The fact is that abnormal people are pathetically respectful of normality. Rhodes once told a bishop that his church was "up the mountain," and, in laying the foundation stone of a Presbyterian Church, admitted that he did not "care to go to a particular church even on one day in the year, when I use my own chapel at all other times." Yet he envied General Booth his religion. "Happy? I happy? Good God, no! . . . I would give all I possess to believe what that old man believes." And he insisted—since such things pleased the world—that the school children of Rhodesia should be taught religion.

When, therefore, Rhodes fashioned his successor, he compounded him of the obvious characteristics of the ideal Englishman; he forgot that the empire-makers have been, not the decent fellows, but men rather sickly, imaginative, and artistic, never at one with their youthful contemporaries, not always very nice in their dealings—as likely as not prosecuted for their peccadilloes or done away with for their unbearable transcendence. He did not take his examples, as in his own life, from Alexander, Cæsar, or Napoleon; nor yet from Raleigh, Clive, Hastings, Disraeli. He ignored himself.

CHAPTER ، 3 4

RHODES AFTER THE RAID

I

"IT WAS," writes the editor of his speeches, "a Rhodes less impassive and more human . . . a modern man like themselves who had known failure and suffering" that, in the year following this third heart attack, faced a Chartered audience in London. Rhodes had resembled once, says this authority, "an old Roman emperor born with the single ambition to annex and administer the habitable world, and careless alike of the praise or blame of lesser mortals." There had been those, he says, who could see nothing in him but brutality, cynicism, and the incarnation of unscrupulous power. . . .

The Raid had revealed his weakness, and the Matabele *indabas* his humanity. It was, indeed, a new Rhodes who, reëlected to the Chartered board, stood before his shareholders (his shareholders once again, and as wild for him as ever), and begged them not to "go and gamble over the shares. It is a great mistake. You do not know the worry it gives to those who are responsible for your interests. I know exactly what you have spent, and I feel perfectly certain that in my lifetime I will return good interest on that. But I do hate to read the lists, and see at times that people have gambled these shares up without warranty for it, because it is in the prospective that they have dealt rather than in the present. You will excuse me saying that frankly."

Yes, it is a new Rhodes, a troubled, divided Rhodes, a Rhodes speaking, as he says, to two audiences: one in London and one in Rhodesia, torn between his settlers and his shareholders, his dreams and his directorate, his beautiful hypotheses and the little ugly facts. He comforts his people, out of his desire, with this, and warns them, out of his conscience, of that. He says, "I have not lost my faith in the minerals," and adds: "I have always spoken with extreme caution; I do not want you to gamble in these shares." He believes "absolutely in the minerals," yet "it will take time to develop them." He sees his way to balancing expenditure and revenue. He has plans for getting in more money. The country, he persists, is a fine country. Didn't Lobengula, the greatest chief in Africa, the greatest African king, know a fine country when he saw one? There must be minerals; he cannot believe that so many excellent engineers can all be telling untruths. . . .

Now he has put in railways and telegraphs, he is civilizing the country. It is not true about the swamps. Rhodesia is a white man's country, it is the finest country in Africa; surely the settlers alone are an asset, and will one day, when they have self-government, repay the shareholders what they have spent in acquiring and developing the country. Ten millions, Lord Grey thinks that may be, but he himself thinks six millions. Moreover, let his audiences, both here and in Rhodesia, understand that not the shareholders or the pioneers must pay for this development of a land from barbarism to civilization, but its eventual fortunate citizens. . . .

And so, one day, everything will come right. "I do not want to be pessimistic, because I am an optimist." Only, in the mean-

384

time, no gambling. He cannot say it often enough: no gambling, no gambling.

Everything will come right—*alles sal recht kom*—it is the creed of South Africa. And yet there are South Africans, Rhodes continues, "who want the country" (his Rhodesia) "damned; who want it to be a hopeless country; . . . who get up every morning and wish that their Hinterland, instead of being a success, should be a failure; and every report they can get to the discredit of the country they are delighted with. Fancy your discovering a new country lying at your back, and a section of you wishing that it might be a hopeless failure!"

Surely England, surely his shareholders, are not going to let it be a hopeless failure. How can one prevent a country from being a hopeless failure?

Well, why does one come to England between one's work in Rhodesia and an election at the Cape—after a heart attack, and with one's mind full of testaments and death? The truth is, one needs money.

Railways. There must be railways. Railways, says Rhodes, are his right hand. Only a few months ago the railway from the south had reached Bulawayo. Hundreds of people had been invited to celebrate the occasion. The High Commissioner had come, the Governor of Natal, six members of the Imperial Parliament. Stanley, the explorer, was there to report it for an English paper, and "Few events of the century," he wrote, "surpass it in interest and importance. It marks the conclusion of an audacious enterprise which less than ten years ago would have been deemed impossible, and only two years ago as most unlikely. It furnishes a lesson to all colonizing nations. It teaches methods of operation never practised before. It suggests large and grand possibilities." . . . and so on, to a climax in which he prophesied that Bulawayo would become the Chicago of South Africa, and Rhodesia overtake, and even exceed, the population of the Transvaal. . . .

And now, having brought the railway to Bulawayo, Rhodes wants to get it to Lake Tanganyika, which will cost two million pounds. He has come to England for that two million pounds. And must they, he asks his shareholders, borrow two million pounds at five per cent when England, that has such excellent credit, can get money for three per cent? They have cost England nothing, they ask her for nothing, but may they not just expect to lean on her credit—in return for which comfort they will give her an Africa wholly linked up by rail? "You get the railway to Lake Tanganyika, you have Her Majesty's sanction for the railway to Uganda, and then you have Kitchener coming down from Khartoum." . . .

Is it the Raid? Has everything been spoilt by the Raid? Are those lovely times past when Rhodes had but to ask and it was given? "I think," says Rhodes, wistfully, "the two objections to the idea are that it is unusual and that Mr. Rhodes is in it." . . .

And then, railways apart, there are other things, other liabilities, other needs. The Duke of Abercorn, who has thought it, he says, his duty to remain at the helm, stands up. He begs to propose that the capital of the company be increased to five million pounds by the creation of one million five hundred thousand new shares at one pound each.

The shareholders will do anything when Rhodes is there. Raid or no Raid, they are still his to command. They sanction the issue.

CHAPTER · 35

UNION! UNION! UNION!

I

AN ELECTION is being fought in South Africa when Rhodes returns from telling his Chartered shareholders of those South Africans who want the country damned and their Hinterland a hopeless failure. And during this election he goes, the leader now of the Progressive Party, from platform to platform, saying the same things to the electors: There are many who "would welcome with delight the morning paper that told them the mines (of Rhodesia) had collapsed." . . . "Did you ever hear, in the history of the world, of a Hinterland to a country being obtained, and yet a section of the country saying everything they possibly could to damage it?" It is a distressed, maddened, sleepless Rhodes that goes, with his clogged arteries, stumping the country, hardly able to speak of more than one thing—a union of South Africa with Rhodesia in it. And almost Rhodesia comes now before union. He is out to save the child of his name, his Rhodesia. He is failing, he will soon be gone, and who then will care for his Rhodesia? If he could depart with the knowledge that it had a home!

It is the middle of 1898, and Rhodes is forty-five. He looks sixty. His hair is grey, his face purpling, his body thickening.

His breath is growing heavier, his clumsy walk clumsier. More often than ever his voice breaks now into its strange falsetto. He cannot restrain his passion. He insults first this one, and then that one. He gives himself away in every direction. He speaks, by turn, in humility and arrogance. He explains and demands, he pleads and threatens. . . . But yet it is a significant ruin which faces the diggers in the schoolrooms—the only places of assembly—along the Vaal River. There is still that big body, that brooding eye, that great brow, that fire, that energy, which make him noteworthy among men.

Union. Union. Union. "I could have had a happy, a pleasant, and a great time given to few in the development of a new state representing eight hundred thousand square miles of Her Majesty's Empire, but the picture would not be complete unless that state kept in complete harmony, in complete unison with the South."

And do they refuse to unite because they hate him? Are their hearts, he asks in those words, hardened against him? "My life is a temporary one, but the country will remain after me; and if you do not go there, your children will and must." . . . "I do not think anyone will suggest that there is any personal advantage which I could obtain by being returned. I wish to be returned for a bigger idea than personal advantage." . . . "The Bond leaders ask you to believe that I am the most dreadful man in the whole country. . . . What have *they* done for you?" . . . "Sit down and think that the man whom they denounce so vehemently has done more for you in a practical way than anyone else in South Africa." . . . "Ask yourselves whether it is a good policy that you should drive out of public life a man who has been largely instrumental in

doing work from which you have so greatly benefited." . . .
"Do you think you are wise in howling against Rhodes?"
. . . "Give me your confidence because your Hinterland is
at stake, and I am the only man who can work the North with
the South." . . . "Whatever your personal feelings may be
regarding me, you will get the country and I shall get only
six feet by four."

It is the old over-repeated little painful joke.

Or do they distrust Rhodesia? Do they think he wants the
Cape to take Rhodesia because it is a failure? Then let the
Cape not unite with Rhodesia before it becomes a gold-produc-
ing country. He has heard it said he wants to *sell* Rhodesia—
he wants to sell it, so the story goes, for twenty million pounds.
"We don't propose to sell Rhodesia or put it up to auction.
We think it is a much better country than this, and having
got it we mean to keep it."

Certainly he thinks it a much better country than any other
man's country. Hasn't it every child's unique quality of being
its parent's own child? . . .

Or do they charge him with race feeling? Is it race feeling
that hinders union? "Race feeling I cannot have in me because
my feeling is that the best man must come to the front whatever his race may be. And this is not an electioneering speech,
for I am expressing ideas that are many years old." . . . "You
cannot live on race feeling. It will not give you new lands for
your children; it will not feed your people; it will not give you
clothes to wear." . . .

"Take the North," he pleads, "that new state which has got
its own railway built, which has borrowed nothing from you
and asked for nothing." . . . "The North is my thought. Co-

operation is my thought—federalism and the Union of South Africa." . . .

Useless! Neither his humility nor his pride, not his prayers nor his promises, can help him. The Boers are with him, he insists. Whatever may have been his mistakes, the large mass of them are still with him. He tells an unlikely story of how, after the Raid, a Dutch commandant in Rhodesia said to him: "We forgive you everything. We know you wanted the Union of South Africa." He says the Dutch are coming to Rhodesia, and he is making them happy in Rhodesia. Nothing helps. Fires occur in his grounds at Groote Schuur, his trees are cut down, the animals of his zoo injured, a charge of bribery is brought against him which fails on a technicality.

Even Jameson is against him: "Rhodes has done absolutely nothing but go backwards," he writes to his brother. "The election has been badly organized. I hate it all and hate the people more than ever—would clear out by the next boat, but have not pluck enough to acknowledge myself beaten."

It is not with Jameson, as with Rhodes, a wild effort to save his own begotten. He cannot bear Rhodes' panderings to the Dutch. He is not prepared to sink his British pride. He wants, not union, but dominance. He is all for race feeling. He finds Milner "the only really healthy personality in the whole crowd."

Rhodes himself is elected, but his party is defeated. Narrowly. Yet narrowly is enough. He says he does not despair. He departs for the North, crying: "We shall not relax our efforts until by our civilization and the efforts of our people we reach the shores of the Mediterranean."

And he struggles on. But his eye is now on a day and a hope beyond his own existence.

It falls to Jameson, after the death of Rhodes, to bring the

Progressives into power and to be a member of that Convention which creates the Union of South Africa.

Time has, forever, the last laugh. Not merely Jameson as leader, Jameson and Union. The joke does not end here. It happens that, by Rhodesia's own will, just precisely Rhodes' North is excluded from this Union.

CHAPTER · 36

"COLOSSUS!"

I

THERE is not even time enough left Rhodes now to make an anti-climax of his end—forgetting death, man's final humiliation, the dragging hence of a whimpering child that will not go and must—forgetting common death as a part of life. True, there is one grotesque incident: Rhodes meets, after much initial scheming on her side, a middle-aged Polish princess, once wealthy, divorced, still fairly handsome, still not without amorous hope and the remnant of charm. She arranges to find herself a passenger on the ship that takes him to Africa, to sit at his table, and to interest him in her conversation. In South Africa she comes often to Groote Schuur; talks international politics to him; writes international politics for foreign papers; edits something of an Imperial journal herself; acts occasionally as his hostess; goes riding with him; becomes utterly tedious to him; tells people they are to be married, or, alternatively, that she is his mistress—both of which stories his intimates deny; forges his name for twenty-nine thousand pounds, is prosecuted, convicted, sentenced to one and a half years' imprisonment, and released, on grounds of ill-health, after nine months in a Cape Town gaol; threatens, after Rhodes' death, to sue his trustees for four hundred thousand pounds damages; writes a book about Rhodes and her own reminiscences.

And it remains to this woman to speed Rhodes' end. He is infuriated by the scandals that link his name with the forger's; insists, against medical warning and the pleas of his friends, on hurrying out from England to attend the prosecution, and on his death-bed gives evidence against her.

It is the only mark any woman makes on Rhodes' life.

That life, for the rest, continues its unswerving course from the 1898 elections to its conclusion. "I do not falter," he says, and truly. He works, still, for his Rhodesia; strives to fructify its earth, since there is, as he points out, a bottom to every mine; plans a school system for it, since education, he maintains, is the whole difference between barbarism and civilization; tries to lure to it black labourers and white settlers; never goes out or rides out but he has a purpose beyond the mere activity—a farm to see, a mine, a kraal, a white man or a native. During the Boer War he is persuaded to head a prayer for the suspension of the Cape Constitution, yet despite this weary yielding, he schemes still a Union of South Africa; advocates equal rights for every civilized man south of the Zambesi, and designs the new Groote Schuur to be the home of the future Union's Prime Ministers. This distinction might once have fallen to him and, through his own act, now cannot; but he looks at what he calls the comparative, and, thinking of his will, sees himself guiding a union far beyond the limits of South Africa—a union of blond men, fostered by that land which, twenty-five years ago, Ruskin had called upon the youths of Oxford to make once more "a royal throne of kings, a sceptred isle, for all the world a source of light, a centre of learning and of the arts, faithful guardian of time-tried principles." . . . "Wake up, Grey!" Rhodes cries one night. "Have you ever thought how lucky you are to have been born an Englishman when there are so many millions who are not born Englishmen?"

II

The year 1899 finds him back in England to get that money from the Government for his Cape to Cairo railway. He does not get it. He has to tell his shareholders—as ever, his own—that the Imperial Government "do not see their way" to giving him the money for the railway to Tanganyika. He has suggested an alternative plan, and the Government "do not see their way to accede" to that. Nor is two million pounds, after all, enough. He needs three million pounds. "How are we going to get three million pounds?"

Beit has offered to lend him half a million; he can find half a million in the City; he himself will provide two hundred thousand ("I should have liked to take more, but during the last ten years I have devoted my mind to politics, and politics and the accumulation of money do not run together"), and, for the rest, will the shareholders come forward? Will they lend him another million or two at four per cent? There are still a number of unissued Chartereds. They shall be allotted to those shareholders who lend him money for his railway.

A Shareholder: At par?

Rhodes: No, at five pounds a share.

It is a haughty Rhodes speaking, a Rhodes whose gold mines in the North have begun to produce, whose new issue of Chartered has been over-subscribed—a Rhodes who has discovered anew (reluctant English Government or not) that he can deal with people.

The Kaiser, no other, is Rhodes' latest triumph. Rhodes has visited the Kaiser in his flannel suit, laughed with him about the Raid telegram, talked about his telegraph through German East Africa, and, glancing at his watch, said: "Well, good-bye. I have to go now. I have some people coming to dinner." Future generations, thinking in one thought of royalties and unicorns, will never understand the significance of these things, nor Rhodes' achievement in coming away from such a meeting with his telegraph assured. He adds a codicil to his will: the Kaiser is personally to choose five Rhodes Scholars a year.

III

But the most moving of his triumphs still awaits him. The man who was rejected by one Oxford college to be accepted by another with the words, "All the colleges send me their failures," this man is now honoured by Oxford with the D.C.L. degree. And not only that. The other recipient of a degree, *honoris causa*, is Kitchener, and it is Rhodes the assembly, shouting Colossus, chiefly acclaim. "Not mere undergraduates," he tells an enchanted audience when he gets back to Cape Town, "but Masters of Arts, gentlemen with grey beards, because, after the day's proceedings, the undergraduates numbered four hundred and the others five thousand."

Ecstasy swells in him at the recollection. He is not only Rhodes the empire-builder—Rhodes of the gold and diamonds, Rhodes the millionaire, Rhodes the politician, Rhodes of Kimberley and Cape Town and Rhodesia and England's future —he is also Rhodes the young man who journeyed from the Diamond Fields to Oxford and heard with awe the words of Ruskin. He is even Cecil John, a hero-worshipping schoolboy, a schoolboy worshipping—whom? Why, all the other Rhodeses the child Rhodes has fathered. He cannot contain his exultation: "I went to Oxford with the great general on whom the eyes of the world were fixed. . . . I can assure you, gentlemen, they gave me a greater reception than Lord Kitchener."

Even at Oxford he cannot dissemble his pride: "There have been not a few men," he says at his old college, "who have done good service to the State, but some of whose actions have partaken of the violence of their age and are hard to justify in a more peaceful and law-abiding age. It is among these men that my own life and actions must be weighed and measured; and I trust to the justice of my countrymen."

He cannot but feel that if he gets this justice, if his life and actions are fairly measured, his place in the world's history will be a high one.

How long does Rhodes expect to be remembered? According to Jameson, four thousand years. "I give myself four thousand years."

"It was not a boast," says Jameson; "he would not have said it at all if I hadn't asked him, and he seemed to be stating a fact like a fact in history. It did not seem to have any personal meaning."

A man does not know himself, said Rhodes in the days of his troubles. But the first sign of a great man, we have here held, is that he knows his destiny. Keats foretold his epitaph as: "Here lies one whose name was writ in water." Does this not mean he believed it should be writ enduringly?

Rhodes makes no such pitiful equivocations. He boldly decrees brass for his name: "Here lie the remains of Cecil John Rhodes"—no date of birth, no date of death, no name of country or begetter. . . . Rightly or wrongly, but superbly, he declares himself, like the greatest of the Cæsars, an immortal.

C H A P T E R ' 3 7

"BAYETE!"

I

THE South African War and the last chapter of Rhodes' life run together. The war began on October 11, 1899.

Rhodes had never believed such a thing could happen. There is his remark that a native chief in Samoa might as soon make trouble for the British Empire as the Transvaal. "I am sure," he says again, "that the President is going to give Her Majesty the terms which Her Majesty demands." . . . "It is only a temporary trouble in South Africa," he maintains. "Kruger will, at the final push, give anything . . . nothing will make Kruger fire a shot." . . . "There is not the slightest chance of war."

No, he could not believe it. He could not believe Kruger would fight any more than he could believe people would cease to mark their betrothals with diamonds, or Rhodesia fail to dominate South Africa, or the British Empire the world.

Yet he had not been back in South Africa three months, after being honoured at Oxford, when war was declared.

He hastened immediately from Cape Town to Kimberley. It was the last thing anybody in Kimberley wished. If there existed a person in Africa the Boers were desirous of taking, it was Rhodes. If there existed, therefore, a very magnet for danger, it was Rhodes. "Under all circumstances," wired the harassed, yet polite, mayor of Kimberley, "would ask you kindly postpone coming."

But Rhodes knew his place. His mines were in Kimberley. He arrived in Kimberley on the last train to reach the town before it was besieged; he arrived, indeed, after the Boers were already encircling the town because, owing to an accident, the train had been delayed.

Jameson was in Ladysmith, another besieged town—again to the chagrin of its inhabitants. The third besieged town was Mafeking, on the way to Rhodes' North.

Even apart from the increased danger Rhodes brought to Kimberley, he brought troubles. As he despised soldiers, he could not submit to their methods in warfare. As he was the autocrat of Kimberley, he insisted on ruling it, whatever the military might decree.

He benefited the town in a Rhodes-like way: fed the poor; against military authority, sent women and children down the mines for shelter; raised and equipped a volunteer corps and a corps of native runners; and had a twenty-eight-pound gun made in the de Beers workshops by an engineer who read up the process in an engineering journal. But he so maddened the officer in command with his orders and criticisms, that, in the end, they were not on speaking terms; he was very nearly arrested for his various misdemeanours; French was even asked to arrest him when he relieved Kimberley; Methuen sent a message, saying, "On my entry into Kimberley, Mr. Rhodes must take his immediate departure." He wrote to Roberts, telling him peremptorily to relieve the town: "Your troops have been more than two months within a distance of little over twenty miles from Kimberley, and if the Spytfontein hills are too strong for them, there is an easy approach over a level flat. . . . It is absolutely necessary that relief should be afforded this place." Another two months, however, passed before the town's relief and Rhodes' forgiving offer to Roberts and Kitchener to forward them supplies, provided "I have full power and no one to interfere with me. . . . Reply sharp, as otherwise I am going to Cape Town."

Apparently, and perhaps unfortunately, they were not prepared to give the conduct of the war over into Rhodes' hands. He spent another two years waiting for his death, now in Cape Town, now in Bulawayo, now in London. In London they said he might live a little longer if he would rest. But he refused to rest. In a flood of passion he suddenly rushed back to Cape Town to give the evidence about the forged bills.

He found he could not breathe in his cabin, and a bed was made for him on a table in the chart-room. All the portholes were left open for air and he caught a cold. There was a storm, and he was thrown from his table and so injured that for days he could not move. He knew he was dying. He spoke of the days soon to come when he would not be there, of the things to be done in which he would have no part. He hoped for peace with the Dutch. "They are a fine people and you must work with them. We have to work together."

II

The people who saw him on his return from Cape Town were more than moved, they were shocked to speechlessness. He was repulsively bloated, with wild grey hair, heavy, straining eyes that asked those terrible questions the mouths of the dying dare not utter, the shape of his face lost in its swelling, his skin a livid purple.

He could not live in Groote Schuur; it was too hot that February. He walked up and down the rooms as he had done after the Raid, and gaped at windows for air.

They took him to a little iron-roofed cottage at Muizenberg, and tore a hole in a side of it that he might get air. In bed he gave the evidence about the forgeries.

He had come back to Cape Town in utter fury. But what now did he care for twenty-nine thousand pounds, or Polish princesses, or scandals, or the men who hovered about him, or the crowds waiting in the road outside for news of his death. He had compared himself, after the Raid, with Job. He might have said now, in the words of Ecclesiastes:

"I made me great works; I builded me houses; I planted me vine-yards;

"I made me gardens and orchards, and I planted trees in them of all kind of fruit;

"I made me pools of water, to water therewith the wood that bringeth forth trees; . . .

". . . I had great possessions of great and small cattle; . . .

"I gathered me also silver and gold, and the peculiar treasure of kings and of the provinces; . . .

"So I was great. . . . .And whatsoever mine eyes desired I kept not from them; I withheld not my heart from any joy: for my heart rejoiced in all my labour; and this was my portion of all my labour.

"Then I looked on all the works that my hands had wrought, and on the labour that I had laboured to do: and, behold, all was vanity and vexation of spirit, and there was no profit under the sun. . . ."

Rhodes had millions. He was the great Empire-maker, the great Enemy, the Colossus. But now he needed a little air and could not get it.

They say his last words were: "So much to do, so little done." But, in fact, his last words were more simply human, more poignant, than these. He said to one of his secretaries: "Turn me over, Jack."

Eight men and no women were with him at his death. He was unconscious when a cablegram came from Hofmeyr saying, "God be with you."

III

"I admire the grandeur and loneliness of the Matoppos," says his last will, "and therefore I desire to be buried in the Matoppos on the hill which I used to visit and which I called the 'View of the World' in a square to be cut in the rock on the top of the hill covered with a plain brass plate with these words thereon—'Here lie the remains of Cecil John Rhodes.' "

To this hill, then, his body was taken. It was covered with an old Union Jack from Groote Schuur and escorted by Mounted Police to the Houses of Parliament. Here it lay for a day and a night. "Know ye not," said the Archbishop of Cape Town in his funeral sermon, "that there is a prince and a great man fallen this day in Israel?"

From Cape Town, in a new train Rhodes had ordered that travelling might be made pleasanter to his North—on the maiden trip of this train Rhodes' body was carried to Rhodesia. The train was draped in black and purple. The carriage in which the coffin rested was the old de Beers special car he had always used. The coffin was covered with wreaths brought by people to the wayside stations. Two troopers of the Cape police stood on guard, with arms reversed. At stations and sidings bugles sounded the "Last Post." A pilot engine preceded the train to Mafeking, but from Mafeking an armoured train escorted the funeral train and searchlights rayed the country, for it was still war.

The body of Rhodes passed along the path of his spirit: from Cape Town where he had ruled, through the Western Province of his vineyards, to Kimberley that had begotten his dreams and his wealth, along his own railway in Bechuanaland, through the country of his name, to the hills where he had made peace with the sons of Moselikatze.

A gun carriage, drawn by twelve oxen, carried the coffin up the black slope of his hill. It was lowered with chains into the rock. The hill was swarming with the Matabele he had won and betrayed and won again and succoured. "Our father is dead!" they cried, and gave him, alone of white men before or since, the royal salute of "Bayete!"

CHRONOLOGICAL TABLE

1853

RHODES is born at Bishop Stortford on July 5th. In 1853 also are born his most intimate associates, Jameson and Beit. The independence of the South African Republic dates from the year before Rhodes' birth, that of the Orange Free State from the year after.

1861

Rhodes goes to school at Bishop Stortford.

1870

He is found to have a tubercular tendency, and is sent to join his brother Herbert in Natal. In this year diamonds, discovered in South Africa two years before, appear in large quantities at Kimberley.

1871

Rhodes follows Herbert to Kimberley.

1872

He has heart trouble, and spends eight months on the veld with Herbert.

1873

Rhodes, already on the way to wealth, matriculates at Oxford.

1874

His lung trouble reasserting itself, he returns to Kimberley.

1876–1878

He keeps terms at Oxford.

1877

Inspired by Ruskin's Inaugural Lecture at Oxford, he makes his first will.

1880

He founds the de Beers Mining Company, and is elected a member of the Cape Parliament.

1881

Shortly after the battle of Majuba he enters Parliament; his maiden speech concerns the disarmament of Basutoland, and he takes his pass degree at Oxford.

1882

There are established in Bechuanaland the Boer Republics of Stellaland and Goshen. Rhodes goes to examine the position in Basutoland and there meets Gordon. He makes his second will.

1883

Rhodes visits Stellaland, becomes inspired with thoughts of the North, and sees in the two new Boer Republics a hindrance to Northward progress.

1884

Basutoland is transferred to Imperial control. Rhodes becomes, for a few weeks, Treasurer of the Cape. He visits Bechuanaland on a Delimitation commission, falls out with the missionary Mackenzie, and is henceforth against all missionaries. He becomes aware that other European countries are marching down Africa and towards Bechuanaland, and asks that General Warren be sent to occupy the country.

1885

Rhodes meets Kruger for the first time in the company of Warren and Mackenzie, and makes a bad impression on Kruger. South-

ern Bechuanaland becomes a Crown Colony. Northern Bechuanaland becomes a British Protectorate. Rhodes attacks Warren in
Parliament. He finds himself, over the Bechuanaland business, more
in sympathy with the Cape Dutch leader Hofmeyr than with
British soldiers and missionaries, and his association with Hofmeyr
begins.

1887

Gold having been discovered on the Witwatersrand in the previous year, and Johannesburg founded, Rhodes establishes his Goldfields Company.

1888

Rhodes impresses the value of the North on the Cape Governor,
Sir Hercules Robinson, and the Moffat treaty is made with Lobengula, King of the Matabele. Rhodes sends his partner Rudd to get a
mining concession from Lobengula over all his territories. He
amalgamates all the diamond mines of Kimberley, and founds the
de Beers Consolidated Mines Company. He makes his third will.

1889

Rhodes donates £10,000 to the Irish Party. . . . He is granted
a mining, trading and administrative charter over Lobengula's
dominions and the British South Africa Company, called the Chartered Company, makes its triumphant appearance.

1890

Rhodes takes office as Prime Minister of the Cape. His pioneers
plant their flag in Mashonaland. He demands that the Cape railway
go north instead of east. He acquires concessions over Barotseland
and Manicaland, and makes an attempt on Gazaland. He is lion-
ized in England.

1891

He sends Jameson as administrator to Mashonaland; establishes
stability in the Cape with his Bank Act; obtains "enormous subscriptions" for a university at the Cape; scotches a Dutch republic
in Manicaland; negotiates with Kruger, who tells him that ill-
gotten gains are accursed, to take Lourenço Marques from the

Portuguese; wants Pondoland annexed to the Cape; offers to run Bechuanaland for England if England will give him £50,000 a year; arranges to connect the Cape railway through the Free State with Johannesburg; begins to build railways in his new territories; obtains Imperial sanction to his further territories; talks tariffs to the British government; attempts to link himself for Imperial purposes with other British colonies; donates £5,000 to the British Liberal party; buys the Lippert Land Concession over Lobengula's Dominions; visits his North. The year 1891 is the apex of Rhodes' life. At the end of the year he falls from a horse, he also has influenza, his heart begins to trouble him again, and he feels henceforth that his life is to be short and he must hurry. He makes his fourth will.

1892

He begins to build his house, Groote Schuur. Assisted by Hofmeyr, and Hofmeyr's followers, the Afrikander Bond, he passes the Franchise and Ballot Act—anti-native in tendency. He meets his Chartered Shareholders in England for the first time and entrances them. He talks to Stead, a new friend, about world-dominion by blond men. He presses his Imperial and tariff views on Gladstone, and demands the British retention of Uganda, in which Rosebery supports him. . . . In Johannesburg there is trouble between Kruger and his non-Dutch citizens, the Uitlanders, and the Uitlanders form their National Union.

1893

Certain of Rhodes' more austere Ministers refuse to serve him because he will not abandon a fourth minister, not so austere, and he forms a new Cabinet. In Mashonaland, for the sake of economy, Jameson is running the country on forty, instead of seven hundred police. At Fort Victoria there is trouble between the Matabele and the Chartered Company, Lobengula is still in authority over Matabeleland, a war, longed for by the Mashonaland Europeans, results and Matabeleland is taken. Rhodes makes his fifth will.

1894

Rhodes puts Sigcau, the Paramount Chief of the Eastern Pondos, in his place, and annexes to the Cape both Eastern and Western

Pondoland. The British, as he desires, proclaim a Protectorate over Uganda—Uganda is on his way to Egypt. He passes the Glen Grey Act, which is his solution of the Native Problem. It appears that the Witwatersrand gold reef does not extend, as was hoped, to either Mashonaland or Matabeleland. Jameson and Rhodes encourage disaffection among the Uitlanders.

1895

Rhodes is gazetted a Privy Councillor. Tongaland is annexed to the Cape. Charterland becomes, officially, Rhodesia. Kruger seeks to stop the entry of British goods into the Transvaal, and there is almost a war with England. On December 29th, Jameson raids the Transvaal. Rhodes has assisted his preparations.

1896

On January 1st Jameson surrenders to the Boers. Hofmeyr and his Afrikander Bond turn against Rhodes. Henceforth his support comes from the Jingoes. He resigns as Prime Minister of the Cape and Managing Director of the Chartered Company. The Matabele rise. He enters among them in the Matoppos, wins their confidence, and makes with them an enduring peace. He chooses his burial-place near Moselikatze in the Matoppos.

1897

He answers before Cape and British Committees of Inquiry for his participation in the Jameson Raid. His railway reaches, amid Imperial celebrations, Bulawayo.

1898

Rhodes is restored to his position on the Chartered Company. He leads the newly-formed Progressive (Jingo) Party in his last election at the Cape. He preaches Union and his North.

1899

Rhodes and the Kaiser charm one another. He gets a telegraph agreement from the Kaiser. He is honoured with the D.C.L. Degree at Oxford. The South African War breaks out, and Rhodes, much to their discomfort, insists on joining the citizens of Kimberley a day before its siege. He falls out with the military authorities. He offers the natives Equal Rights. The Rhodes Scholarships (including now five to be allocated by the Kaiser) are the feature of Rhodes' sixth and last will.

1900

Kimberley is relieved. Rhodes' heart is now diseased beyond hope.

1901

The Transvaal and Orange Free State are proclaimed British.

1902

On March 26th, two months before the end of the Boer War, Rhodes dies at the Cape, and his body is taken by train to his tomb in the Matoppos.

SOURCES

THERE are a number of men living who knew Rhodes and worked with or against him. Many of these have frankly and generously searched their memories or notes for the sake of this book, and their testimony is beyond question. Since, however, some of them do not wish their names mentioned, it has been thought best to identify only published authorities and to class all personal information under the title "private source."

The speeches collected by *Vindex* are the storehouse in which most of Rhodes' sayings here quoted were found. One could not describe the Jameson Raid without Sir Percy Fitzpatrick's *Transvaal from Within*. The extent to which exploration has been lightened through the guidance of Messrs. Walker, Williams, Hofmeyr, Hyatt, Colvin, Hole, and John Harris may be judged by the number of times their names are given as references; and Rhodes' experiences in the Matoppos are largely drawn from the material in the books of Sir J. G. McDonald and Mr. Vere Stent.

Published works on Rhodes abound: lives and impressions and newspaper articles beyond count. He is the hero of several novels. He figures in practically every book concerning the South Africa of the eighteen-eighties, the eighteen-nineties and the early years of the twentieth century, and often in the books dealing with the English public life of his period. He is the dominant figure in South African histories. Government Blue-books of his time are full of him. Many of these authorities have been consulted—if not for facts, then for background or comparison, and also the lives of other empire-builders—not necessarily English. More might have been consulted but for the consciousness that too rich a mixture chokes an engine, and that there comes a time when one must be getting along. Only those works on which this book directly depends are named below. These are:

Angove, John,	*In the Early Days*
Baker, Herbert,	*Article in "Nineteenth Century"*
Blunt, Wilfrid S.,	*Diaries*
Bryce, James,	*Impressions of South Africa*
Butler, William,	*Autobiography*
Cohen, Louis,	*Reminiscences of Kimberley*
Colvin, Ian,	*Life of Jameson*
De Waal, D. C.,	*With Rhodes in Mashonaland*
Encyclopædia Britannica	*Rhodes, by Lady Lugard, and various historical and geographical articles*
Fitzpatrick, Percy,	*Transvaal from Within*
	South African Memories
Fort, Seymour,	*Life of Beit*
Froude, Anthony,	*Two Lectures on South Africa*
Fuller, Thomas,	*Cecil John Rhodes*
Gardiner, A. G.,	*Life of Sir William Harcourt*
Garrett, F. E.,	*Story of an African Crisis*
Gretton, R. H.,	*A Modern History of the English People*
Harris, David,	*Pioneer, Soldier and Politician*
Harris, John H.,	*The Chartered Millions*
Headlam, Cecil,	*The Milner Papers (South Africa)*
Hensman, Howard,	*Cecil Rhodes*
Hobson, J. A.,	*The War in South Africa*
Hofmeyr, J. H. (with F. W. Reitz),	*The Life of Jan Hendrik Hofmeyr*
Hole, Hugh Marshall,	*The Making of Rhodesia*
	The Jameson Raid
Hyatt, Stanley Portal,	*The Northward Trek*
Johnston, Harry,	*The Colonization of Africa*
Jollie, Ethel Tawse,	*The Real Rhodesia*
Jourdan, Philip,	*Cecil Rhodes*
Kruger, J. S. P.,	*Memoirs*
Le Sueur, Gordon,	*Cecil Rhodes*
McDonald, J. G.,	*Rhodes: A Life*

412

MacNeill, J. G. Swift,	*What I Have Seen and Heard*
Michell, Lewis,	*Cecil John Rhodes*
Morley, John,	*Life of Gladstone*
Selous, Frederick C.,	*Sunshine and Storm in Rhodesia*
Spender, J. A.,	*Life of The Right Hon. Sir Henry Campbell-Bannerman*
Spengler, Oswald,	*Decline of the West*
Stanley, H. M.,	*Through South Africa*
Stead, W. T.,	*The Last Will and Testament of C. J. Rhodes*
Stent, Vere,	*Some Incidents in the Life of Cecil Rhodes*
Thorold, Algar,	*The Life of Henry Labouchere*
Trollope, Anthony,	*South Africa*
Vindex,	*Speeches*
Walker, Eric A.,	*A History of South Africa*
	Life of Lord de Villiers and His Times
William, Basil,	*Cecil Rhodes*
Wills, W. A., and Collingridge, L. T.,	*The Downfall of Lobengula*
Wilson, Sarah,	*South African Memories*
Woolls-Sampson, A., and Hay, Ian,	*Anti-Commando*

GOVERNMENT REPORTS

Bechuanaland

The Position when Rhodes took his first step North, C. 5918.

Mashonaland and Matabeleland

Rhodes' Concessions over Lobengula's Dominions and his occupation of Mashonaland, C. 5918, C. 5524.

Rhodes' Occupation of Matabeleland, C. 7171, C. 7196, C. 7284, C. 7290, C. 7555.

Economic Commission

Report of 1932, as it concerns Rhodes' handling of the natives, U.G. 22.

Report of Select Committee (Cape), A.6. 1896.
Report of Select Committee (England), 311, 311-1, 311-2, C. 7333.

OTHER REPORTS

The Chartered Company's Doings, Reports of the B.S.A. Company.
The Chartered Company's Ownership of Rhodesia, Privy Council's Report of Lord Cave's Commission (*Times,* April, July, 1918).
A Few Notes on Sir Sidney Shippard, South African Law Journal (1902).
The Rhodes Scholarships, Rhodes Scholar Record.

The References are given according to chapter, section, page and paragraph (§). The Paragraphs (§§) are numbered, not according to section, but according to page. The pages of the references are not given that there may be no confusion with the pages of this book, but most of the works cited have indexes.

The two books of Sir Percy Fitzpatrick are quoted as Fitzpatrick's Transvaal (T'vaal); of Colonel Marshall Hole as Hole's Raid, and Hole's Rhodesia; and of Professor Eric Walker as Walker's History and Walker's de Villiers.

REFERENCES

CHAPTER I

Section I, P. 1, § 1, Meredith's Letters. P. 1, § 2, Jourdan. P. 1, § 4, Le Sueur. P. 2, §§ 1, 2, 3, 4, Le Sueur.
Section II, P. 4, § 2, Le Sueur.
Section III, P. 4, §§ 1, 2, Hensman. P. 5, §§ 3, 4, Le Sueur. P. 6, §§ 2, 3, Private Source. P. 7, § 1, Kruger. P. 7, § 2, Michell.
Section IV, P. 7, §§ 5, 6, Michell. P. 7, § 6, Williams. P. 8, § 1, Stead.

CHAPTER II

Section II, P. 12, § 1, Trollope. P. 12, §§ 2, 3, Williams. P. 12, § 4, Williams. P. 13, § 2, etc., Angove.

Section III, Pp. 14, 15, Walter's History.

Section IV, P. 16, § 1, Le Sueur. P. 16, § 3, Gretton. P. 17, § 1, Colvin. P. 17, § 5, McDonald.

Section V, P. 18, § 1, Trollope. P. 18, § 2, Private Source.

Section VI, P. 19, § 3, Froude. P. 19, § 4, Trollope. P. 20, § 2, Cohen.

CHAPTER III

Section I, P. 22, § 2, Michell. P. 22, § 3, Cohen. P. 23, § 2, Le Sueur. P. 23, § 4, Michell, Fitzpatrick's Memories. P. 24, § 1, Michell. P. 24, § 4, Private Source. P. 24, § 6, Private Source. P. 24, § 7, Stead.

Section II, P. 26, § 1, Jourdan. P. 26, § 3, Williams. P. 26, § 3, Michell.

Section III, P. 27, § 2, Williams. P. 27, § 3, Williams. P. 28, § 1, Woolls-Sampson and Hay.

Section V, P. 29, § 2, McDonald. P. 30, §§ 3, 4, Williams.

Section VI, P. 30, § 5, Private Source. P. 31, Private Source.

CHAPTER IV

Section I, P. 33, § 2, Hensman. P. 33, § 3, Hensman. P. 33, §§ 4, 5, Williams.

Section II, Pp. 35, 36, Stead.

Section III, P. 36, § 2, Garrett. P. 36, § 4, Stead. P. 37, § 2, Stead. P. 38, § 1, S.A. Law Journal (1902). P. 38, § 3, Fuller, McDonald. P. 39, § 6, Fuller.

Section IV, P. 40, § 1, Williams. P. 41, § 2, Spengler.

CHAPTER V

Section I, P. 43, § 2, Encyc. Brit.

Section II, P. 45, § 6, Encyc. Brit. P. 45, § 7, P. 46, § 1, Hofmeyr. P. 46, § 3, Kruger. P. 46, § 5, Kruger.

Section III, Pp. 46, 47, Trollope. P. 47, § 4, Williams.

Section IV, P. 48, § 6, Gretton. P. 49, § 1, Morley. P. 49, § 2, Kruger. P. 49, § 3, Kruger, Morley. P. 50, § 1, Kruger.

Section V, P. 50, Hensman, Michell. P. 51, § 4, Williams. P. 51, § 5, Vindex.

CHAPTER VI

Section I, P. 53, § 2, Kruger, Hofmeyr. P. 52, § 2, Hofmeyr.
Section II, P. 54, § 3, Vindex. P. 54, § 4, Walker's History.
P. 55, § 1, Walker's History, Vindex.
Section III, P. 55, § 2, Walker's History. P. 56, § 1, Kruger.
P. 56, § 4, Encyc. Brit. P. 57, §§ 3, 4, Vindex.
Section IV, P. 59, § 2, Samuel Butler's Notebooks. P. 59, § 4,
Private Source, Vindex. P. 60, § 1, Vindex. P. 60, § 3, Michell.

CHAPTER VII

Section I, P. 64, § 2, Vindex.
Section III, Pp. 65, 66, 67, Hyatt.
Section IV, P. 67, § 4, P. 68, § 1, Fuller. Pp. 68, 69, 70, Vindex.
Section V, P. 71, §§ 1, 2, Trollope. P. 72, § 1, Vindex. P. 72,
§§ 1, 2, Vindex. P. 73, § 2, Vindex.
Section VI, P. 73, 74, Hyatt. P. 74, § 4, Williams. P. 74, § 5,
Hofmeyr. P. 74, § 6, McDonald. P. 74, § 7, Vindex, Private Source.
P. 75, § 1, Vindex. P. 75, § 4, Vindex. P. 75, § 5, Headlam. P. 76,
§ 1, etc., Kruger. P. 76, § 2, Private Source.

CHAPTER VIII

Section I, P. 78, §§ 1, 2, Walker's History. P. 78, § 3, Walker's
History, Hyatt.
Section II, Pp. 79, 80, Walker's History. P. 80, § 1, Johnston. P.
80, § 2, Johnston. P. 80, § 3, Walker's History.
Section III, P. 80, § 4, Hyatt, Williams. P. 81, § 1, Hyatt,
Vindex, Williams, McDonald, David Harris. P. 82, § 3, Kruger.
P. 82, § 4, Walker's History, Hyatt. P. 82, § 5, Walker's History,
Vindex. P. 83, § 2, Williams.

CHAPTER IX

Section II, P. 86, §§ 1, 2, Gretton. P. 86, § 4, Hole's Raid. P. 87,
§ 2, Vindex. P. 88, § 1, Kruger, Williams.
Section III, P. 88, § 3, Fort, Colvin.

CHAPTER X

Section I, P. 90, § 1, Hole. P. 90, § 2, David Harris. P. 90, § 3,
Colvin, David Harris. P. 91, § 1, David Harris, P. 91, § 3, Colvin.
P. 91, § 4, Cohen, P. 91, § 5, Colvin. P. 92, § 1, Fort.

Section II, P. 92, § 4, David Harris. P. 93, § 1, Trollope, Colvin. P. 94, §§ 1, 2, Colvin. P. 94, § 3, William Butler. Pp. 94, 95, Williams. P. 95, § 6, Williams. P. 96, § 1, Williams, David Harris. P. 96, §§ 2, 3, Vindex. P. 97, § 2, Vindex. P. 97, § 6, Fort quotes Frank Harris. P. 97, § 1, Vindex. P. 98, § 1, Vindex, Michell, Colvin. P. 98, §§ 3, 4, 5, etc., Vindex. P. 99 § 5, Private Source. P. 99, § 6, Vindex, David Harris. P. 100, § 1, Vindex. P. 100, § 2, Colvin. P. 100, § 3, David Harris.

Section IV, P. 101, § 4, Michell. P. 101, § 6, Vindex. P. 102, § 1, Michell. P. 102, § 2, Williams, David Harris. P. 102, §§ 3, 4, Walker's de Villiers. P. 103, § 1, Walker's de Villiers. P. 104, § 1, Vindex. P. 104, § 4, Williams, Vindex, Private Source.

CHAPTER XI

Section II, P. 106, § 5, Hyatt, John Harris. Pp. 107, 108, Hyatt, John Harris.

Section III, Pp. 108, 109, Hyatt, John Harris. P. 109, § 3, Wortham's Delightful Profession. P. 109, § 4, P. 110, § 1, Le Sueur.

Section IV, P. 112, § 1, Gibbon's Decline and Fall. P. 111, § 1, Gibbon's Decline and Fall.

Section V, Hyatt.

CHAPTER XII

Section II, P. 114, §§ 2, 3, P. 115, §§ 1, 2, Kruger. C. 5918. P. 115, § 3, Vindex.

Section III, Pp. 116, 117, C. 5534.

Section IV, Colvin, Hole's Rhodesia.

Section V, P. 119, § 4, Hole's Rhodesia. P. 120, § 2, C. 5918, Private Source. P. 120, Private Source, C. 5918. Pp. 121, 122, C. 5918.

Section VI, Pp. 122, 123, C. 5918. P. 123, § 4, Walker's History.

CHAPTER XIII

Section I, Pp. 124, 125, C. 5918. P. 125, § 8, Williams. P. 127, § 3, Vindex. P. 127, § 1, Stead. P. 127, § 2, C. 5918.

Section II, Private Source.

Section III, P. 129, § 4, Hole's Rhodesia. P. 130, § 2, Colvin. P. 131, §§ 4, 5, P. 132, §§ 1, 2, Hole's Rhodesia. P. 132, C. 5918, John Harris. P. 133, John Harris.

Vindex, P. 172, § 4, Fuller. P. 172, § 5, Baker. P. 173, §§ 1, 2, 3, 4, Baker, P. 174, § 2, Baker. P. 174, § 3, McDonald.

CHAPTER XVIII

Section I, P. 175, § 2, Garrett. P. 176, § 1, Fuller, Private Source. P. 176, § 2, Garrett, Vindex, Williams, Stead. P. 177, § 2, Blunt, Meredith.

Section II, P. 177, §§ 4, 5, Vindex. P. 177, § 6, Spender. P. 178, § 2, Vindex, Hofmeyr. P. 179, § 1, Vindex. P. 179, § 3, Walker's History. P. 179, §§ 4, 5. P. 180, §§ 1, 2, Walker's History. P. 180, § 4, etc., Kruger. P. 180, § 5, Vindex. P. 181, § 1, Williams.

Section III, P. 181, § 3, Vindex. P. 182, § 1, Fuller, C. 1171. P. 182, Fitzpatrick's Memories, C. 7171. P. 183, § 1, Private Source. P. 183, § 3, McDonald. P. 183, § 5, Privy Council Report (1918). P. 184, § 1, Privy Council Report (1918), Vindex. P. 185, § 1, Private Source.

Section IV, P. 185, § 2, Vindex. P. 185, § 3, Jollie, Hyatt, Hole. P. 186, § 1, Williams, Vindex. P. 187, § 1, Vindex, Fuller, Private Source. P. 187, § 1, Michell. P. 187, §. 2, Michell. P. 188, § 3, Vindex.

Section V, P. 188, § 4, de Waal, Vindex. P. 189, §§ 1, 2, 4, Vindex. P. 189, § 5, Walker's History, Vindex. P. 190, § 2, Walker's History, Vindex. P. 190, § 3, Vindex. P. 190, § 3, Vindex.

CHAPTER XIX

Section I, P. 192, § 3, Stead. P. 193, § 1, Thorold. P. 193, Vindex. P. 194, §§ 2, 3, 4, Vindex.

Section II, P. 195, § 1, Stead. P. 195, Stead. P. 196, § 3, Vindex, Stead.

Section III, P. 196, § 5, Vindex. P. 197, § 1, Gardiner. P. 197, § 2, Vindex. P. 197, § 4, Hofmeyr. P. 198, §§ 1, 2, 3. P. 198, § 4, P. 199, §§ 1, 2, 3, Vindex.

Section IV, Vindex.

Section V, P. 200, § 2, Blunt, Vindex. P. 201, § 1, Vindex. P. 201, § 2, Walker's History.

Section VI, P. 202, § 1, Walker's de Villiers, Hofmeyr. P. 202, §§ 3, 4, Hofmeyr. P. 202, § 4. P. 203, §§ 1, 2, Walker's de Villiers. P. 203, § 3, Williams.

CHAPTER XX

Section I, Walker's History.

Section III, de Waal.

Section IV, P. 207, § 1, de Waal. P. 207, § 3, C. 7171.

Section V, P. 208, § 1, C. 7171. P. 208, § 2, Hole's Rhodesia. P. 209, § 1, Kruger, C. 7555. P. 209, § 2, Thorold.

Section VI, P. 211, C. 7171. P. 211, § 3, C. 7171. P. 212, § 1, Michell, C. 7171. P. 212, § 2, Private Source.

Section VII, P. 214, § 1, C. 7555. P. 214, § 4, Wills and Collingridge, C. 7555. P. 214, § 5, C. 7196. P. 214, § 6, C. 7171, C. 7196. P. 215, § 1, Michell. P. 215, § 4, Michell.

CHAPTER XXI

Section I, P. 216, § 2, Hole's Rhodesia, John Harris. P. 216, § 3, C. 7171. P. 217, § 1, Hole's Rhodesia. P. 217, § 2, Hole's Rhodesia, John Harris, Wills and Collingridge.

Section II, P. 217, §§ 4, 5, C. 7196. P. 218, § 1, Hole's Rhodesia, John Harris. P. 218, § 2, John Harris. P. 218, § 3, Hole's Rhodesia, Williams. P. 218, § 4, C. 7196.

Section III, P. 218, §§ 5, 6, C. 7196. P. 219, § 1, Hole's Rhodesia. P. 219, § 2, C. 7196, Blunt. P. 219, § 4, C. 7290, Vindex. P. 220, §§ 1, 2, 3, Hole's Rhodesia.

Section IV, C. 7294.

Section V, P. 222, § 2, McDonald, Hole's Rhodesia. P. 222, § 3, Hole's Rhodesia. P. 223, §§ 1, 2, 3, Hole's Rhodesia.

Section VI, P. 223, § 4, John Harris. P. 224, §§ 1, 2, John Harris. P. 224, §§ 3, 4, Vindex. P. 225, § 1, Vindex. P. 225, § 2, Privy Council Report, John Harris, Vindex. P. 226, § 3, Jollie.

Section VII, P. 226, § 4, Vindex. P. 226, §§ 5, 6, Fitzpatrick's Memories. P. 227, § 1, Hole's Rhodesia. P. 227, §§ 3, 4, Hole's Rhodesia. P. 228, § 1, McDonald. P. 228, §§ 2, 4, Hole's Rhodesia. P. 228, § 5, de Waal.

Section VIII, P. 229, § 8, Vindex. P. 230, § 1, B.S.A. Report.

CHAPTER XXII

Section I, P. 231, § 1, B.S.A. Report. §§ 2, 3, 4, 5, P. 232, §§ 1, 2, Walker's History. Pp. 232, 233, B.S.A. Reports and Walker's History.

Section II, P. 234, § 4, B.S.A. Report. P. 234, § 5, Private Source. P. 235, § 1, C. 7290.

Section III, Pp. 235, 236, Vindex. P. 237, § 6, Hofmeyr, Vindex. P. 239, § 3, Private Source.

Section IV, P. 240, § 1, Michell. P. 240, § 4, Jourdan. P. 240, § 6, Spengler.

Section V, P. 241, § 4, Spengler. P. 242, § 2, Vindex. P. 242, § 3, Williams. P. 242, § 5, P. 243, §§ 1, 2, Vindex. P. 243, § 4, Jourdan, Michell. P. 243, § 4, Williams, B.S.A. Report. P. 246, §§ 2, 4, Stead.

Section VI, P. 247, § 1, Fuller. P. 247, § 2, Spengler.

CHAPTER XXIII

Section I, P. 248, Vindex. P. 249, § 1, Walker's History, Hofmeyr. P. 250, § 1, Hofmeyr. P. 250, § 2, Vindex. Pp. 250, 251, Vindex.

Section II, P. 252, § 3, Vindex, Walker's History. P. 252, § 3, Vindex. P. 253, § 2, Walker's History, Hofmeyr. P. 253, § 3, Vindex. P. 254, § 3, Hofmeyr.

Section IV, P. 255, § 9, Vindex.

Section V, P. 256, §§ 2, 4, Vindex. P. 256, § 6, Darwin's Descent of Man. P. 257, § 2, Vindex. P. 258, § 3, Vindex.

Section VI, P. 258, §§ 5, 7, Hofmeyr. P. 259, § 1, Vindex. P. 259, § 2, Hofmeyr.

Section VII, P. 259, § 5, Williams. P. 260, § 2, Walker's de Villiers. P. 261, §§ 2, 3, Williams. P. 261, § 4, Walker's de Villiers, Vindex. P. 262, § 1, Vindex. P. 262, §§ 2, 3, Walker's de Villiers.

CHAPTER XXIV

Section II, P. 265, Vindex. P. 266, § 4, P. 267, §§ 1, 2, Vindex. P. 234, § 5, Williams. P. 267, §§ 3, 4, Vindex. P. 267, § 5, Private Source. P. 268, § 3, Vindex.

Section IV, U.G. 22 (1902).

CHAPTER XXV

Section I, P. 273, § 1, Hofmeyr, Williams. P. 273, § 2, Williams. P. 274, § 1, Vindex. P. 274, § 2, Vindex.

Section II, P. 275, § 1, Vindex.

Section III, P. 276, § 1, Vindex. P. 276, § 2, Walker's History.

P. 276, § 3, Williams. P. 276, § 4, Kruger. P. 277, § 3, Williams, Hole's Raid, Walker's History. P. 277, § 4, Michell. P. 277, § 6, Williams, P. 278, §, 1, Walker's History, Williams.

Section IV, P. 278, § 3, Walker's de Villiers. P. 279, § 1, Fuller, Fitzpatrick's Transvaal, Kruger. P. 279, § 4, Kruger. P. 280, § 1, Walker's History. P. 280, § 2, Vindex.

Section V, P. 281, § 4, Walker's History. P. 281, § 5, A.6 (1896). P. 282, § 1, Hole's Raid.

Section VI, P. 282, § 3, Bryce. P. 283, § 1, McDonald, Fitzpatrick's Transvaal.

CHAPTER XXVI

Section II, P. 285, § 6, Bryce. P. 286, § 1, Fitzpatrick Transvaal, Kruger. P. 287, § 1, Bryce. P. 287, § 2, Fitzpatrick's T'vaal. P. 288, § 2, Private Source.

Section III, § 2, Vindex. P. 289, Fitzpatrick's T'vaal.

Section IV, P. 290, §§ 1, 2, Kruger. P. 291, §§ 3, 4, Fitzpatrick's T'vaal. P. 292, Hobson. P. 293, § 2, Fitzpatrick's T'vaal.

Section V, P. 293, § 3, Bryce. P. 294, § 1, Private Source. P. 294, §§ 1, 2, 3, Fitzpatrick's T'vaal.

Section VI, P. 295, § 1, Bryce. P. 295, § 4, Williams, Hole's Raid, Fitzpatrick's T'vaal. P. 296, § 2, Michell, Vindex, Walker's History. P. 297, § 1, Hole's Raid. P. 297, § 2, Fitzpatrick's T'vaal.

Section VII, P. 298, § 1, 311 (–1, –2, Raid Inquiry, England), Vindex. P. 298, § 3, Williams, Fitzpatrick's T'vaal. P. 298, § 4, Vindex. P. 299, § 1, Vindex.

CHAPTER XXVII

Section I, Fitzpatrick's T'vaal.

Section II, P. 303, § 4, Williams, Victoria's Letters, B.S.A. Report. P. 304, §§ 3, 4, Colvin.

Section III, P. 304, § 5, P. 305, §§ 1, 2, 3, Raid Inquiry (311, –1, –2). P. 305, § 5, Walker's History, B.S.A. Report.

Section IV, P. 306, §§ 2, 3, 4, Williams, Walker's History. P. 307, § 2, Walker's History.

Section V, Fitzpatrick's T'vaal.

Section VI, Pp. 308, 309, 312, Fitzpatrick's T'vaal. Raid Inquiry (311, –1, –2). P. 311, § 3, Fitzpatrick's T'vaal. P. 311, § 4, Colvin, Raid Inquiry (311, –1, –2), Fitzpatrick's T'vaal. P. 312,

§ 1, Colvin, Fitzpatrick's T'vaal. P. 312, § 3, P. 313, §§ 1, 2, 3, Fitzpatrick's T'vaal. P. 313, § 5, Williams. P. 313, § 6, Williams. P. 314, §§ 1, 2, 3, Fitzpatrick's T'vaal.
Section VII, Fitzpatrick's T'vaal.

CHAPTER XXVIII

Section I, P. 317, § 2, C. 7933. P. 318, § 1, Hole's Raid. P. 318, §§ 2, 3, C. 7933. P. 319, § 1, Fitzpatrick's T'vaal, Cape Inquiry (A–6), Blunt.

Section II, P. 320, § 2, Cape Inquiry (A–6). P. 320, § 5, Mc-Donald, Cape Inquiry (A–6). P. 320, § 6, P. 321, § 1, etc., Cape Inquiry (A–6).

Section III, P. 321, § 11, Raid Inquiry (311, –1, –2), McDonald, Blunt. P. 322, § 2, Private Source. P. 322, § 3, Fitzpatrick's T'vaal. P. 322, § 4, Colvin, Hole's Raid. P. 323, § 1, Hole's Raid.

Section IV, P. 323, § 2, Fitzpatrick's T'vaal. P. 323, § 3, Colvin, Hofmeyr. P. 324, § 1, Fitzpatrick's T'vaal. P. 324, § 2, Fitzpatrick's T'vaal, S.A. Law Journal (1902).

Section V, Fitzpatrick's T'vaal.

Section VI, Raid Inquiry (311, –1, –2), Hole's Raid.

Section VII, P. 325, § 6, Fitzpatrick's T'vaal. P. 326, §§ 1, 2, Fitzpatrick's Raid. P. 326, § 3, Fitzpatrick's T'vaal. Private Source.

Section VIII, P. 326, § 4, Fitzpatrick's T'vaal. P. 327, § 1, Fitzpatrick's T'vaal, Walker's de Villiers. P. 327, §§ 2, 3, P. 328, § 1, Fitzpatrick's T'vaal. P. 286, § 4, Private Source.

CHAPTER XXIX

Section I, P. 329, § 1, Private Source. P. 329, § 2, Fitzpatrick's T'vaal, Private Source. P. 330, §§ 1, 2, Hofmeyr, Thorold. P. 330, § 3, Hofmeyr. P. 331, § 2, Williams, Gardiner. P. 311, §§ 4, 5, Hofmeyr.

Section II, P. 332, §§ 1, 2, 3, 4, 5, Hofmeyr. P. 332, § 6, Jourdan. P. 332, § 7, Colvin. P. 332, §§ 8, 9, Hofmeyr. P. 333, § 2, Hofmeyr, Vindex. P. 333, § 3, Hofmeyr. P. 333, § 4, Colvin. P. 333, § 4, Michell, Vindex. P. 334, § 1, Vindex, Private Source.

Section III, P. 335, § 1, Michell, Hofmeyr. P. 335, § 2, B.S.A. Report. P. 335, § 3, Blunt, B.S.A. Report. P. 336, § 1, Hofmeyr. P. 336, § 2, P. 337, § 1, B.S.A. Report.

Section IV, P. 337, §§ 2, 3, Hofmeyr. P. 337, § 4, Fitzpatrick's T'vaal, Hofmeyr. P. 338, § 1, Fitzpatrick's T'vaal. P. 338, § 2, Colvin, Hofmeyr.

CHAPTER XXX

Section I, P. 340, § 1, Selous.
Section II, P. 341, § 2, Bryce. P. 342, § 2, Bryce. P. 343, §§ 1, 2, Selous.
Section III, P. 344, § 1, Le Sueur. P. 344, § 2, Jollie. P. 344, §3, McDonald. P. 344, § 4, Gardiner. Pp. 345, 346, Gardiner.
Section IV, P. 346, § 1, Gardiner. P. 346, § 2, McDonald.
Section V, P. 347, § 1, Vindex. P. 347, § 2, Jourdan, Vindex. P. 348, § 1, B.S.A. Reports.
Section VI, P. 349, § 1, McDonald.
Section VII, Pp. 349, 350, McDonald. Pp. 350, 351, 352, 353, 354, 355, Stent. P. 355, last § in section, Selous.
Section VIII, P. 355, McDonald. P. 355, §§ 12, 13, McDonald. P. 356, § 1, McDonald, Hole's Rhodesia. P. 356, § 2, Jourdan. P. 357, §§ 1, 2, Jourdan. P. 357, § 3, McDonald. P. 358, § 1, Williams.

CHAPTER XXXI

Section I, McDonald.
Section II, McDonald.
Section III, P. 362, § 3, Williams. P. 362, § 4, Cape Inquiry (A-6). P. 362, § 5, P. 363, § 1, Vindex. P. 363, § 2, Fuller.

CHAPTER XXXII

Section I, P. 364, § 1, Gardiner. P. 364, §§ 2, 3, 4, P. 365, § 1, B.S.A. Reports. Pp. 365, 366, 367, B.S.A. Report.
Section II, Pp. 367, 368, B.S.A. Report.
Section IV, P. 369, § 2, Gardiner, Blunt, MacNeill. P. 370, § 1, Private Source. P. 370, § 2, Gardiner.

CHAPTER XXXIII

Section I, P. 371, § 1, Headlam. P. 371, § 2, Vindex. P. 372, §§ 1, 2, Vindex. P. 373, § 1, Spengler.
Section II, P. 374, § 1, Vindex. P. 375, § 1, McDonald. § 2, McDonald, Michell. P. 376, § 1, Fuller. P. 376, § 2, Bryce. P. 376,

§ 3, Michell. P. 377, § 1, Private Source. P. 377, § 2, Vindex. P. 378, Stead.

Section III, Pp. 379, 380, 381, Rhodes Scholar Book. P. 381, § 1, Private Source.

Section IV, P. 381, § 3, Williams, Vindex.

CHAPTER XXXIV

Section I, Vindex.

Section II, Vindex.

Section III, P. 385, § 4, Stanley. P. 386, § 1, Vindex. P. 386, § 2, Vindex. P. 386, § 3, P. 387, § 1, B.S.A. Report.

CHAPTER XXXV

Pp. 388, 389, 390, 391, Vindex. P. 391, § 2, Colvin. P. 391, Vindex.

CHAPTER XXXVI

Section I, P. 393, § 1, Jourdan, Le Sueur. P. 394, § 1, Jourdan, Le Sueur. P. 394, § 2, McDonald. P. 394, § 3, Williams.

Section II, P. 395, § 1, Vindex. P. 395, §§ 2, 3, 4, 5, Vindex. P. 396, § 1, McDonald.

Section III, P. 396, § 2, Williams. P. 396, § 3, P. 397, § 1, Williams. P. 397, §§ 3, 4, Fitzpatrick's Memories.

CHAPTER XXXVII

Section I, P. 399, § 2, Vindex. P. 399, § 4, Michell. P. 399, P. 400, § 4, David Harris, Hensman. P. 400, § 4, Williams. P. 401, § 2, Fitzpatrick's Memories.

Section II, P. 401, § 3, P. 402 §§ 1, 2, Le Sueur. P. 403, Penultimate §, Private Source. P. 403, last §, Hofmeyr.

Section III, McDonald.

Index

429

431

433

Inheritors of Rhodes' estate, 7
Innes, Sir James Rose, 18, 143, 202
Inquiries into the Rail
   Cape Town, 320-21, 362
   London, 178, 238, 305, 336-7, 362,
      368
Inyanga Farm, 171
Irrigation, 375
Irish Party, 127, 178
Isaacs, Barnett (alias Barney Barnato)
   —See Barnato
Isaacs, Rufus, 15
Isaiah quoted, 34
Israelites compared with Boers, 85
Italy in Africa, 55

Jameson, Sir Leander Starr (Dr. Jim)
   accompanies Pioneer Column, 137
   administrator in Rhodesia, 188, 189,
      339
   arrested for gun-running, 123, 147
   banqueted, 297
   camp at Pitsani, 304, 307, 308, 312,
      316, 321, 323
   charm, 190, 205
   dealings with Lobengula, 137, 138
   description of, 130
   diamond magnates confer at his house,
      101-2
   disheartened, 391
   exploits, 296
   forgiven by Rhodes, 23, 130
   Gazaland mission, 149
   Johannesburg visits, 281, 283, 295,
      301-2, 308
   in England, 296
   Kimberley days, 23-4
   Ladysmith, 400
   National Convention, 339, 392
   opinion of Milner, 391
   Prime Minister, 339
   quits medical practice, 137-8
   recreation, 131
   See also Jameson Raid, below
Jameson Raid, 301-339
   alluded to, 39, 41, 48, 68, 234, 289
   amnesty, 337
   Boers on the path, 323, 324
   "Border" police force, 305
   Chamberlain's alleged complicity, 368,
      369, 370

Jameson Raid—(Continued)
   effect on Rhodes, 200, 224, 228, 255,
      274-5, 319, 332, 373-4
   England's sympathy, 325, 327, 330-1
   flag question, 313
   Harcourt's indictment, 178, 344, 364,
      368
   High Commissioner's action, 324, 326,
      328
   Hofmeyr's attitude, 68, 324, 330, 331,
      333, 337
   hooted, 326
   inquiry in Cape Town, 320, 362
   inquiry in London, 178, 238, 305, 337,
      344, 362, 368
   instructions to Jameson, 313-15, 319,
      370
   intelligence departments, 311, 319,
      368
   Johannesburg plans, 301-2
   jumping-off place, 302-3
   Kruger cognizant, 320
   letter of invitation from Johannesburg,
      308-310
   letter of invitation read to troops,
      323
   letter to Harcourt, 25, 345
   not a cause of the Boer War, 373
   number of followers, 322
   only failure in Rhodes' system, 82
   Pitsani Camp, 304, 307, 308, 312,
      316, 321, 323
   premature action hinted at, 315
   reformers, q.v.
   repudiations all round, 329-331
   Rhodesia Horse, 282, 295, 297
   rising postponed, 314-5
   sealed document deposited, 370
   sentences on Reformers, 338-9
   Shepstone precedent, 46
   shipped for trial, 337
   suggested connection with affairs of
      chartered company, 234
   sure of success, 322
   surrender, 326
   what emerged from the Inquiry, 369
   wires supposed to be cut, 320
Jerusalem, 238
Jesuit example, 37, 146, 195, 196, 246
Jewish friends, 248
   See Barnato, Beit
Jewish physiognomy, 16

435

446

447

448

Printed in the United Kingdom
by Lightning Source UK Ltd.
9503400001B